KU-210-230

AA

100 WEEKEND WALKS IN BRITAIN

Produced by AA Publishing

Copy Editor: Penny Hicks
Designers: Design 23

Contributors: Steve Ashton, Chris Barber, Jackie Bates, Kate Chevalier, Paddy Dillon, Heather Freeman, Susan Gordon, Des Hannigan, Leigh Hatts, Tony Hopkins, Charlie Hurt, Peter Lambley, Helen Livingston, Cameron McNeish, Andy Murray, Brian Pearce, Ben Perkins, Mark Richards, Erica Schwarz, Roger Smith, Roland Smith, Rebecca Snelling, Colin Speakman, Donald Stokoe, Clive Tully

First edition 1994
First paperback edition 1995

ISBN 0 7495 1052 8

Published by AA Publishing (a trading name of Automobile Association Developments Limited, whose registered office is Norfolk House, Priestley Road, Basingstoke, Hampshire RG24 9NY; registered number 1878835).

Colour separation by Daylight Colour Art Pte, Singapore
Printed by Graficromo, Cordoba, Spain

Essential Information for Walkers

All the routes have been carefully researched, but despite our best efforts to ensure accuracy, changes may occur at any stage during the lifetime of the book. Landscapes change: features mentioned as landmarks may alter or disappear completely, and paths may become muddy or overgrown.

It is important to note that some of the routes pass close to dangerous features in the landscape and need care, especially if children are with you. Our walks follow public rights of way and established paths, tracks and bridleways wherever possible, but the routes sometimes include stretches along a road. Some of the routes are around the coast. Please remember that, although exciting places to visit, cliffs are by their very nature dangerous, so stay away from the edge. Walking on the seashore, be aware of the tide: it can rise with surprising speed. When seas are rough, keep well away from the water.

The walks have all been carefully selected to take you through attractive and varied areas of the British countryside, and to be enjoyable both for experienced and occasional walkers. While the approximate distance is always stated, the time taken to do the walk will vary with the individual. Do wear sensible clothes for the conditions; and you will need comfortable footwear that will withstand wet and possibly muddy or slippery conditions.

With the information for each walk, we indicate the conditions you should expect – for example, whether it is a gentle stroll on reasonably level ground, or a more challenging walk on rougher terrain. If a walk includes any particularly steep hill stretches, or other hazards such as stiles, we have indicated this. Where possible we have also listed nearby facilities for refreshments, and the nearest public access toilets. Listing in this guide does not imply AA inspection or recognition, although establishments may have an AA classification.

The National Grid reference for the start of each walk is given below the walk number; this relates to the larger scale Ordnance Survey maps (1:50,000 and 1:25,000), which walkers may like to use in addition to the maps in this book.

Places are suggested where you may be able to park. These have all been checked by our researchers and were found to be practicable. However, these suggestions are not a guarantee of any right to leave a vehicle parked, and if no distinct car park exists, walkers should park carefully and considerately where they can. Remember that it is the responsibility of the individual to ensure that their vehicle is safely and not illegally parked, and that it does not obstruct other traffic or access.

Respect the country code and keep dogs strictly under control. Please keep to the designated paths, and if you open a gate, please close it after you. Be particularly careful not to discard cans, bottles or food because these are a hazard to wildlife as well as being an eyesore. Do not discard lighted cigarettes, matches or anything else that could cause a fire.

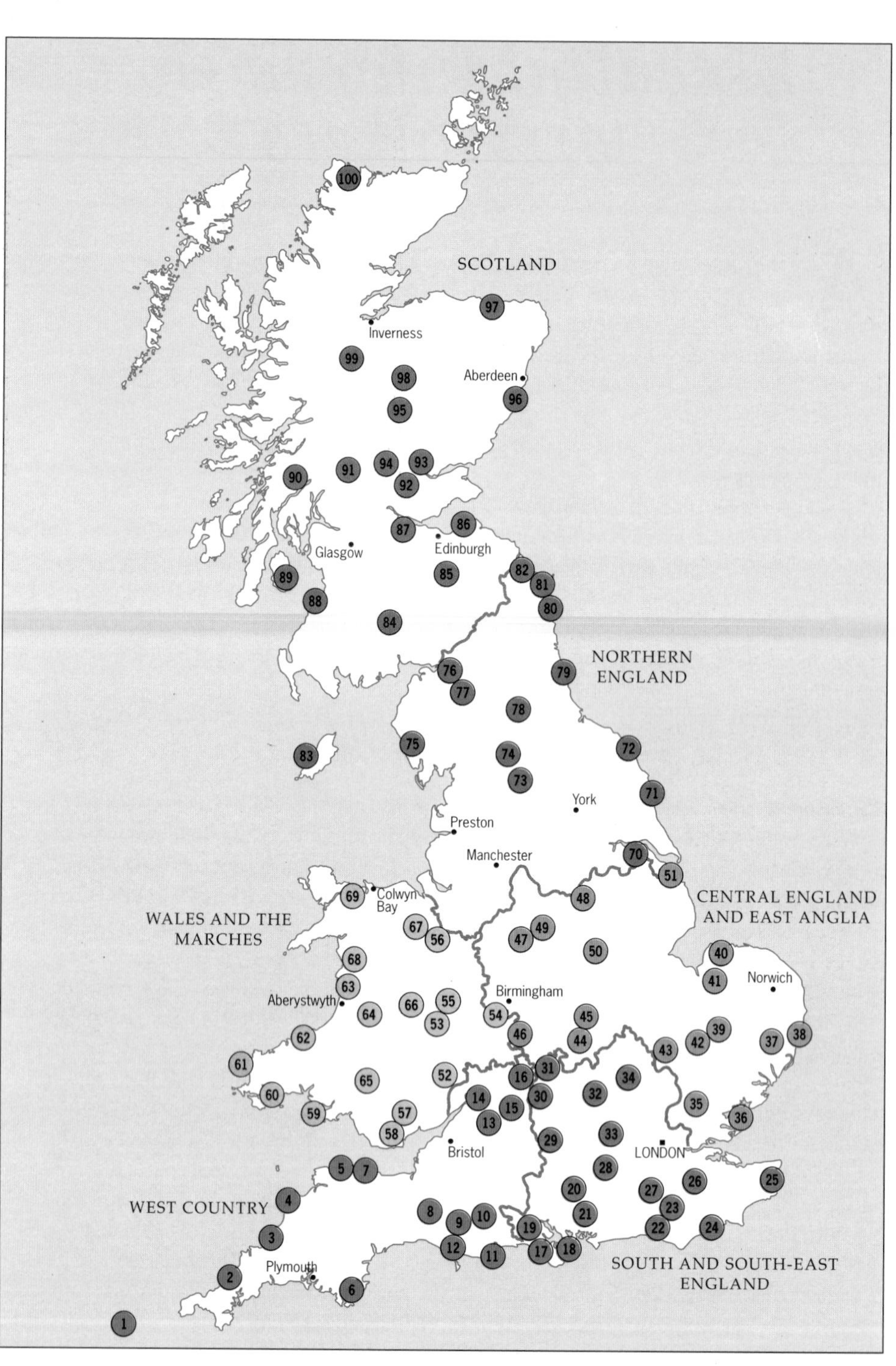
SCOTLAND
Inverness
Aberdeen
Glasgow
Edinburgh
NORTHERN ENGLAND
York
Preston
Manchester
Colwyn Bay
WALES AND THE MARCHES
CENTRAL ENGLAND AND EAST ANGLIA
Norwich
Birmingham
Aberystwyth
Bristol
LONDON
WEST COUNTRY
Plymouth
SOUTH AND SOUTH-EAST ENGLAND

The Walks

Introduction

by Paul Sterry

One of the great pleasures of walking in the countryside is discovering a new landscape and the wildlife that goes with it. Yet it is possible to walk for several miles and apparently see very little. It is only when somebody points out a clue that you realise you may have been missing all sorts of interesting things. This introduction is designed to give you a few of those clues, to help you really enjoy and make the most of your walks.

While many of the walks in this book pass through nature reserves and national parks – areas where plants and animals are particularly encouraged to flourish – others simply take you through attractive scenery, but all the walks unashamedly celebrate the traditional landscape and wildlife of Britain.

The wildlife heritage of Britain is extraordinarily rich and diverse, and a naturalist's interest in plants and animals can be satisfied almost anywhere in these islands. All you need is a keen eye, a sense of curiosity and an ability to interpret the landscape and wildlife around you.

This introduction sets the scene for the walks, and provides background information for the habitats and wildlife you are likely to encounter. Because some plants and animals are habitat-specific – that is, they occur only when certain conditions of landscape, climate and food source are met – the distinctions between these wildlife communities are highlighted in the text. Information is also provided on how to get the most from your observations, so that you can become your own nature detective. If you were not already interested in natural history, the walks will whet your appetite for wildlife watching. Using the book as a guide, weekend walkers will soon discover that an interest in natural history can really enhance your day out in the country.

Keeping Your Eyes Open

Follow the routes in this book and nature will be all around you –but there are ways to increase the range of things you see and improve your chances of seeing them. All you need to know is how, where and when to look, and the following guidelines will make your task easier.

Choosing Your Equipment

Before you set out on a walk, consider the sort of equipment you might need. The items should be appropriate both to your particular interests and the character of the walk, of course, and above all, they should be portable. There is nothing worse than being burdened by a rucksack full of overweight and unnecessary equipment!

For the birdwatcher and anyone who wants to observe shy creatures such as deer over a distance, the most obvious piece of equipment is a pair of binoculars which should be both of a reasonable magnification and lightweight for carrying. When purchasing a pair for the first time you should bear in mind the set of two figures that accompany all

binoculars – typical examples might be 8x30 or 10x40. The first number in the couplet refers to the magnification (that is, eight and ten times respectively), and the second indicates the light-gathering capacity of the lenses: the higher the figure, the brighter the image you will see.

At first, it might seem that a high magnification and bright image are obvious specifications to aim for. However, the larger the magnification and the brighter the image, the heavier and more unwieldy the binoculars become. Try a few pairs out in the shop, and aim at compromise with a lightweight pair and a specification of around 8x30. Dedicated birdwatchers invariably include a telescope and tripod among their armoury of equipment but for the purposes of the more casual observer they are unnecessary.

For a closer look at plant life, the choice of equipment is even simpler. A small hand lens is all you need to view floral details in close-up, and also comes in useful when observing insects and other invertebrates. If a pair of binoculars is all you have with you at the time, and you need to scrutinise a flower or leaf, try turning the binoculars the wrong way round to look at the fine detail. You will be surprised at how effective this can be.

Several mammals and birds eat hazelnuts, and the husks can tell you whose dinner it was. Clockwise from top right, these nuts have been opened by a dormouse, a water vole, a nuthatch, a squirrel, a bank vole and a wood mouse.

The ability to identify and name the plants and animals that you encounter is part of the fun, and a good set of field guides can help here. There are excellent books available covering almost every aspect of British natural history, and there is a particularly wide – indeed, bewildering – choice relating to birds, wild flowers and trees. Some are illustrated with photographs, others with artwork. Whichever you prefer, try to select a guide which does not go into more detail than you actually want – this will only complicate matters. Included in this proviso must be a consideration of the geographical area that the book covers – so do not buy a guide that covers the whole of Europe if you are only interested in British wildlife.

Using your field guide, try to identify the plant or animal in question on the spot. Failing that, why not take a photograph for subsequent scrutiny? Most modern 35mm SLR cameras are suitable, and you will need a close-up lens for flowers or a telephoto lens for birds and mammals. This also removes the temptation to pick or collect from the wild, an activity that should be avoided at all costs.

Fieldcraft Skills

Although you will have no difficulty in seeing wildlife along the walks in this book, a knowledge of the techniques and fieldcraft employed by experienced observers can be useful. A lot of this is just common-sense although some of the following tips may be less immediately obvious to the less experienced naturalist.

The approach to birdwatching depends on factors such as the habitat in question, the season, and the type of birds you are likely to encounter. Take, for example, birdwatching in a deciduous, or broad-leaved, woodland. In the spring, the different bird songs give the best clues as to the species present. Singing male birds, while initially difficult to locate among the emerging leaves, can be tracked down by following the source of the sounds. From dawn until about eight o'clock in the morning is the best time of day for most species, after which they often cease singing and concentrate on feeding.

Nightingales, which may be heard on several of the walks in this book, will sing at almost any time of day and often at night as well. On a stroll in the late evening through woods, you may also hear the familiar sounds of tawny owls and the strange, grunting calls of the woodcock.

Go birdwatching in a winter woodland, however, and you will need a different approach. Many of the small songbirds gather together in mixed feeding flocks that roam nomadically through the trees. For long periods of time you will not see a single bird but do not get disheartened. All of a sudden, a noisy flock will come into range. Birds from the flock can sometimes be lured closer by making a 'pssshh' sound with clenched teeth and pursed lips. Make sure your walking companions know your intentions beforehand, however!

Around the coast, you need to employ different techniques again. Some of the walks visit seabird colonies, which are at their busiest from May to July. Generally speaking, the birds nest on inaccessible ledges and are confident of their invulnerability. Consequently, the birds often appear almost indifferent to human onlookers; all you need is the common-sense not to approach the cliff edge too closely for your own safety.

On saltmarshes and estuaries, at their best in terms of numbers and variety of birds in the winter months, a different strategy is needed. The birds are often rather wary of human figures in this otherwise rather featureless landscape. Use the cover of bushes and hedges adjacent to the mudflats and keep low down. If you can interpret a tide-timetable with confidence, this can also be useful. Find a comfortable spot near the high-tide line and sit there on a rising tide. The water will gradually push the birds towards you and if you remain still, you will get excellent views.

When viewing mammals, remember that they have a keen sense of smell. Approach deer, for example, from a down-wind position and try to keep below the skyline if possible. With both mammals and birds, however, it is often just as much fun to look for their tracks, trails and signs. With some nocturnal animals, this may offer the only likelihood of detecting their presence in an area.

Tracking

Some of our larger mammals leave conspicuous tracks which can be readily identified when found along muddy paths. Roe deer, for example, leave neat slots made by their hooves. These are smaller but more regularly encountered than those of fallow deer; and red deer prints may be encountered as well. Beware of confusion with the tracks of domestic sheep.

Other commonly encountered tracks are those of rabbits, grey squirrels and foxes. The latter are superficially similar to those of dogs, so beware of possible confusion between the two. Badgers too leave broad prints in muddy soil. Follow their trails and you may find a badger latrine or tufts of hair caught in the lowest strand of a barbed wire fence. If you come across a badger sett, however, leave it well alone. Badgers desert their homes if disturbed by human scent.

Food remnants and other signs of feeding can also provide valuable clues to the inhabitants of the countryside, particularly those that are shy or unobtrusive. Mice, voles and squirrels all have distinctive ways of eating hazelnuts and acorns – the shape of the nibbled hole and the size of the teeth marks can tell you a great deal. Pine cones too are eaten in a variety of ways according to the species carrying out the nibbling.

Don't forget to keep an eye open for droppings and pellets, which are excellent clues to the other users of your path. The droppings of rabbits and deer are easily identified. Equally so are those of foxes, which are deposited in conspicuous places on paths and rides in order to advertise the boundaries of a territory.

Using Your Senses

While we identify things around us by sight, using our other senses – particularly smell and hearing – can provide vital information about

certain species. Bird calls are obvious examples where sounds can be diagnostic: with practise, most people can identify a reasonable number of our native birds by sound alone. Some insects, particularly grasshoppers and bush crickets, are also notable songsters.

The use of smell is normally associated with the identification of plants, both from the flowers and from scents derived from crushed leaves. It becomes particularly important in the identification of fungi – and the sickening aroma of the stinkhorn fungus in hedgerows and woodlands between May and October is not easily forgotten. The pungent, musky smell of foxes, used to mark territories, is another distinctive aroma of the country.

Animals have their different methods of opening conifer cones to reach the seeds within. Diagonally left from top right, these are pinecones nibbled by mice, woodpeckers, crossbills and a squirrel. The four spruce cones below (clockwise from bottom right) show the undamaged state, and evidence of squirrels, woodpeckers and crossbills.

Adults tend to take most notice of plants and animals at eye level, but as anyone who has taken a country walk with children will tell you, by paying less attention to other levels in the terrain, we miss all sorts of interesting things. Children are invariably better than adults at spotting interesting plants and animals at ground level, and it is worth training yourself to scan the ground at your feet as well as the tree canopy above. Ground level searching can be particularly fruitful on an autumn walk in woodland. Try lying on the ground and looking around for fungi – you will be amazed at how many more species and specimens you see at this level.

A few creatures leave clues which tell us about their homes. Lucky observers may find the round nests of harvest mice, woven out of shredded grasses and sited among meadow plants. Along the hedges, look for bramble leaves marked with white scribble marks: these are the homes of leaf miner caterpillars which actually live between the leaf surfaces. Logs and fallen branches on woodland floors are also good hunting places. Turn them over to find slugs, snails, woodlice and centipedes but remember to turn them back again when you have finished.

Walking for Pleasure

Walking in the countryside can be enjoyable at a variety of levels. A casual stroll through pleasant terrain can be restorative and relaxing – the ideal way to unwind after a busy working week. However, taking a more focused interest in the plants, animals and scenery along your route can add another dimension to your outdoor pursuits. Whichever walks you follow and whatever your interests, with an eye for natural history you will never get bored!

WALK 1

CORNWALL
SV903105

Isles of Scilly: A Scillonian Stroll

A delightful walk on St Mary's, the largest of the Scilly Isles, through quiet water meadows and on to a safe beach, then out to Peninnis Head with its fantastically shaped boulders. The walk can easily be included as part of a day-trip from the mainland.

Information

The walk is just over three miles long
Level on the inland section and moderately undulating on the coast
Some road walking on pavements
Café/restaurant at Old Town
Dogs are banned from Old Town beach and Porthcressa beach from May to September

START
Hugh Town is the main settlement on St Mary's. Start the walk from the top end of High Street by the Bishop and Wolf pub.

DIRECTIONS
Where the road forks in front of the pub, take left fork and keep left at the next fork by the telephone boxes. Walk along The Strand, past the Customs House on the left, and continue uphill past the school and on down the left-hand pavement of Telegraph Road. At the end of the houses after 250yds, at a junction with a side road to the left, cross the road and go over a broken stone stile onto a signed path through the Lower Moors Nature Reserve. Where the path leaves the Reserve (after about ½ mile) continue along a road between bungalows to Old Town. Cross the road to the beach.
From the far left (east) end of the beach go down slipway steps and follow the sandy track along the beach to pass the church. Climb rocks at end of beach onto the open cliff and follow the path. Explore the rocks of Carn Leh before continuing along the coast path, taking the lower left fork after about 500yds to reach Peninnis Lighthouse. The surrounding rocks include the large protruding flat rock known as Pulpit Rock. Continue along the coast path from the lighthouse for about ½ mile to Porthcressa Beach. The start point is reached by walking down the road that passes behind the information office and toilets on the beach front and then along Silver Street to High Street.

Birds Galore
Small islands are often a paradise for birds, but the Scilly Isles are very special. They are particularly famous as staging posts for migrating birds during spring and autumn, when rare species can sometimes be spotted. At all times of the year there are

What to look out for

There is a variety of birds to be seen in the Lower Moors reed beds, with a bird hide just off the path. The marine life of these islands is among the best in Britain, and at Old Town Beach there are a number of fascinating rock pools containing small fish like blennies as well as sea anemones, starfish, porcellain crabs and lots more.

Porth Cressa and Hugh Town from Peninnis Head

numerous seabirds including herring gulls, shags and oystercatchers with their distinctive black and white plumage and orange beaks. In Lower Moors there are snipe, moorhens and mallards. A notable feature of Scillonian birdlife is the remarkable tameness of resident songbirds such as the song thrush and robin.

Peninnis Rocks

The fantastically shaped granite rocks and headlands at Peninnis have been sculpted by wind and water. Though the hollows in the rocks are caused by rain water, which has slowly worn out the basin shapes over many centuries, local legends suggest they may have been created by Druids for blood sacrifices! Individual rocks in the area have wonderful names like Kettle and Pans, and Tooth Rock, while caves and inlets include Big and Little Jolly, Sleep's Abode and Izzicumpucca. Watch out for seabirds, such as gannets, flying past the headland.

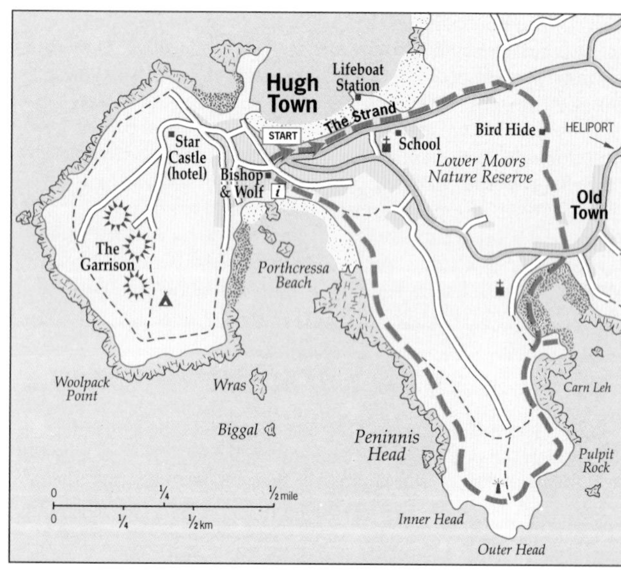

Crantock and The Rushy Green

WALK 2
CORNWALL
SW776606

This walk includes the wide open spaces of Crantock beach and its undulating dunes. The village of Crantock, with its many fine features, is also visited.

START
West Pentire is reached by turning off the A3075 just over a mile south of Newquay. There is a large car park.

DIRECTIONS
Down the road from the car park entrance turn left at the junction, signposted 'Vugga Cove'. Go through a gate just past some houses and follow the broad track. Bear sharp right and go through gate. At fork, go right and down over a stile. After about 50yds, descend a short flight of stone steps. Continue along the coast path and at a slight incline turn left and cross

Piper's Pool and Crantock Bay

Information

The walk is three miles long
Level most of the way but with one or two short inclines and one flight of steps
No road walking other than in Crantock and West Pentire villages
A few stiles to cross
Picnic on beach
Pubs and refreshments at Crantock and West Pentire
Seasonal toilets at Crantock beach; all year toilets at Crantock

below a putting green. After 100yds cross a granite stile and turn left at a fork to reach Pusey's Steps. The main path crosses a plank bridge then climbs the flight of steps (good views). Continue along the cliff-top path and round the impressive Piper's Pool. Continue along cliff path and over a stile. At the far bottom corner of a field, the adventurous can drop 20ft down a sand dune onto the beach; otherwise continue round to the right to reach the beach by a gentler slope. At the far end of the beach go up a wide break by a metal sign ('no river bathing') and down into the car park. Near the entrance on the right, by a National Trust marker, go up a path onto The Rushy Green. Follow a direct line across dunes aiming for a pink house with glass roof domes. To pass behind the house, follow a sandy path to a junction marked by two small fins of granite, then turn left through the zig-zag gate. At Boskenna House continue along the track (Green Lane). At road junction turn right into Crantock.
Retrace your steps to the pink house. Turn left at the junction by the zig-zag gate.

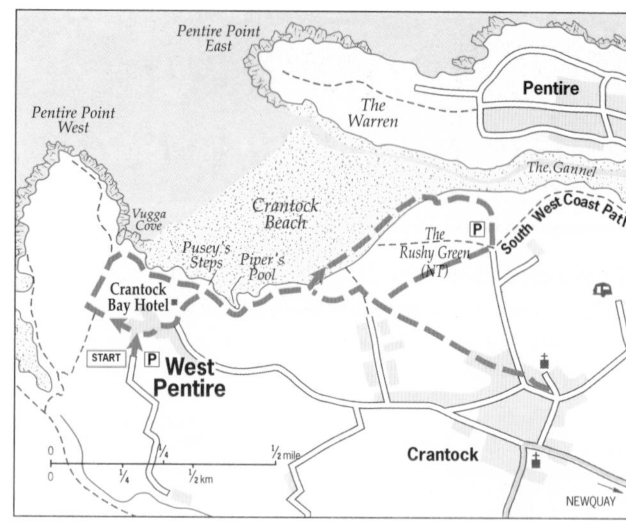

Continue to a second junction and turn right then immediately left. At the field edge turn right and follow the path round the field back past Piper's Pool. Turn left at a junction after Pusey's Steps and follow a surfaced path to the road by the Crantock Bay Hotel. Cross the road and turn right for the car park.

Pusey's Steps

This rocky access to the beach was reputedly used by a priest, Dr Pusey, who lived in the old Manor House at West Pentire, and who may well have been involved in the prolific smuggling which went on hereabouts. His ghost, said to be fairly active around dusk, is considered to be friendly!

Burnet rose

Crantock

This delightful old village was a major commercial centre and port long before Newquay developed. Schooners off-loaded just across the river, and barges would then transport the cargo for several miles up river. The Gannel is a lovely river but a dangerous one – warning notices against swimming should be heeded.

What to look out for

The Rushy Green has a mass of flowering plants typically found in sand dunes, including marram grass, sea stock and sea sandwort. In the centre of Crantock are a holy well and the charming Round Garden; behind the church find the old village stocks and learn about the resourceful wickedness of an 18th-century smuggler!

The Valency Valley

WALK 3
CORNWALL
SX101913

A woodland walk along the banks of the Valency River to the enchanting Minster Church, with quiet lanes and field paths on the return.

START

There is a large car park at Boscastle. The walk starts from its far end where a gate leads on to a grassy play and picnic area.

DIRECTIONS

Cross the play and picnic area to its far left-hand corner. Go through the kissing-gate, then follow the path alongside the river, passing through another two kissing-gates on the way. After ¾ mile go right, over a footbridge. A fairly steep path leads up to a welcome seat. Continue uphill, then bear right at a fork to reach Minster Church. After visiting the church go through a gate a the far side of the churchyard to the lane and turn right. Continue along the lane past a charming house on the left at Trecarne Gate. Halfway down the hill where the lane bends left, cross a stile into a field (signed 'Public Footpath'). Keep straight ahead into a second field. At its bottom left-hand corner go through a kissing-gate, then turn right to pass a duck pond beside a cottage.

Follow the track, bearing left at a fork, to where it comes out between houses onto High Street. (The Napoleon Inn is a short distance up to the left.) Turn right and go down High Street and the linking Fore Street, Dunn Street and Old Road and so back to the harbour and car park.

The Valency Valley

The Valency Valley is a wonderfully romantic place, made more so by its connections with Thomas Hardy, the novelist and poet. Hardy came as a young

This duck pond is towards the end of the walk

Information

The walk is two and a half miles long
Level walking for the first half, a steep section to the church, then mainly downhill
One stile to cross
Some quiet lanes to walk
Dogs should be kept on a lead for the short field section
Pub and toilets at the top of High Street, the lane leading back down to Boscastle

architect to assist in restoration work on St Juliot Church at the head of the valley in 1872. He fell in love with the vicar's young sister-in-law, Emma Gifford. They walked up and down the Valency Valley to Boscastle on numerous occasions and later married. Sadly the marriage proved unhappy, yet after his wife's death Hardy wrote many intense and bitter-sweet love poems about their idyllic days in the Boscastle area. Even the smallest incident was dwelt upon – the couple once lost a picnic tumbler in the stream and Hardy included this in a poem called *Under the Waterfall.*

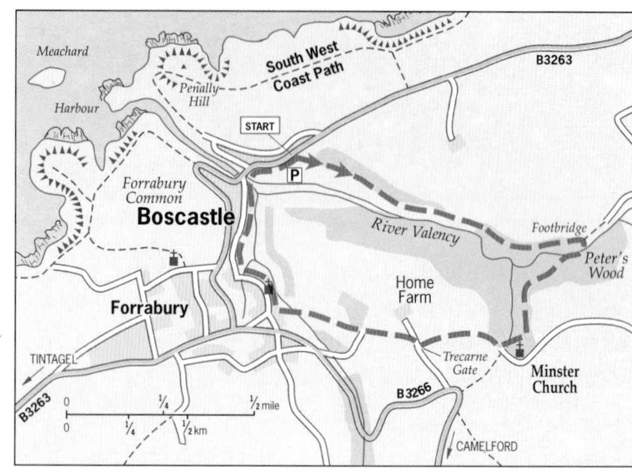

Boscastle's Minster Church

Minster Church
The handsome old church of St Merteriana, locked into its hillside amidst ash trees and sycamores, is splendidly isolated from any traditional settlement. It sits amidst a mosaic of daffodils and bluebells in spring. The site once housed a pre-Norman chapel, and then a 12th-century monastic priory. Minster has many fascinating details. Look for the famous scissors in the tower wall. There is no explanation for them, other than that they may have come from a more ancient building.

Wren

What to look out for

There are many woodland birds, including willow warblers and blackcaps during the summer. Grey wagtail and dippers are also present along the course of the river, and look out for butterflies. Peter's Wood, through which the path climbs to Minster Church, is predominently oak, with an abundance of woodland flowers such as dog mercury and lesser celandine.

WALK 4
DEVON
SS226247

Hartland Quay and Coast

Information

The walk is two and a half miles long
Mainly easy walking. There is a slight incline between Dyers Lookout and Stoke
Several stiles
Dogs should be on leads at start of walk
Good picnic area at Dyer's Lookout
Cream teas at Stoke during the season
Toilets at Stoke
Hartland Quay Hotel serves bar meals; children welcome
Small museum at Hartland Quay

START
From the A39 turn onto the B3248, signed Hartland. Pass through the villages of Hartland and Stoke, following signs for Hartland Quay. There is a car park just inside the toll-gate and this is where to start (other car parks lower down give easy access to the pub and museum).

A visually exciting walk from the dramatic headland of Hartland Quay to the quiet cove at Dyer's Lookout. The route then turns inland through woods and fields to Stoke village before returning to Hartland Quay.

DIRECTIONS
From the toll booth turn left, crossing a stile beside the Old Rocket House. Follow the coast path (keeping well in from the cliff edge) across open ground to pass a ruined building, keeping to the main footpath for approximately ¼ mile. Where the path descends to Dyer's Lookout bear inland, following 'Coast Path' signs. Go through a gate. Turn left, cross over a stile and cross the Abbey River to gain the track that curves round to the left above an isolated cottage. Go through a kissing-gate to reach a flat grassy area above the beach (short stony descent to the beach to right of an old bench looking seaward). Retrace your steps to cross the Abbey River. Turn inland along the public footpath and follow the tree-shaded path (can be muddy). Continue uphill alongside open fields. Just before the road turn sharp left over a stile and down a narrow path between hedges. Go through a gate and cross a stile, then go over another stile into the churchyard.
From the churchyard return to the field where the path from Dyer's Lookout joins from the north. Continue straight ahead along the left edge of the field to reach the car park.

Old Rocket House and the Pleasure House
The Old Rocket House was built in 1892 to house the wagon and rocket equipment of the newly formed Hartland Life Saving Apparatus Company. The team gave outstanding service during many shipwrecks on this notorious coast.

What to look out for

There are many seabirds such as gannets, guillemots and fulmars, to be seen offshore. Kestrels may often be seen hovering just above the cliff edge, and peregrines are not uncommon. Dyer's Lookout is a good place to look out for grey seals. In clear weather you should be able to see the island of Lundy which lies about ten miles north-north-west.

Dusk at Dyer's Lookout

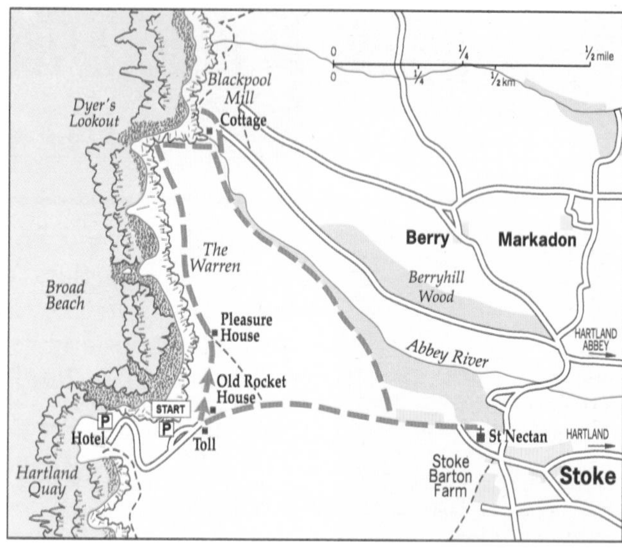

The roofless building just beyond the Rocket House is called the Pleasure House, believed to have been built as a summer house in the 18th century. The large archway is said to have been incorporated so that a coach could be backed inside. The cliff top between the Rocket House and Dyer's Lookout was a rabbit warren in the 19th century.

Church of St Nectan

The 128ft tower of this 14th-century church is one of the highest in Devon. St Nectan was a 5th-century Welsh saint and legend has it that one day, when he was out looking for his cattle, robbers attacked him and cut off his head. Undaunted, St Nectan tucked his head under his arm and walked the mile or so back to his holy well at Stoke, where he finally expired. The church and churchyard of St Nectan have many memorials to shipwrecked sailors. The western end of the graveyard is called Stranger's Hill and it is here that unidentified victims of shipwrecks lie buried.

The view from Dyer's Lookout, with Lundy on the horizon

Heddon's Mouth

WALK 5
DEVON
SS665482

A woodland and riverside walk to the lovely beach at Heddon's Mouth, with wildlife interest well maintained between the contrasting environments of oak woodland and seashore.

Information

The walk is two miles long
A straightforward and generally level walk along wide paths with some short inclines
Very short road section; care needed on corners
Good picnic area on river bank
Pub and café at Hunter's Inn
Toilets at Hunter's Inn Shop
Dogs must be kept on leads

START

All the roads to Hunter's Inn are single track with passing places, and include a 1 in 4 (25%) hill; great care needs to be taken. From Combe Martin, turn off to the north along a side road just before leaving the village; from Lynton turn north off the A39 at Martinhoe Cross.

DIRECTIONS

Follow the track to the right of the Hunter's Inn. Go through a gate and follow the path bearing left at a fork. At the next fork, just past a wooden seat, either path can be taken: the left branch leads above the river while the path to the right climbs slightly on its way through the woods before the two link up again at a footbridge. Cross the footbridge and turn right to follow the river downstream before passing through a gate; at the junction with another path turn right. The path again follows the river downstream to reach a grassy open space just before another footbridge. Continue along the left bank above the river to the old lime kiln. The beach is easily reached from here, but be aware of the tide and don't wander far. Return to the nearest bridge. Cross over and follow the path upstream over a stony section, to reach the higher bridge. Cross this second bridge, then pass through the gate. Turn left at the junction and follow the path. On reaching the road turn left

The valley of the River Heddon

The old lime kiln at Heddon's Mouth

and walk back towards Hunter's Inn.

Heddon's Mouth

There are few beaches along the wild North Devon coast and places like Heddon's Mouth have provided access to and from the sea for hundreds of years. The main trade was in coal and limestone, brought by ship from Wales for the kiln. Heddon's Mouth was also used by smugglers. The name Heddon comes from 'etin', the ancient name for giant.

Heddon's Mouth is in the joint ownership of the National Trust, Devon County Council and the Exmoor Society. The Exmoor Society was formed in 1958 after a successful campaign by lovers of the moor to prevent an area of the high moor called The Chains from becoming a conifer plantation.

Lime Kilns

The well-preserved lime kiln above Heddon's Mouth beach is typical of many round the Devon coast, many of them sited at coves and beaches where coal could be easily landed. Limestone was also brought in if there was no convenient local supply. The coal and limestone were burnt in layers utilising a simple draught system and the resulting lime was used by farmers to sweeten the acidic soil.

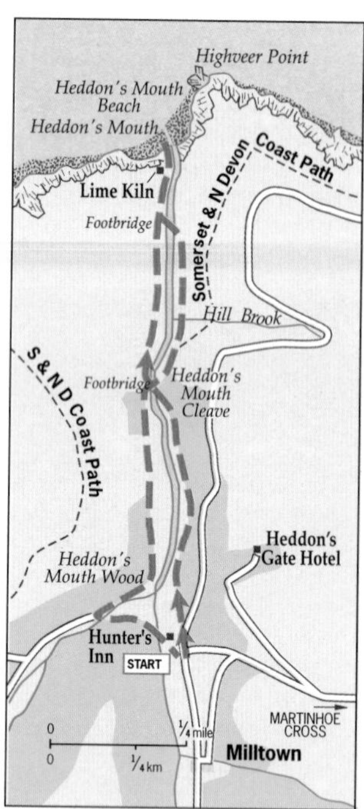

What to look out for

You cannot miss the handsome peacocks at Hunter's Inn and the woods are full of less exotic but still fascinating bird life.
Fast-moving dippers, with their distinctive white breasts, frequent the River Heddon.
Butterflies, such as pearl-bordered fritillaries, inhabit the woodlands, and look out along the coast for the stiff-winged fulmar, a rather gull-like seabird.

WALK 6
DEVON
SX828442

Slapton Ley Nature Ramble

This is a good wildlife walk through part of the Slapton Ley Nature Reserve, offering the opportunity to observe many interesting birds. Slapton Village has a quiet charm.

START
There is a large car park at the northern end of Slapton Ley on the A379, halfway along the shingle ridge.

DIRECTIONS
Cross the busy road at the northern entrance of the car park and turn right to join the path alongside the Ley. Turn left at the road leading inland to cross Slapton Bridge. Turn left through a gate into the Nature Reserve and take the path by the stone fishing hut.
Follow the path alongside the Ley over stiles and pass an old pillbox, later crossing over a 'tree' bridge. Keep on the path to a fork. Keep left and after about 100yds go

Information

The walk is just over two miles long
Easy walking with only one slight incline
Short road section through Slapton Village
Several stiles
Dogs must be kept on leads in Nature Reserve
Pubs in Slapton
Pleasant picnic spots alongside the inner Ley

A family of swans at Slapton Ley

What to look out for

Slapton Ley is host to thousands of birds, including huge flocks of gulls that often roost in the inner bay of the Ley. Buzzards may be seen circling above the woods and fields, and the grey heron is a regular feeder. Many smaller birds frequent the area: reed and sedge warblers sing from the reedbeds during summer, and kingfishers are year-round waterside residents. Wildfowl are abundant in winter. The waters of the marshy borders are ideal for insects like water boatmen and pond skaters, and several species of damselfly and dragonfly are present.

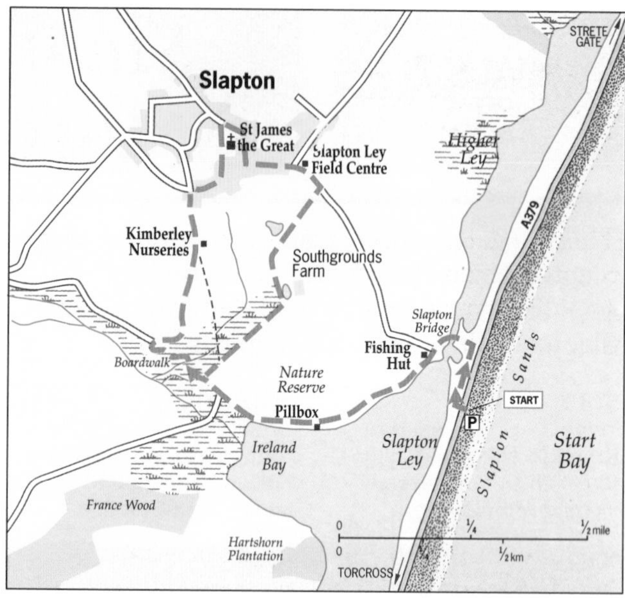

along a short boardwalk. Go over a stone stile. At a junction in an open area, bear right and follow the path through woods, turning left just before a gate and stile. Walk along a boardwalk through the reed beds and at the end turn right, signed 'Slapton Village', to go through fields, passing the Kimberley Nurseries before reaching a road. Turn right into Slapton Village, then turn left up a narrow lane leading to the church. Leave the churchyard by its top gate (pubs to left and right), go right, then left and up past the post office. Continue past the Slapton Ley Field Centre on your left, then turn right down a lane signed 'Southgrounds Farm'. Cross a stile on the right and follow a public footpath sign. After about 100yds go down past a fenced-in duck pond below the farmhouse with a lovely old dovecote on its far bank.

Turn right beyond the duck pond to reach a stile and the junction with the boardwalk section of the path. Continue directly ahead and retrace your steps alongside Slapton Ley to the car park.

Peaceful Slapton village was once a military training ground

Slapton Ley
This impressive lake, originally a bay of the sea, is now penned in by a huge shingle ridge which built up at the end of the last Ice Age between what are now Strete Gate and Torcross. Streams feed the Ley and its rich waters, reed beds and mud banks are valuable feeding grounds for migrating and over-wintering birds.

Slapton Village
During World War II Slapton Sands was used for training thousands of American soldiers in preparation for the Normandy Landings. Because of these exercises the village was evacuated until after the war, and many of the houses in the village now have rendered walls, hiding damage from the shelling. A simple obelisk on the edge of Slapton Sands commemorates the US troops who trained so hard here.

WALK 7
SOMERSET
SS864488

Exmoor: Porlock Bay

This is a varied walk, incorporating a village as well as seaside, marsh and woodland with lots of wildlife interest. On a clear day you can see as far as Wales.

START
Porlock Weir is two miles west of the A39 at Porlock. There is a large car park by the beach, opposite The Ship Inn.

DIRECTIONS
Take the road back towards Porlock. At the end of the railings descend the steps and turn right along the pebble beach (an alternative, easier path is soon reached behind the ridge). After a mile pass a memorial to 11 US airmen who died when their plane crashed on the marsh in 1942. Cross a stile and continue to a gate in the fence and sign for Porlock. Turn right and cross Porlock Marsh, entering the lane at the next gate.
Follow signposts, keeping to the edge of the fields (5 gates). Continue up the lane and turn right along Porlock High Street. At the end of the street turn up the road marked 'Toll Road', passing the Village Hall on the right.
After the last house turn right down the footpath, following signs 'Porlock Weir'. The path leads through woods then behind some beautiful gardens at West Porlock.
After 1½ miles, cross a stream, pass a hut, cross a minor road and turn left at the main road. Take the next left turn into Porlock Weir's back street; a right turn leads back to the car park.

The harbour at Porlock Weir

Information

The walk is just over four miles long
It is mostly level and dry; large beach pebbles require surefootedness
There are few stiles
Porlock has many cafés and pubs; the Ship Inn at Porlock Weir has tables outside and there is a tea shop
The harbour and beach are suitable for picnicking

Porlock Weir
The harbour was built along a natural creek and was mainly used by herring fishermen until the early 19th century, when it was enlarged and lock gates

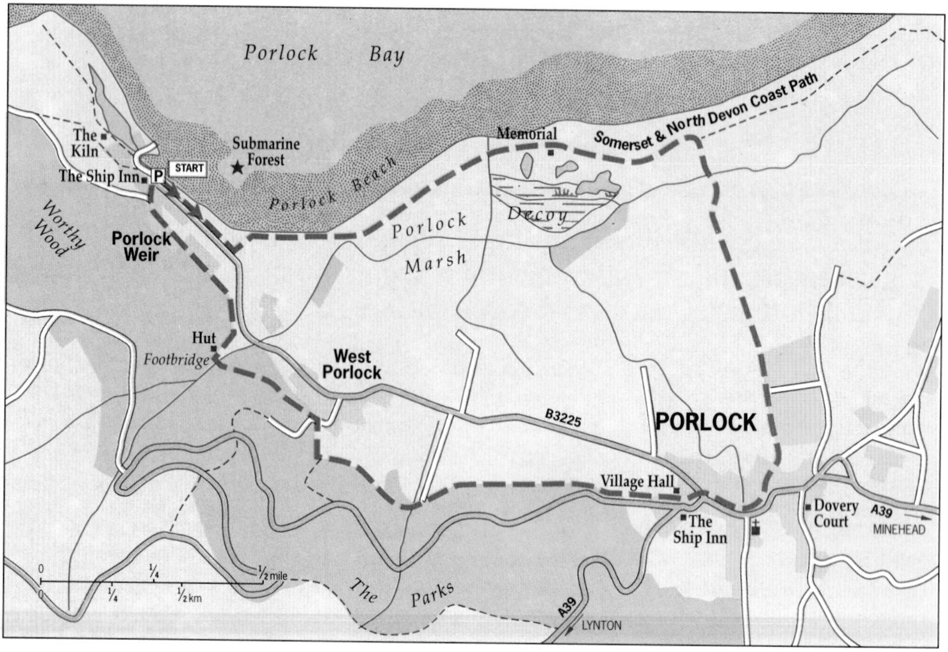

added. These held water in the harbour for cargo boats to be loaded at low tide. The gates are now mainly used to let water out at low tide to scour the channel through the pebble ridge. The harbour was intended for use as an ore port, but mainly exported livestock and tan bark from the surrounding woods. Coal and limestone were imported from South Wales for burning in the kiln, now converted into a house.

Porlock Marsh
In medieval times the bay extended inland as far as Porlock. As the pebble ridge built up and streams silted up behind it, the marsh was formed, though it has since been artificially drained. There was once a duck decoy here and wildfowling continues, as does reed cutting for thatch.

Porlock
This interesting village, with its thatched cottages, medieval manor house and church, is worth exploring. Southey wrote about the Ship Inn, and his brother-in-law, Coleridge, is said to have written part of *The Rhyme of the Ancient Mariner* there.

Curlew

What to look out for

Beachcombing is rewarding here, and the peat, clay and tree stumps of a submerged forest can be found just beyond the pebble ridge at low tide. The marsh usually has curlew, grey heron, shelduck and many other water birds in winter. It is a route for migrant birds such as swallows, wheatears, warblers, sandpipers and finches, which stop off to rest along the coast. The mixed woodland is home to a small herd of wild red deer.

Ham Hill

WALK 8
SOMERSET
ST479168

This walk is partly within a country park, with superb views over the surrounding countryside, and has the added attraction of a ruined priory.

Information

The walk is just over three miles long
Mostly level and dry, with a gradual climb at the end
A few stiles
Dogs should be kept on leads except on the hill
Pub with garden at start of walk; others in Stoke sub Hamdon
Ice cream van sometimes at top of Ham Hill Road
Picnic places on Ham Hill
Toilets near start of walk

START

Ham Hill is five miles west of Yeovil off the A3088, or eight miles east of Ilminster off the A303. Approaching from the Yeovil and Montacute direction, turn left along the High Street in Stoke sub Hamdon as signposted. At the top of the hill turn left again for the car park next to the Prince of Wales pub and Ranger's Office.

DIRECTIONS

Take the path on the far side of the pub, towards East Stoke and Montacute. Keep straight ahead, ignoring the waymarked left turn. Keep along the edge of the old quarry pits, veering left through scrub. Keep ahead where other paths join from the left and between overgrown quarries, following the kiln waymarks. Cross the road and take the path immediately opposite.

Pass above an old lime kiln and turn left into the car park, then take the next path left, signposted 'Ham Hill Road'. Keep right after the masonry works. By the road turn right through the gateway signposted 'Norton Covert' and left along the edge of the overgrown field.

Meadow buttercup

Cross the stile at the end (down to the left is the site of a deserted medieval village). Descend a few yards and take the next path up to the right, following the ditch between the hill fort embankments. Keep ahead for about ¼ mile, with a fence on the right for the last part. At the end of the fence there is a junction of paths. Turn left down a steep path through the trees. Turn right up the road, then left along the bridleway. Keep ahead through the gateway and through the field to the gate at the far end. Turn left down the pavement.

At High Street detour left then right down North Street for the Priory, 100yds on the left. Return to the High Street, turn left and continue for ½ mile, then turn right, signposted 'Ham Hill'. At the

What to look out for

The overgrown quarries provide a wonderful habitat for wild flowers and butterflies.
Elsewhere on the walk are meadows full of flowers, and the woods include many trees and shrubs, such as dogwood and the wayfaring tree.

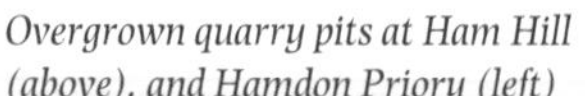

Overgrown quarry pits at Ham Hill (above), and Hamdon Priory (left)

end of the lane, cross the stile and follow the combe upwards. Take the stile ahead at the top, continuing ahead and taking the second right turn to return to the car park.

Ham Hill
Archaeological finds indicate that Ham Hill was settled from Neolithic times, and on its summit is the largest (200 acres) hill fort in Somerset, dating from the Bronze Age. The fort was occupied in the Iron Age, then the Romans took it over. The quarries date back to the Roman era, continuing in importance through Saxon and medieval times, only ceasing production during the present century.

Stoke sub Hamdon Priory
Now a National Trust property, the Priory was part of the manor of Stoke – five priests were retained here to pray for the lords of the manor and their friends. After the Dissolution it was plundered for building materials. Today the remains of several farm buildings and part of a hall can be visited.

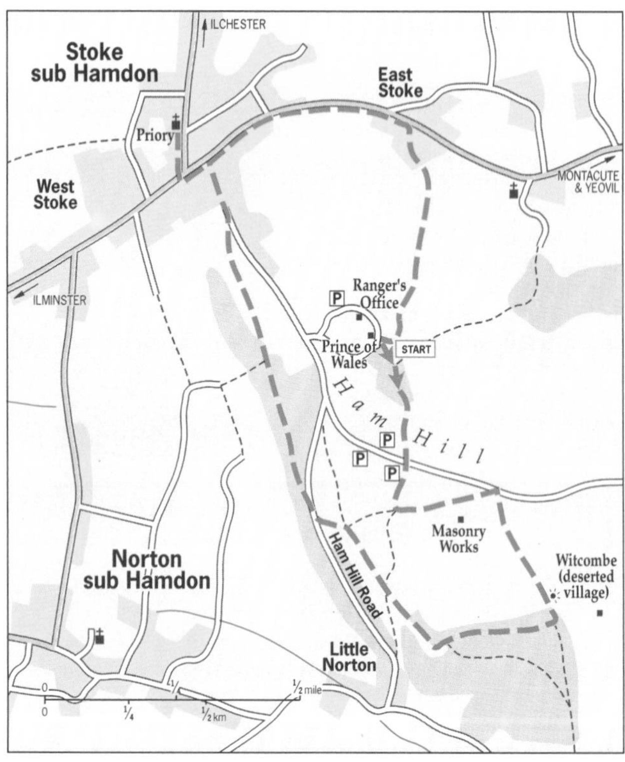

Minterne Magna and Dogbury Hill

The walk makes a gentle ascent of Dogbury Hill, with its woodland and earthwork remains, offering fine views of Blackmoor Vale and of Minterne House.

WALK 9
DORSET
ST 659043

Information

The walk is about two miles long
Fairly gentle ascent and descent of Dogbury Hill, otherwise level
No road walking
One stile
Picnic places in woods on Dogbury Hill
Pubs and cafés in nearby Cerne Abbas

START
Minterne Magna is on the A352, about nine miles north of Dorchester and ten miles south of Sherborne. There is parking opposite the church on the main road through the village.

DIRECTIONS
Cross the road and take the bridleway to the right of the church. Cross the ford by the stone bridge and follow the track round to two gateways. Go through the right-hand gate and start to climb. Shortly, go left through the blue, waymarked gate. Walk straight ahead and soon go through another gate. Follow the track, bearing slightly left, keeping parallel to the stream in the trees on the left. Go through another gate and aim for the grey roof visible ahead. At the house, turn back right, up the hill, aiming for the stile. Cross the stile and immediately go

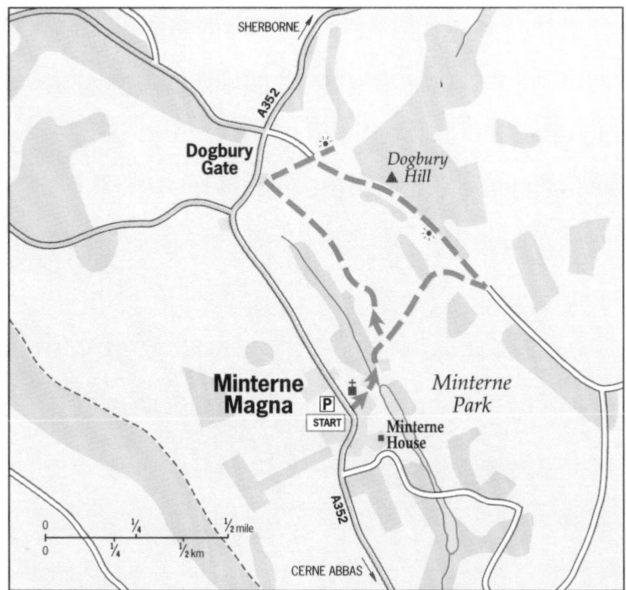

through another gate on to a track. Cross the track and go through a gate, then walk on for a few yards to get a magnificent view of Blackmoor Vale. Retrace your steps to the track and turn left.

Follow the broad track through Dogbury Camp, whose earthworks are hidden in the trees on either side. Continue on the track for just over ½ mile (views of Minterne House to the right).

Go through the second gate on the right, directly opposite a small gate, and double back to the right through a thistley field towards another gate. Go through this gate and head diagonally downhill to the left, to a small wooden gate and then yet another gate. The well-defined track then goes straight down through the field to another small wooden gate. Continue on down, joining the route near the start and retracing your steps to the car park.

What to look out for

In the woods on Dogbury Hill there are the embankments of an Iron Age camp (probably unfinished) which was one of many in the area.

Minterne House and Gardens
Minterne House is a splendid example of the work of Leonard Stokes, an architect of the Arts and Crafts movement, who built the mansion for the Digby family in 1904. The gardens had been landscaped with lakes, streams and cascades at the end of the 18th century, and are a fine setting for the outstanding collection of rhododendrons and rare plants and trees brought back from various late 19th- and early 20th-century expeditions to China and Tibet. The gardens are open daily (closed in winter).

The Cerne Giant
A mile or two down the A352 is the famously well-endowed, club-bearing and aggressively all-male hill figure – 180ft tall. Cut into the turf of the hillside about 1500 years ago, he is generally considered to be connected with ancient fertility rites. There is an excellent view of him from the lay-by at the turn-off to the village of Cerne Abbas.

Minterne House and its lovely landscaped gardens

Fontmell Down

WALK 10
DORSET
ST869185

Fontmell Down, in the care of The National Trust, is one of the most superb stretches of chalk downland left to us. In summer months walkers tread the carpet of wild flowers accompanied by myriad butterflies, and the views are magnificent. About half-way, the walk passes near Compton Abbas airfield, busy with light aircraft.

Information

The walk is three miles long
There is a fairly steep climb onto and down from the Down, otherwise reasonably level. Can be muddy
Road walking through the quiet village lanes
One stile
Tearooms in Compton Abbas, on the main road. Café and toilets at the airfield (open daily, all year). Pub and tea rooms in nearby Fontmell Magna

START
Compton Abbas is on the A350, three miles south of Shaftesbury. There is parking in the large pull-in on the east side of the A350, in front of the church.

DIRECTIONS
From the parking area, go carefully as if to turn right on to the main road, but immediately go up a few steps and through a small metal gate on to the grass beside the church hall. Keep left of the hall, follow the path through some trees and down some steps. Turn immediately right down a leafy track known as Watery Lane (a mass of snowdrops in February). Turn right at the junction for a few yards. At the footpath sign 'Gore Clump 1½m', turn left down a narrow footpath. At the gate at the end, follow the blue waymark and go straight up the right-hand side of the field and then left along the top of it, under the trees.

Go through gate by National Trust sign 'Fontmell Down' and follow broad track rising slightly to the right. This eventually leads to a gate and a stile. Ignore these and continue along edge of fence until second stile. Cross it and head diagonally left towards the signpost visible across the field. At the sign keep straight on to meet the road (good view on right), down into Longcombe Bottom.

(To visit the airfield, about 200yds distant, cross the road with care and follow the sign. Retrace your steps to this point.)

To continue on the walk, use the National Trust footpath

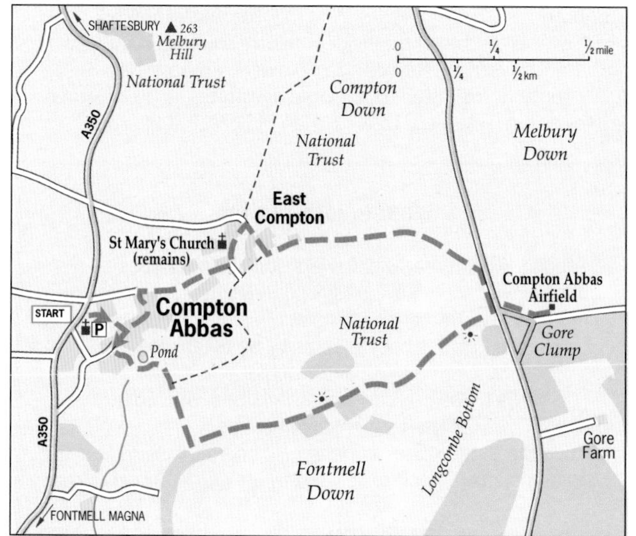

Fontmell Down overlooks the beautiful Blackmoor Vale

that runs along the west side of the road and emerge at a car park where there is an information board. Take the track at the far side of the car park, signed 'Not suitable for motors', and follow it steeply downhill. Eventually it becomes a road. Follow the road as it turns sharp right, with a track turning to the left. Keep on the road.

At a junction, turn left, immediately passing a farm with a dovecote on the right. Pass East Compton's old church tower in a graveyard, also on the right. Follow the road for some way, passing houses on the left, until reaching junction. Turn left, passing post box and follow the bend to the right. At the fork turn right into Watery Lane and retrace your steps to the start of the walk.

The Old Church, East Compton

The tower is all that remains of the 14th-century church. In 1906 the writer Frederick Treves described a pear tree blossoming on its summit and it was only when the tower needed restoration work in very recent years that the tree was removed to ensure the tower's safety. Nearby, among the gravestones, is the stump of an old preaching cross.

What to look out for

Around 90 different wild flowers and up to 25 species of butterfly typical of chalk grassland thrive here, including the characteristic chalkhill, common and small blues.

Field guides should certainly be taken in late spring and summer.

Birds to look out for include kestrels, buzzards, skylarks and yellowhammers.

Outside the gate to East Compton old church, look out for the stone mounting block once used by less agile horseriders.

Dancing Ledge

WALK 11
DORSET
SY999787

On one of Dorset's most beautiful stretches of coastline, the highlight of this walk is a very special place which is accessible only on foot – a broad, flat shelf of rock, left by quarrying and lapped by the sea.

Information

The walk is one and a half miles long
No road walking
A few stiles
About half the walk is on level ground, but the slope down to Dancing Ledge is fairly steep. Small children and the less agile may need help
Low tide is the best time to visit Dancing Ledge. For tide times telephone Swanage Tourist Information Centre – 0929 422885
The Ledge is ideal for picnicking
Coffee shop and pub in Langton Matravers

START

Langton Matravers is about one and a half miles west of Swanage. Turn down Durnford Drove, off the B3069 through the village, and go up the hill through the gate at the end, passing a large house, then through another gate and along a very rough, stony track to Spyway Barn car park (small charge), the start point for the walk.

DIRECTIONS

Study the map of the Dorset Heritage Coast, then go through the waymarked gate and head across the field to the gate and stone stile in the middle of the drystone wall. Cross the next field, go through the stone gateposts and down the slope towards the sea. In late spring and summer listen for the song of skylarks. On a clear day there are especially fine views westwards of one of the very best stretches of Dorset coast, towards the strip lynchets, or terraces, of St Aldhelm's Head.

Follow the track steeply downhill to meet the Dorset Coast Path at a group of three stiles. Cross either of the two stiles facing the sea and climb down to Dancing Ledge. Once you have exhausted its delights, climb back up to the stiles. Follow the sign 'Langton 1¼', heading up the hill to a stile visible in the gorse. At the top, at the waymarked sign 'Langton 1', follow the track with a wall on the right, Sea Spray House on the left and evidence of old

Dancing Ledge from the Dorset coast path

What to look out for

The limestone grassland is excellent in summer for flowers, butterflies and other insects, especially grasshoppers and bush crickets. Butterflies may include the Lulworth skipper, found only in this area. Guillemots and razorbills are among the sea birds which frequent the coast here and nest on the cliff ledges during the summer months. At Dancing Ledge the rock pools are full of life, and there are a number of huge ammonites embedded in the limestone. Sometimes abseilers can be seen descending the cliff and on the upper ledge there is a cave left by quarrying. The drystone walls and old quarries along the route make good fossil-hunting grounds. Dinosaur footprints may not be two-a-penny, but fish bones and sharks' teeth are within the bounds of possibility.

Just one way of getting down to Dancing Ledge

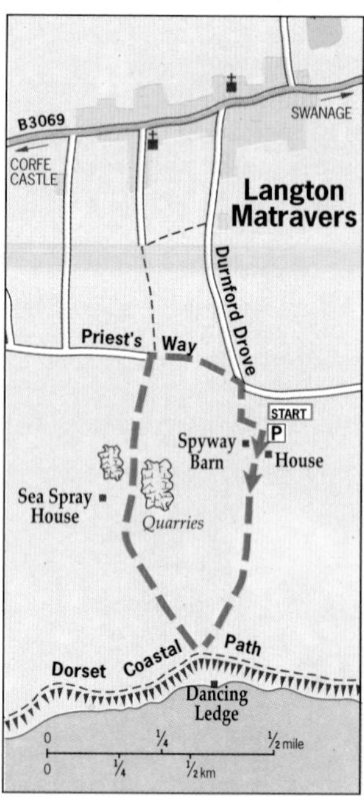

quarries on either side.
At a gate and stile, turn right on to the Priest's Way, a medieval trackway supposedly used by the priest from Worth Matravers on his way to take mass at the church in Swanage. Keep straight on, through a gate and stile by the National Trust 'Eastington' sign. At the junction with the track from the village to Spyway Barn, signed 'Langton' to the left and 'Dancing Ledge' to the right, turn right and return to the car park.

Quarrying at Dancing Ledge

The Isle of Purbeck has been extensively quarried over the centuries for its limestone, much in demand by architects for the construction of such grand buildings as St Paul's Cathedral in London and the closer Corfe Castle. Reminders of this industry remain all around the area, including a number of caves in the cliffs along this stretch of coast, such as Tilly Whim and Winspit. At Dancing Ledge, quarrying cut back the cliffs, leaving broad shelves or 'ledges'; the 'dancing' part of the name comes not from any human recreation here, but from the dancing action of the waves over the lower ledges at high tide.

WALK 12
WILTSHIRE
SU098719

Winterbourne Monkton

The steep climb up Windmill Hill can be very bracing on a windy day, but combined with a visit to Avebury, this walk will provide an interesting and rewarding day out.

Information

The walk is about three miles long
Level ground with just one gentle hill
A lot of stiles
No road walking
New Inn in Winterbourne Monkton has a garden with play equipment; also pub, restaurant and café in Avebury
Windmill Hill suitable for picnics

START

Winterbourne Monkton is a mile north of Avebury. On entering the village look for a turning to the left marked Manor Farm and Church. Follow the road through the farm, past the church. Immediately on the left next to the church is a concrete yard where you can park.

DIRECTIONS

Turn left out of the yard and on the corner turn right down a footpath which reaches a footbridge. (To visit the village of Winterbourne Monkton cross the bridge.) Continue straight on to the left of the footbridge over rough ground to reach a stile. Follow the direction of the arrow across the field to another stile. Do not cross this stile, but turn to the left and head for a stile with a signpost on the opposite side of the field. Cross this and drop down the bank on to a farm track and turn right. Continue along the track for about ¾ mile, passing a barn on the right, to a junction of several paths, then turn left. Reach a stile leading onto Windmill Hill. Head straight up to the top where there are fenced-off mounds (good views). Proceed in the same general direction, past the mounds, to leave the area over a stile behind the last mound. Continue until the path becomes a tarmac track at the bottom of the hill. Go

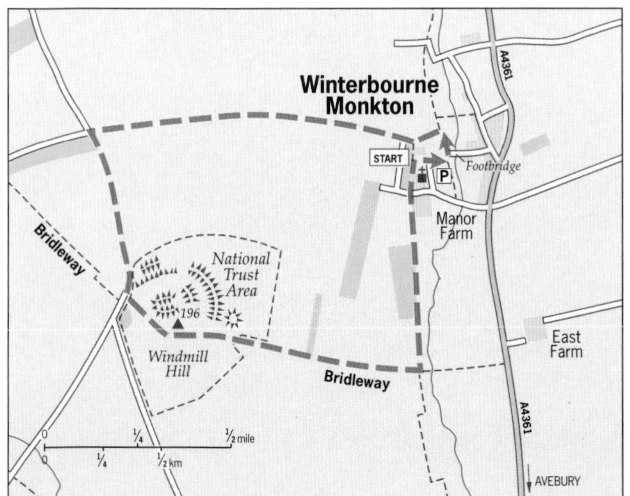

Skylark

through the gate and almost immediately turn left into a field. Cross the field and continue to follow the footpath signs, crossing over a further four stiles and muddy farm tracks. Pass the farm on your right and continue ahead to the road. Turn right to reach the car park.

What to look out for

On a clear day the stone circles of Avebury can be seen from the top of Windmill Hill. Listen for skylarks and watch for kestrels on your route.

Looking back along the walk from Windmill Hill

Windmill Hill

About 5,000 years ago Windmill Hill was occupied by a large Neolithic settlement and excavations of the site by Alexander Keiller in the 1920s yielded rich pickings. The vast amount of bones (human and animal), beads, pots, flint implements etc that were found in the ditches gave a clear picture of the community's way of life, and this is well documented in the Keiller Museum in Avebury. The 20 or so acres enclosed by three circles of ditches and banks are not in the care of the National Trust or English Heritage.

Avebury

A mile from the start of the walk lies the fascinating village of Avebury and a visit here before or after the walk provides enough of interest to fill the rest of the day easily. As well as the famous stones, there is Avebury Manor (National Trust) and the thatched Great Barn, housing a shop and the Museum of Wiltshire Folk Life. Displays here illustrate dairying and the work of the thatcher, saddler, shepherd and wheelwright. The Alexander Keiller Museum displays archaeological finds.

Malmesbury

WALK 13
WILTSHIRE
ST933875

This undemanding walk starts from the historic town of Malmesbury which, with its narrow, hilly streets, ancient stone buildings and numerous craft and antique shops, is a fascinating place to explore on foot.

Information

The walk is two miles long
Level, easy walking, apart from the steps leaving the town
A few stiles
Refreshment facilities in Malmesbury
Picnic site by weir, near station car park
Toilets in Malmesbury

START
Malmesbury is west of Swindon on the A429. Start the walk from the Station Road car park.

DIRECTIONS
From the car park follow the signpost to the town centre. Cross the River Avon and go up the steps at the back of the abbey then turn right into the abbey garden. Walk across to the far right corner by the Old Bell Hotel. Cross the road and turn left. Go underneath the large mirror and follow the lane. Turn right at the bottom of the steps and continue down the lane ('Burnivale') until the path opens into a wider lane. Here turn left down the lane towards the river and go over two bridges, passing the weir on the left. After crossing a metal stile turn almost immediately to the left, away from the river bank. Cross a small flat stone bridge and follow a clear path to the right to reach a farm lane. Turn left, pass a barn on the right, and continue ahead. Pass to the right of an old stone building and through the gate. Cut diagonally across the field to the tree in the top right-hand corner opposite. Cross the improvised stile to the right of this and head towards the big Dutch barn. Follow the diagonal path across to the farmyard. Go straight through the yard and turn sharp left down the farm road.
At the bottom go through the gate on the left and follow the path round the bottom of the field. Just before the old buildings passed earlier, turn right across a stile and turn left at the bottom of the field. Go through the gap at the bottom of the wall, over the stone slab bridge, and retrace your steps back up to the abbey and the car park.

Malmesbury
Built on a hill by the River Avon in Saxon times, Malmesbury is now officially recognised in the Guinness Book of Records as the oldest borough in England. At the

Fishing for tiddlers near the bridge

top of the town is the famous 12th-century abbey; only the nave remains today, but at one time it had a spire as high as St Paul's Cathedral.

To learn about the history of the town, visit the Athelstan Museum in Cross Hayes. There is a tourist information centre nearby.

Malmesbury is another Wiltshire town that has retained its blind house. In fact, there are two here – one on either side of the arched gateway leading from the market place into the abbey grounds.

The abbey at Malmesbury

What to look out for

Evidence of prisoners' desperate and futile attempts to escape can be seen in the scratched stone by the keyholes of one of the 'blind houses'.

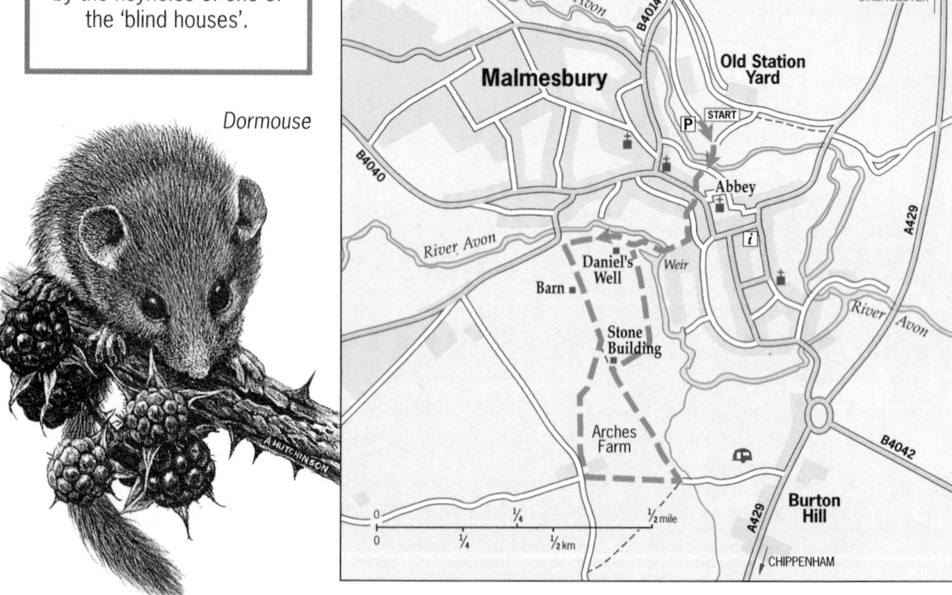

Dormouse

WALK 14
GLOUCESTERSHIRE
SO832086

Haresfield Beacon

This walk takes in two contrasting spurs of the Cotswold escarpment – the open aspect of the Shortwood spar, overlooking Standish Woods, and the narrow, steep Haresfield Beacon, almost craggy by comparison, offering far-reaching views across the Severn valley towards the Forest of Dean.

START
The Cripple Gate National Trust car park is situated two miles north of Stroud, accessible from the A4173 Gloucester road at Edge. From here travel south following the Haresfield Beacon signs.

DIRECTIONS
From the squeeze-stile, beside the National Trust information panel in the car park, follow the track south-west to the Topograph Viewpoint. Take track due north and just before reaching the wall, turn left down a woodland track parallel to the road.
At the foot of the incline cross a stile. Continue for about 20yds and fork left, following the wall/fence round and up to a stile. Keep to the wall at the foot of the steep Haresfield Beacon bank for about ½ mile. Eventually the path turns to the right and where you see a stile on the left, take the path slanting sharply right on to the tip of the ridge. A grass path climbs the ridge steadily through the light thorn scrub, ascending quite steeply to the beacon site and trig point via rampart ditches. Follow the southern rampart of the hill fort eastward to a stile. Join the fenced path beside a field (good views). Where the principal promontory fort ditch cuts across the neck of the ridge the path encounters a hunting-gate and wall squeeze-stile, then winds down through more broken ground to the road.
(To extend the walk turn left at the collection box,

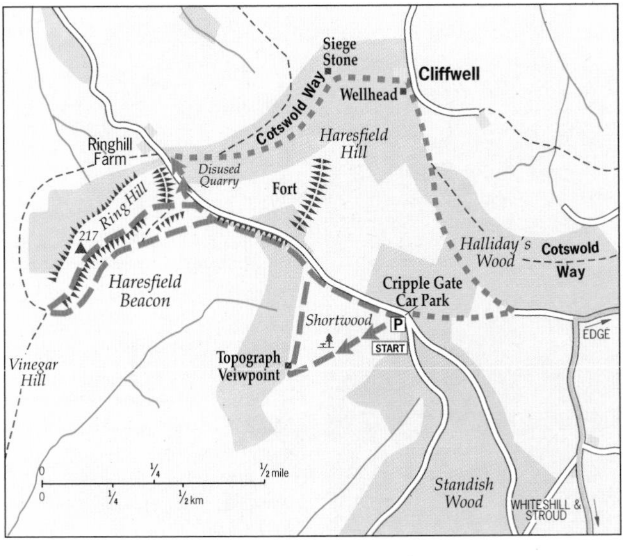

Information

The walk is two miles long, three with optional extension
Firm paths, with one brief, but steep ascent on to Haresfield Beacon
A few stiles
No road walking
Dogs must be on lead
Pub (Edgemoor Inn) on Cotswold Way, a quarter of a mile south of Edge on the A4173
Picnic places on grassy Shortwood spur

following the road as far as Ringhill Farm. At the farm turn right following 'Cotswold Way' signs. Continue along the path, passing the Siege Stone, dated 1643, commemorating the siege of Gloucester. On reaching the road and wellhead, turn right and continue along the road for about ½ mile. Turn right at the sign for Haresfield Beacon and return to the car park.)

What to look out for

There is much wildlife in the old scarpland, grassland and beechwood. Notable birds include wood warblers and spotted flycatchers in the woods, while skylarks prefer more open terrain. The occasional buzzard may be seen wheeling overhead. Look out for butterflies and wild orchids.

For the main walk bear immediately right down the steps next to the National Trust collection box, signposted 'Cotswold Way'; this path slants left and shortly rejoins the outward path, rising to the stile. Ascend the incline, maintaining course at the top and walking parallel to the wall over the Shortwood pasture to reach the car park.

Shortwood Topograph

This unusual relief plinth stands in the midst of three Cotswold escarpments of precious unimproved calcareous grassland and beech woodland. The view extends over Standish Woods, the twin towers of the de-commissioned Berkeley Nuclear Power Station, three loops of the Severn, the Forest of Dean and the Black Mountains.

Haresfield Beacon

At the 50-mile mid-point of the Cotswold Way between Chipping Campden and Bath, the Beacon is surmounted by Ring Hill camp and the old Ordnance Survey triangulation station, made obsolete now by satellite mapping. The narrow ridge bears the scars of many centuries of surface quarrying.

Haresfield Beacon is perfect for kite flying

Colne Valley

WALK 15
GLOUCESTERSHIRE
SP103077

The near perfect harmony of Cotswold villages within their landscape present a quintessentially English rural scene. Though the walk starts little more than a mile from the tourist rendezvous of Bibury, we find peace and beauty in full measure.

START
Ablington is a mile west of A433 at Bibury. Park safely and considerately in the village, then commence the walk at the old mill on the east side of the Coln bridge. Alternative parking is available at Swains Bridge at Coln Rogers.

DIRECTIONS
Follow the lane leading north-west beside attractive gardens overlooking the mill-stream, beyond a gate the track proceeds past kennels, swinging up round a walled enclosure. The track descends to a gate then runs directly across the side valley, rising to a gate. With drystone wall to the right, advance to a gate and enter Potlicker's Lane. From Lampits Farm this green track carries regular traffic. Meeting the minor road go forward finding a narrow path leading left by the grove and down into the valley. At the foot of the lane, beside the Village Hall, go right, crossing the broad Swains Bridge. At the road fork bear left, towards Lower Farm (Stratford Place Stud) and turn left, crossing the open gravel yard to the steps to the right of the barn. Pass along the bank above a drystone

Winson church, Saxon in parts, has some fine table tombs in its churchyard

Information

The walk is three and three quarter miles long
Gently undulating, but with muddy patches in wet conditions and one section overgrown with nettles in summer
Road walking only in villages
Dogs must be kept on leads
Several stiles and gates
Pubs and café at Bibury, ice cream at the Trout Farm, refreshment van regularly at Arlington Mill
Picnics in dry valley below Ablington Downs

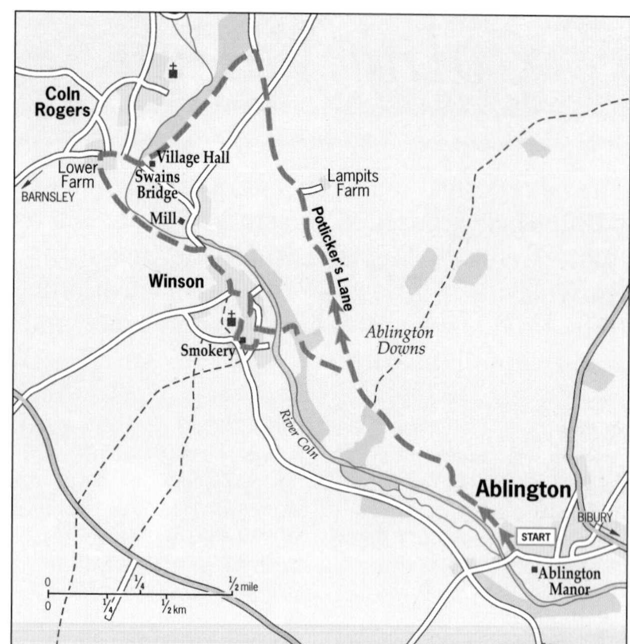

wall to a stile in the curve of the paddock fencing, proceed downwards via a gate and cross the low fence stile. Passing through the old hedge line, keep right upon the bank (ignore track to a gate beside Winson Mill) and continue above the mill to a gate, joining the road directly into Winson to your right. Go left at the road junction to the triangular green. Keep right, past the church, then left by the Coln Valley Fish and Game Company (the 'Smokery'), descending the narrow lane bearing left to find a white wicket gate on your right and concrete footpath marker. Cross the paddock to a second wicket gate, then cross the stile footbridge and go through the poplar grove, passing up through the larch plantation to a gate. Do not go through the gate, but bear right between conifers and fence to reach a gate/stile. Ascend the pasture, crossing to the far corner to a gate to rejoin the outward route at the Ablington Downs dry valley.

Cotswold Villages
Ablington has several classic Cotswold houses of which Ablington House, dating from 1650, must be pre-eminent. Its high pitched gables stand proudly behind a high drystone wall; the 19th-century stone lions came from the Houses of Parliament. Coln Rogers church, though not directly en route, is well worth a visit. It is almost unique in the Cotswolds in that it has a largely intact Saxon chancel and nave and its secluded, almost farmyard setting ensures that it retains its centuries old tranquillity. Winson is a compact village centred upon a small green which is dominated by the Georgian manor and the Saxon/Norman parish church. Notice the table tombs and old school house in the churchyard.

What to look out for

In the intriguingly named Potlicker's Lane you can judge the age of the hedgerow by the variety of woody species of tree, thorn and shrub that flourish within it. During the drive from Bibury notice the quaint signpost at the first junction in Ablington 'Bibury 4/3'.

Bourton-on-the-Water

WALK 16
GLOUCESTERSHIRE
SP170208

Information

The walk is three and three quarter miles long
Easy route and level walking, can be muddy after rain
Very little road walking
Excellent for dogs on leads
A large number of stiles and gates
A range of pubs and cafés in Bourton-on-the-Water
Plenty of picnic places

Common vole

A quiet country stroll incorporating a delightful village, pastureland, streams and tranquil lakes. Bourton-on-the-Water, known as the 'Venice of the Cotswolds', has a splendid array of visitor attractions, and no shortage of teas and ice cream.

START

Bourton-on-the-Water lies adjacent to the Fosse Way, five miles north of Northleach, three miles south of Stow-on-the-Wold. Start the walk from the large car park off Station Road.

DIRECTIONS

Follow Station Road north, branching right along Roman Way. Find the stone steps beside Woodlands House at the entrance to Moor Lane. Cross the stile into a pasture field, follow the hedge to a second stile then angle half-right across the marshy ground, crossing a wooden bridge to another stile. Follow the left-hand hedge to the stile and cross a farm track via a kissing-gate. Maintain company with the left-hand hedge via a stile and footbridges over branches of the River Dikler. Crossing a large pasture, pass through two gates and bear left via gates on to the road and turn right into Wyck Rissington. Follow the street, passing the pond and church. Directly after the last building on your right, where the tarmac road bends left, branch right to follow the track, bending right then left through two gates, for a distance of ¼ mile to reach a short pasture lane with an old hedge on the left. At the end go right through the gate, along the bridleway beside the left-hand hedge and along the field edges for ¼ mile. Shortly after a bend, pass through field gate on left, crossing pasture to a second gate, following the right-hand hedge to a metal gate into a field. Continue to a bridle-gate into the lane, going right towards Rissington Mill. Where the shingle track bears right, cross the stile on the left and after the subsequent kissing-gate pass between the garden wall and tennis court to a pair of footbridges across the Dikler. Bear right, initially beside the river, to cross the

What to look out for

In Wyck Rissington church see the carvings of Jester Irland in the porch and the discreet reference to composer Gustav Holst on the organ. Holst lived in the village for a short while in 1892–3, residing at Mace's Cottage (the first cottage on the right on the walk into the village).

Wyck Rissington church

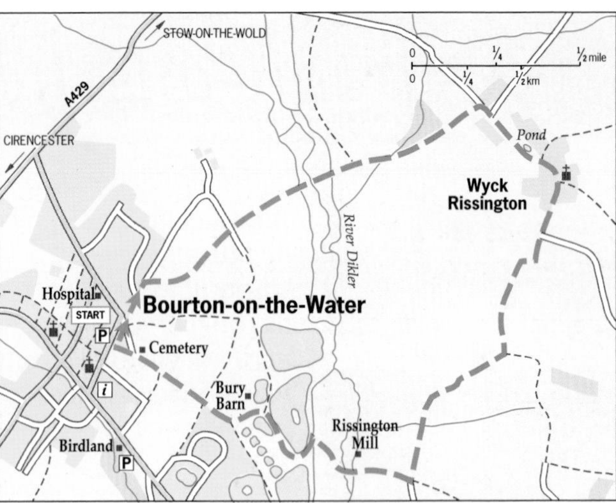

pasture half left to the stile, then cross the long pasture to a wicket gate. A confined path sweeps round beside the lake, and on reaching the lane junction go left to the gate and use the squeeze-gap beside the entrance to Bury Barn. Follow the lane, bearing right (ignore footpath sign) to pass Burghfields Cottage. Take the narrow footpath on your left (opposite the cemetery) to rejoin Station Road for the return to the car park.

Bourton-on-the-Water
This is a pretty village of Cotswold stone buildings and lawns sloping down to the River Windrush. Its many tourist attractions include a one-ninth size model of the village itself, an eight-acre bird garden, a motor museum and village life exhibition.

Wyck Rissington
This charming village has neat cottages picturesquely lining a tapering green. The duck pond has an old cart slipway where, as in Constable's *The Haywain*, wagons were drawn into the water to expand the wooden wheels to fit their metal rims more snugly.

The River Windrush at Bourton-on-the-Water

The River Yar

WALK 17
ISLE OF WIGHT
SZ353895

A walk round the estuary of the River Yar, rich in bird and plant life, also taking in fields, woodland and the route of the old railway line.

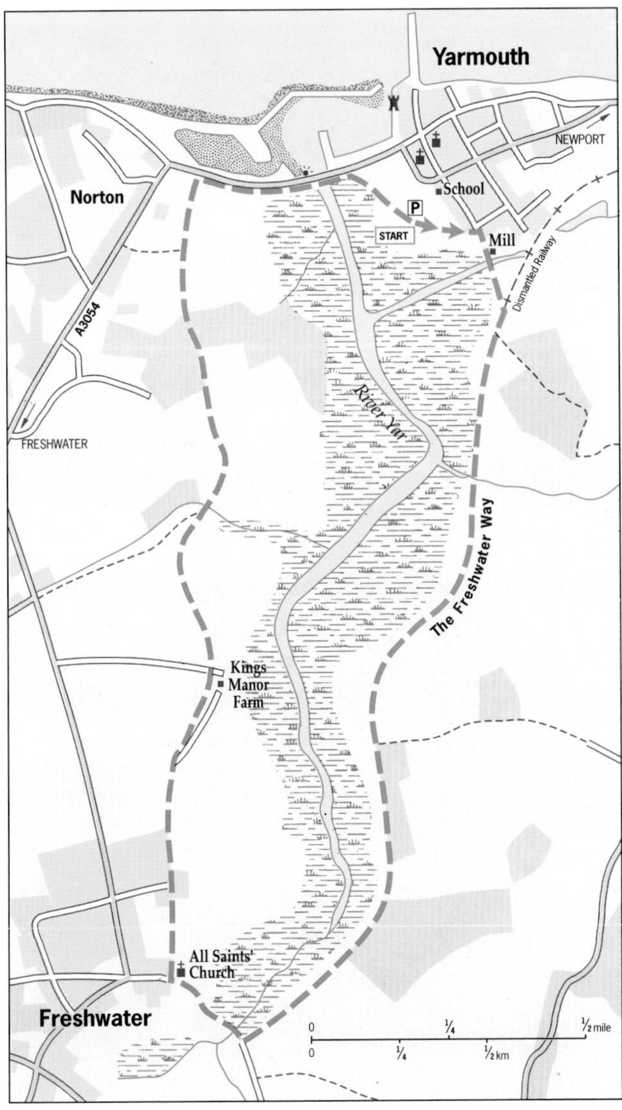

Information

The walk is four miles long
Mostly level ground, but parts can be muddy
A lot of stiles
Pub near the church in Old Freshwater; morning coffee and bar food
Seats along the old railway line and at All Saints' church
Picnic area at the end of the walk, with tables and benches

START
Yarmouth is in West Wight, on the A3054. Start from the large car park just south of the harbour, next to Yarmouth School.

DIRECTIONS
Take the gravelled path from the corner of the car park diagonally opposite the entrance. Walk past the old water mill to join the old railway line, turning right and walking down the side of the estuary for 1½ miles. At the causeway, turn right and walk along the road to All Saints' Church. Take the path between the churchyard and The White Cottage, and follow this path, crossing two stiles. Just before the farmyard, turn left over a double stile and cross the field to another stile and a kissing-gate, with the farm on your right. Walk past the entrance to Kings Manor, over a stile, and along

a farm track. This track rises gently and then falls: look for the path on the right signposted 'Yarmouth', and follow this through a field to a stile in the left-hand corner. Walk straight ahead to a narrow path which goes down through woodland to join a roadway.
Turn left and walk to the main road (A3054). Turn right across the Yar Bridge. Immediately after the bridge take the path to the right which leads you back to the car park.

What to look out for

The estuary is a rich feeding ground for wild birds. Look out for teal, wigeon, grey herons and waders during the winter; terns can be seen during the summer. As well as the birds,there is an abundance of plant life by the water and in the oak woodland. There are wild roses and honeysuckle in the summer, blackberries in the autumn. As you walk over the Yar Bridge, there is a fine view of the harbour and of Yarmouth Castle.

An Ancient Mill
The mill at Yarmouth was built to harness the power of the sea as the tide flowed in and out of the estuary. There has probably been a mill on this site since the time of the Domesday Book. The present mill was built in 1793 and the old sluice gates which controlled the water flowing in from Thorley Brook can still be seen.

A Poet's Family Grave
Alfred Lord Tennyson lived at Freshwater and his wife, Emily, is buried in the churchyard of All Saints' Church, together with other members of their family. The graves are at the eastern edge of this beautiful churchyard.

The old tide mill at Yarmouth Harbour

WALK 18
ISLE OF WIGHT
SZ637892

The Duver at St Helens

'Duver' is a local word, meaning a narrow sandy spit, and this walk begins and ends close to the beach. A fairly short walk, it has the added attraction of walking right across a harbour on the broad top of an old mill wall.

Yarrow

START
St Helens is four miles south-east of Ryde. The Duver lies at the eastern end of the village, off the B3330. The walk starts from the National Trust car park.

DIRECTIONS
Leave the car park and turn left along the roadway. On reaching the boatyard walk to the right across the grass and follow the raised gravel path along the edge of the harbour. Turn left across the old mill wall, continue round St Helens Mill and up Mill Road to the right, which climbs between caravans and houses to the village green. Turn right at the Green and follow the road to branch right and enter St Helens Common. The footpath back to The Duver is signposted right. Follow it down between the trees and across the footbridge back to the car park.

Information
The walk is one and a half miles long
One short section of the footpath is narrow and can be muddy – otherwise an easy route
No stiles
Café on the beach, a few yards from the end of the walk
The sand dunes of the Duver are ideal for picnics

On the Beach
A path leads from the car park directly to the beach, only a few yards away. Steps lead from the sea-wall down to the sand-and-pebble beach. Here there is a café for drinks and ices and an enchanting row of beach huts made from converted railway carriages. At the northern end of the beach is all that remains of the old church of St Helens. The tower appears intact from the land, but if you scramble round to the seaward side you will find only a flat brick wall, painted white to be a landmark for ships.

The harbour at Bembridge borders the early part of the walk

Walking Over the Water
The causeway across the harbour here was once a dam, used to control the flow of water for the old tide mill. As you walk over it, you can see the mill pools, and the gaps where the tide once flooded in to power the mill.

What to look out for

The Duver is a paradise for botanists, and is said to contain nearly one third of the plant species of the whole of the Isle of Wight. In June pink thrift is in bloom, while later in the year, the autumn squill raises slender purple spires. There are many butterflies – look out for the marbled white, the brown argus and the green hairstreak. The short, springy turf is kept neat by the large rabbit population, and benefits low-growing plants such as thyme.

Wilverley Inclosure, The New Forest

This walk follows one of the Forest's lesser-known woodland paths, ending up on an open plain, and is excellent for the whole family.

WALK 19
HAMPSHIRE
SU253006

START
Wilverley Inclosure lies immediately to the east of the A35, six miles south-west of Lyndhurst. The car park is on the eastern edge of the Inclosure, just off the Sway–Burley road.

DIRECTIONS
Go through the Inclosure gates and after about 20yds take the gravel 'drive' to the left, passing a marker post on the right. Shortly reach some recent birch/conifer planting on the left and notice ahead another green and yellow marker post. Fifteen yards before this post, turn right, going up at right angles, then veering slightly left alongside one of the fallen tree trunks. The way may not be very clear at first, but continue uphill, veering slightly right again and out into a glade of beech trees, with larches ahead. Head on through the left side of the glade and turn right onto a track that comes up from the left.
Negotiate two fallen tree trunks before reaching the bottom of the hill. Follow the

The path through Wilverley Inclosure

Information

The walk is two miles long, but can be shortened to one and a half miles or extended to three
Level walking except for one gentle hill
No road walking
No stiles, but there may be fallen tree trunks to cross
From the car park is a short trail for the physically disabled with seats *en route*
Plenty of picnic places
Toilets near Wilverley Plain car park

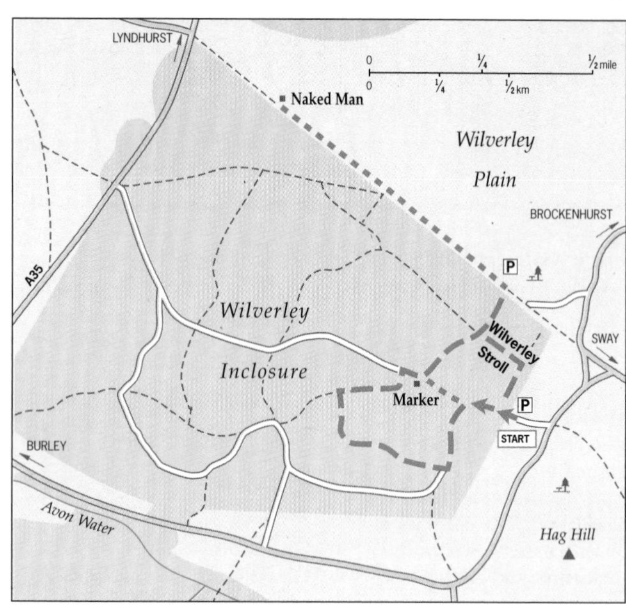

path up again and where it appears to divide at a beech tree, stick to the most obvious path, bearing right through another glade. At a junction, turn right and at the gravel drive turn right again. An information panel here describes the Forestry Commission's conservation practices. Shortly, where another drive joins from the left, note the Victorian Wilverley Inclosure marker. To take the shortest option, continue straight on from here to reach the car park in about 300yds.

To continue to Wilverley Plain, go left along the joining drive to the edge of the Inclosure and out through the gate.

(To see the 'Naked Man' described below, turn left here and follow the edge of the Inclosure for just over ½ mile. Retrace your steps to the gate.)

To return to the car park go back through the gate and take the first track to the left. Turn right at the T-junction for the few yards back to the car park.

The Ancient Forest

Wilverley's 500 acres were first enclosed for tree planting in 1775, when naval shipbuilders needed the oak from 60 acres of trees to construct one large warship. Nowadays, the production of timber remains the Forestry Commission's main concern, but some local residents still have ancient 'Commoners' rights'. These include the grazing of animals and the collection of firewood – you may well see stacks of this 'Assignment Fuelwood'.

The Naked Man

The New Forest provided first-rate cover for smugglers bringing their illicit cargo in from the sea, but sometimes they were caught and punishment was harsh. The Naked Man is a tree stump, all that now survives of a tree from which many a smuggler and highwayman was hanged.

What to look out for

This is one of the best places in the New Forest for fungi in the autumn. Keep an eye open too for wood ants' nests, which may be several feet across. There are often wild ponies around the edges of the Inclosure, and buzzards wheel overhead.

Selborne Common and Romany Workshop

WALK 20
HAMPSHIRE
SU742335

Information

The walk is about two and a quarter miles long
The Zig-Zag is fairly demanding
200 yards of pavement walking
No stiles
Picnic places en route
Pub with children's play area, tea rooms and restaurant in village
Toilets in car park

The Zig-Zag path up the steep side of Selborne Hill makes an adventurous start and finish to the walk and up on the Common are the trees, flowers, birds and butterflies that Gilbert White wrote about in his *Natural History of Selborne.*

START
Selborne is about three miles south-east of Alton on the B3006. There is a car park behind the Selborne Arms on the main road through the village.

DIRECTIONS
Follow the path near the entrance to the car park signposted 'Footpath to Zig-Zag and The Hanger'. Go through a kissing-gate and left to start the climb up the Zig-Zag. Pause now and then to admire the view of the village and the surrounding countryside that opens up as you climb; there is a bench between the 18th and 19th bends, and at the top turn left to find another one.

Turn right around the back of the bench on to a track and keep straight on, ignoring another track off to the left. After a while the woods open out and the grassy Common lies to the right of the path. Diagonally opposite there is a pond once used by grazing cattle – to see it, keep on the main path until it veers to the left and is joined by a track from the right. Take this track, heading for a silver birch, behind which lies the pond.

Retrace your steps to the original path and turn right. The trees close in here. At a four-way crossing of paths with a signpost, go left for a few yards to another four-way signpost. Go left again on a wide track, following the sign 'Selborne via Church Path'. Down in the woody area to the right are badger setts.

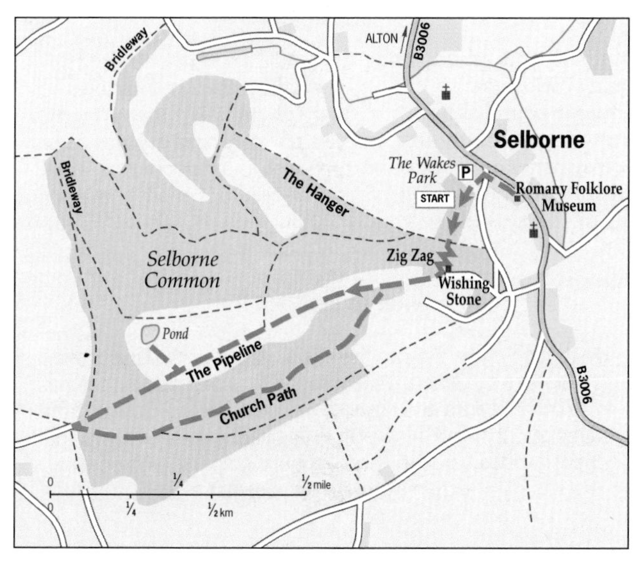

The view over Selborne village from The Hanger

Eventually the wide track comes to an end beside a beech tree. Take the path to the left of the tree, and turn right shortly afterwards to retrace your steps to the top of the Zig-Zag.

Go back down the Zig-Zag and return to the car park entrance, then cross the lane and meet the main road through the village.

Turn right to walk along the pavement for 100yds to see the unique Romany Folklore Museum and Workshop.

Retrace your steps to return to the village centre and the car park.

Romany Folklore Museum and Workshop

Peter Ingram has been restoring and decorating gypsy caravans for over 30 years, and there are always living-wagons in various stages of repair to see. The little museum illustrates traditional Romany life, and the shop sells gypsy crafts as well as lucky charms. The museum is open most days, but to check, tel: 042050 486.

What to look out for

At the top of the Zig-Zag there is a Sarsen or Wishing Stone, placed there by Gilbert White who, with his brother, cut the path in 1753. The flora and fauna of Selborne Hill and Common are especially rich, and it is worth taking field guides with you. The beechwoods harbour wood warblers in spring, and boast a harvest of fungi in autumn.

WALK 21
SUSSEX
SU815126

Kingley Vale

Information

The main walk is four and a half miles long
One long, well graded climb on to Bow Hill
All on clear tracks, except half a mile along a quiet country lane
Muddy in places, but generally well drained chalk
Pub with garden in Stoughton village

Brown hare

From a downland vale this walk climbs gently through woodland to one of the finest viewpoints on the Sussex Downs, then down through the ancient yew forest of Kingley Vale.

START
Park at the Forestry Commission car park and picnic area beside a sharp bend in the unclassified road linking Walderton and East Marden, about a mile north-east of Stoughton. Easiest access by car is from the B2146, Chichester-to-South Harting road, about two miles north of Funtington.

DIRECTIONS
Start the walk from the car park through a double gate and along a roughly metalled Forestry Commission track, heading north-east, with woodland to your right. After ¼ mile keep on main track and go round to the right. After another ¼ mile, at a fork where the main track bears left, go straight ahead, still on a roughly metalled track which soon narrows and begins to climb through thick woodland.
At the point where the track comes out into the open, go straight ahead, now with woods to your left and a wide view along the valley towards Stoughton on your right. In about 100yds fork left on a narrower path through mixed woodland and scrub.
After ¼ mile turn right along a gently descending path through scrub. At a T-junction with a wider track, turn left, still through woodland, mainly mixed beech and yew. After a further ½ mile emerge onto Bow Hill, crowned by four prominent Bronze Age barrows.
(To extend the walk down into Kingley Vale, you can pick up the nature trail, marked by green posts, on the other side of the barrows.)
The main walk follows the track, passing to the right of the barrows. Go forward between mixed yew and scrub, soon on a broad woodland ride (can be muddy). Where the wood ends, turn right at a T-junction and follow a clear track for almost a mile down to the lane at Stoughton.
Turn right through the

What to look out for

A viewing table on Bow Hill provides a guide to the exceptional views which can be enjoyed from this 676ft summit. To the north, various points on the Downs are clearly identifiable, including Butser Hill and Beacon Hill. To the south there is a wide prospect across Chichester Harbour to the Isle of Wight, with the spire of Chichester cathedral prominent in the foreground. Open areas of ground in the brooding yew forest are rich in downland flowers and butterflies.

The village of Stoughton from the track on Bow Hill

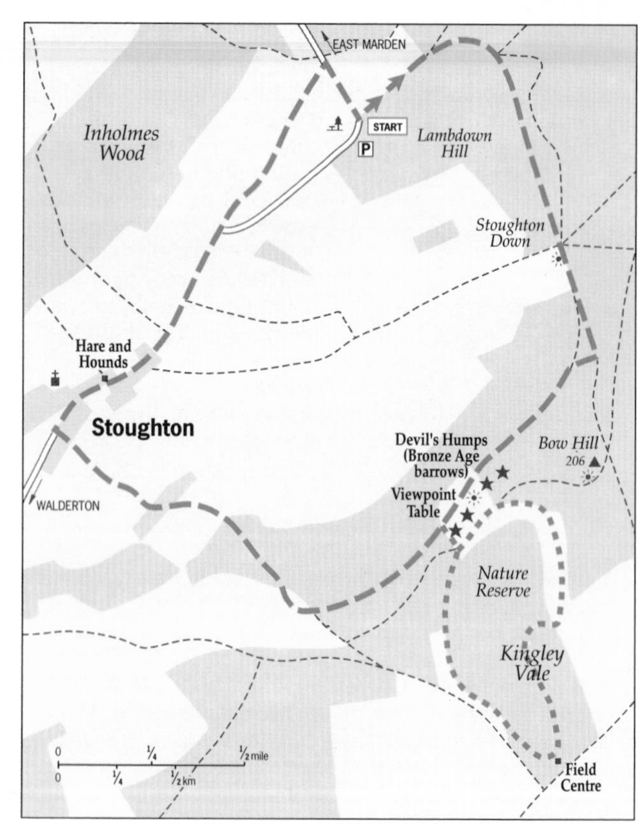

village, passing the church and the Hare and Hounds pub, both on the left.
The car park is now a mile away up the valley. Follow the lane at first, where it bends to the right, go ahead over a stile and beside a hedge on your left. After ½ mile rejoin the lane and turn right for the car park.

Kingley Vale
Kingley Vale is a National Nature Reserve, notable for what has been described as the 'finest yew forest in Europe' with many specimens more than 500 years old. Over 50 species of bird breed within the reserve and, during the spring and summer, a wide variety of wild flowers can be seen, especially in open areas of chalk downland.

Barcombe Mills and the River Ouse

WALK 22

SUSSEX
TQ434147

This is an easy stroll along the banks of the Sussex Ouse, with an opportunity to extend the journey further upstream, either on foot or by hiring a rowing boat at the Anchor Inn.

START
Barcombe Mills can be reached along a lane from the A26 about three miles north of Lewes. There is a large signposted grass car park (may not always be open).

DIRECTIONS
From the entrance to the car park, turn right. In a few yards fork right along a drive at 'No entry for vehicles' sign. In 25yds, just before Pikes Bridge, turn right through a squeeze-stile. After 180yds go left over a stile/footbridge and continue forwards along the right bank of the Ouse. After another 300yds go forward over a stile and across a concrete outflow platform by a pumping station, then walk on with the river on your left and the reservoir bank on your right.
After 300yds turn left over the next bridge and bear left along the river bank for 350yds. Cross a stile by a farm gate and go over bridge. Squeeze past gate and turn right into a farm track. In about 50yds turn right between houses, following a footpath sign along a narrow path through trees. After about 100yds go over stile by a pillbox to rejoin the Ouse, now on your right, and keep to the river bank for ¼ mile. Cross over stile by weir and proceed towards the Anchor Inn.
(From here it is possible to extend the walk along the Ouse, either on foot or by rowing boat, to Isfield and beyond.)
Retrace your steps from the Anchor Inn to bridge by which you crossed the river. Do not re-cross the bridge but continue along the farm track with the Ouse on your left at first. The track leads back to Barçombe Mills. At Mill Farm, a few yards beyond a green gate, turn left down a track in between houses.
(At the next junction, a right turn leads to the Angler's Rest pub and the tea room, restaurant and shop at the old Barcombe Mills railway station. Return by the same pathway.)
To complete the walk, keep

What to look out for

The station buildings at Barcombe Mills, although extensively converted, still retain several old railway notices.
On either side of Pikes Bridge, the brick bridge over the old canal, two former locks have been converted to fish ladders to allow sea trout to pass upstream.

Information

The walk is about three miles long
Completely level, easy walking
No road walking
Several stiles and one gate, which may be padlocked
Pub (Anchor Inn) half way round the walk; another at Barcombe Mills Station, where there is also a tea room and restaurant
Picnics discouraged along the river bank

Goldeneye

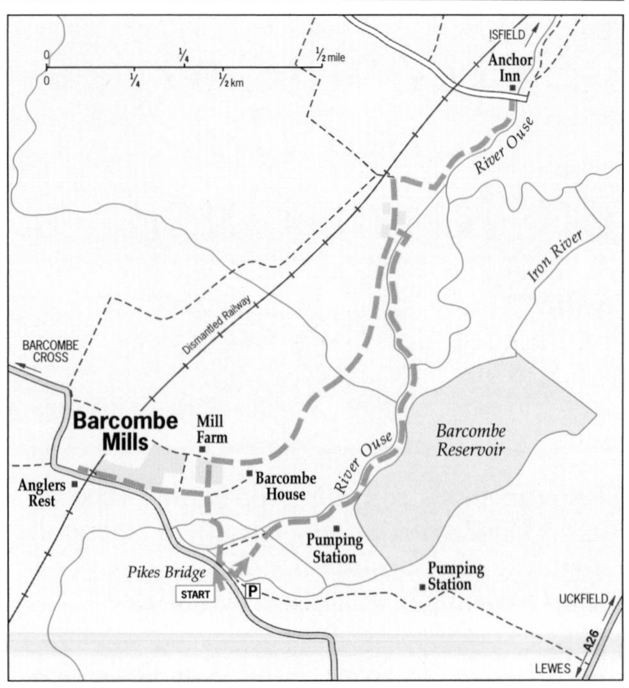

straight ahead past another 'No vehicles' sign. At the gateway to Barcombe House the track crosses, in quick succession, a side stream, the main river, passing the site of the mill, then another stream next to a large trout pool and a weir, before crossing Pikes Bridge to rejoin the outgoing route.

Barcombe Mills

The Domesday Book records a flour mill at Barcombe Mills, but the most recent mill, built in 1870, was burned down just before World War II. Today a grassy mound and two millstones mark the spot. The road past the mill was owned by the miller, who charged one shilling for a carriage and horse, sixpence for two wheels and one horse, one shilling for motor cars and two shillings for steam engines. The sign detailing these charges can still be seen.

The Anchor Inn on the River Ouse

Ashdown Forest

WALK 23
SUSSEX
TQ471325

Through the landscape described by A A Milne in the Winnie-the-Pooh books for children, this walk visits the 'Enchanted Place' described in *The House at Pooh Corner*, climbs gently through Five Hundred Acre Wood, and goes on to 'Pooh Sticks Bridge'.

Information

The walk is three and a half miles long, with a half-mile optional extension to Pooh Sticks Bridge
Most of the walk crosses Ashdown Forest, much of it on open heathland
Several stiles and a couple of gates
No refreshments but plenty of picnic spots

START
Park in the Wren's Warren forest car park to the west of the B2026 about two and a half miles south of Hartfield.

DIRECTIONS
Cross a low wooden barrier in the far left corner of the car park, go forward for a few feet and turn right along a wide forest track.
After about 500yds fork left past some houses to join a lane. Turn left, and shortly, at a road junction, go right. In front of the gateway to Andbell House turn right between staggered rails and along a woodland track.
(To visit Pooh Sticks Bridge, continue along lane past Andbell House and in a few yards turn right along the public bridleway [very muddy] to the bridge. Return the same way.)
After 200yds along the woodland track, turn left along a small unmarked path. Shortly leave the wood via a wooden gate, and cross a meadow to re-enter woodland in the bottom left corner of the field. Walk through the wood, cross a stile then go ahead along the side of the field to the far corner. Cross a stile and go through gate, then walk up a track with woodland on the left. At the junction, go ahead over a stile, and through a small gate to cross a paddock. Go througfh a second gate and cross another stile by a hedge, to reach the B2026. Cross road and follow footpath to descend between banks to a stream. Cross over narrow earth bridge and after another 500yds turn sharply right on the

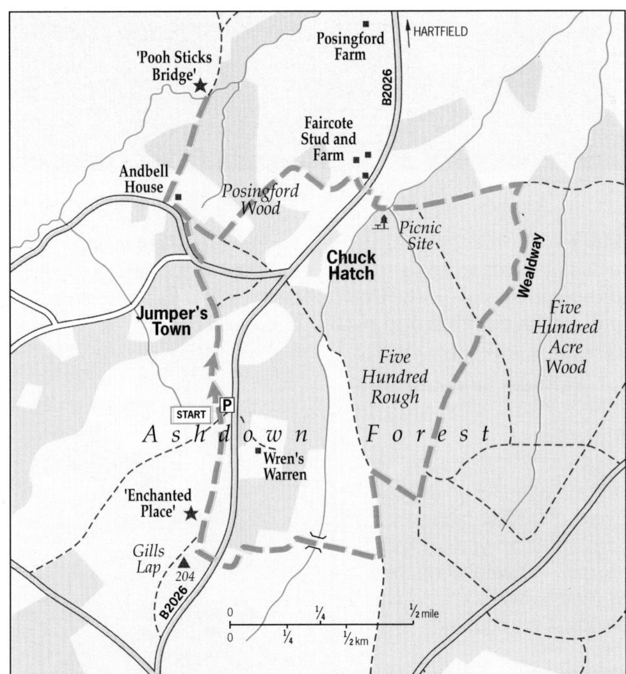

Wealdway, marked by yellow arrows and then wooden posts as it climbs through Five Hundred Acre Wood. Make sure you go through the gateway past a stile.

After about ¾ mile, in a grove of beech trees, turn sharply back to the right on a well-worn, descending path. At a T-junction with a forest ride, with buildings of Wren's Warren across the valley ahead, turn left on a ride across open forest.

After another 300yds or so, turn right on a ride which crosses a valley and climbs towards Gill's Lap. Towards the top, bear left with the ride and, after 100yds, turn right along a narrow path out to the road.

Go through the 'Quarry' car park, almost opposite. Leave the car park over a plank bridge in the right corner. Go forward beside the quarry to join another ride. Turn right and descend (to the left of the track is the site of A A Milne's 'Enchanted Place').

Continue downhill to return to the car park.

The original Pooh Sticks Bridge in Ashdown Forest

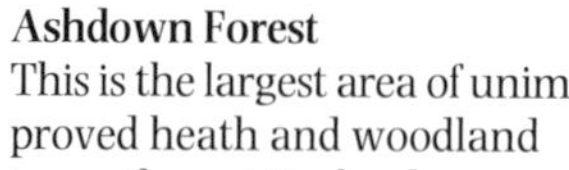

Ashdown Forest

This is the largest area of unimproved heath and woodland in south-east England, covering over 6,000 acres. Much of the ancient woodland was felled to provide charcoal for the iron industry in the 16th and 17th centuries, leaving extensive open areas of gorse and heather with scattered clumps of trees. Timid fallow deer, foxes and badgers thrive here, but are rarely seen by day.

What to look out for

Gorse, heather and bracken predominate on the open heath, with thinly scattered Scots pine and silver birch. Beside the stream in Wren's Warren Bottom you will find mosses, ferns and liverwort. Look out for hovering kestrels, stonechats perched on the gorse, and butterflies, including the silver studded blue, amongst the heather.

White clover

Hastings

WALK 24
SUSSEX
TQ860117

This walk, fairly strenuous but full of variety and interest, lies entirely within the Hastings Country Park, an attractive 580-acre area of undeveloped coastline.

START
The Hastings Country Park lies to the south of the unclassified road linking Ore, east of Hastings, with Fairlight and Fairlight Cove. Park in one of the two main car parks, signposted from the road, near Fairlight church.

DIRECTIONS
From the car park, head for the sea, passing to the left of a row of coastguard cottages.

On nearing the cliff edge, turn right at bollard 14. The path soon descends into Warren Glen, veering inland, with a fine panorama of the low cliffs spread out ahead.

Towards the bottom of the hill, turn left down a flight of steps, and head towards the sea along the floor of the glen. Cross a stream and climb steeply.

At the top of the hill reach bollard 13. For the shorter walk omitting Fairlight Glen, turn right here, along the edge of a wood (directions continue at * below).

For the full walk, go half right, up a flight of steps.

At the top, cross an open area, past bollard 12, keeping a fence on your right, and descend more steps. At bollard 11, turn left and walk seawards. (At the bottom of the hill, a path to the left provides a detour, descending steeply through an area of bare, crumbling cliff to a pebbly beach. Return the same way.)

Continue along the coastal path, going straight on at bollard 10. About two thirds of the way up the hill, turn

Information

The full walk is just over three miles; the shorter version is one and a quarter miles
Several steep climbs and descents, aided by steps; the shorter route eliminates the toughest section
No road walking
A few stiles and a gate
Café behind main car park near Fairlight church
Large grassy picnic area adjacent to seaward car park
Visitor Centre open on weekend afternoons

Gorse in full flower on the cliffs above Fairlight Cove

right at bollard 8, signed to Fairlight Upper Glen. A path winds through woodland, along the side of the glen. At a T-junction with a wide grassy path, turn left and climb steadily. At the head of the glen, just beyond bollard 9, double back to the right, keeping to high ground on the other side of the glen. Back at bollard 11, retrace your earlier route across high ground and down the steps to bollard 13. Here, turn sharp left along the wood edge. *After almost ½ mile, cross a stile and turn right across pasture at the head of Warren Glen to a second stile near a house. Now cross open, undulating ground, aiming for a wireless mast. On

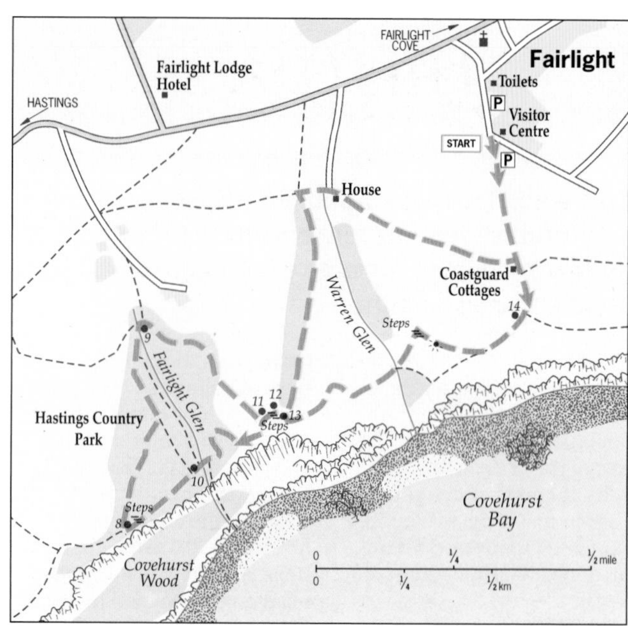

nearing the coastguard cottages passed earlier on the walk, go through a bridle-gate and cross a field to join your outgoing route. Turn left, back to the start.

The Glens

At Fairlight Glen a tiny stream tumbles down the valley through dense, ancient woodland which extends right to the edge of the eroded clay and sandstone cliffs. In the sheltered depths of the glen, the cool and humid atmosphere helps to support a wide variety of ferns and mosses.

The more open slopes of nearby Warren Glen are a mass of bluebells in the spring, and wide tracts of bright yellow gorse are a striking feature in most seasons.

A grassy path on the clifftop

What to look out for

The Hastings Country Park embraces areas of heath, grassland, seashore and woodland, and provides habitats for a wide variety of wildlife. Butterflies observed here include brimstone, peacock, small tortoiseshell and common blue, and a variety of migrant birds pass through the area in spring and autumn; skylarks and corn buntings are resident.

The Pond at Worth

With the Garden of England's best soil and some of its warmest weather, the market garden village of Worth remains a peaceful haven. At the entrance to the village is the famous 'Ham Sandwich' signpost.

WALK 25
KENT
TR332567

START
Worth is a mile south of Sandwich off the A258.
Start the walk by the pond opposite the church. There is parking in The Street between the Blue Pigeons and the post office.

DIRECTIONS
From the pond walk past the church lych-gate and The Blue Pigeons. Keep on the pavement to pass the post office and reach the 'Ham Sandwich' signpost.
Cross the main road at this point and go up the narrow footpath at the side of the driveway opposite. The hedged path runs for 400yds to a junction.
Turn left here, pass Felder Cottage and continue on the track which runs alongside a blackcurrant field. As the blackcurrants give way to apple trees do not swing right into the field with the main track, but keep straight ahead to pass through a gap. The path runs gently downhill to the corner of the orchard.
Turn left onto an enclosed footpath. On reaching a road go directly over and turn left at the side of a driveway on a path marked 'link 6'. The path rises gently and runs between two fields. Continue over the main road on the path by the Upton House lodge.
The footpath follows the side of a field before becoming enclosed and after a double bend enters the churchyard at a kissing-gate. Carry straight on and at a second gate turn left to return to Worth church.

Information

The walk is just under two miles long
Mainly level easy ground
No stiles
Both pubs in Worth have nice gardens, offer bar meals and welcome children
Picnic by village pond

Worth
This is a village of Flemish-style brick cottages. The wood shingle tower on the church has acted for years as a landmark for shipping avoiding the Goodwin Sands. The oldest parts of the church are the Norman pillars on the south side and a Norman archway which can be found through the door on the left in the nave.
The Old Blue Pigeons opposite the church was the original pub; the present day hostelry of the same name now occupies the former rectory next door.
The St Crispin pub dates from 1450 and is said to have been named by veteran soldiers from the Battle of Agincourt, fought on St Crispin's Day in 1415. The village pond

What to look out for

The proximity of the marshes means that lapwings and golden plovers can be seen in winter, as can roaming flocks of finches and skylarks. In summer there are cuckoos and willow warblers. Gulls from the coast two miles away also wheel overhead. Nearby rookeries mean that rooks are common here; jackdaws and magpies are also often seen. Watch out for migrant hawker dragonflies in the autumn.

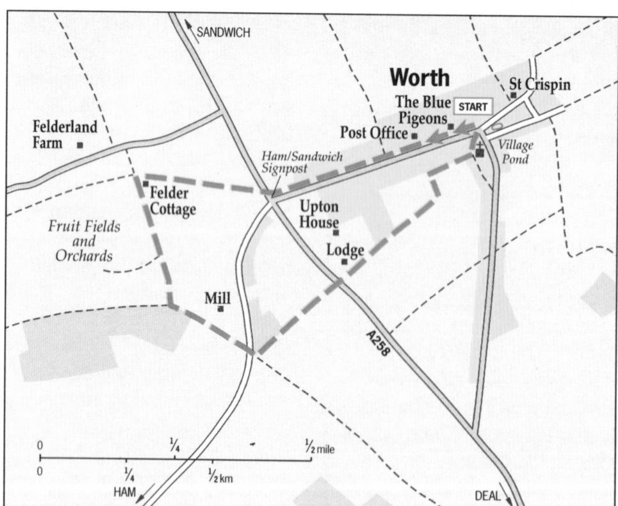

Flemish-style houses at Worth

may be the remains of a sea creek used by Thomas à Becket during his escape to France.

Ham & Sandwich

The two places from the famous signpost are Ham, a hamlet dating from at least the 13th century, and Sandwich, a port whose name means 'settlement on sand'. It was necessary for Sandwich to obtain its water from Worth, and the Delf Stream, dug from springs to the north, runs beside the main footpath.

The Medway at East Peckham

WALK 26

KENT

TQ487667

Information

The walk is around two and a half miles long
Level, easy ground
Several stiles
Pubs in East Peckham: The Merryboys does not allow children inside but there is a garden: bar meals and morning coffee served; The Queen Tavern allows children in at Sunday lunch time and has a garden
Grassy area at lock suitable for picnics

This is a short, pleasant waterside walk that is packed with attractions, including a canal lock, a nature reserve, an island and a unique view of oast houses.

START

East Peckham is four miles east of Tonbridge, off the A26. Start the walk from The Merryboys pub in the village centre. There is a car park in the road opposite the pub and behind the Methodist church.

DIRECTIONS

Walk south past the fish and chip shop to the next crossroads by the Queen Tavern. Turn right to follow a farm track leading to a footbridge. Bear half right to reach Sluice Weir Lock on the River Medway. Cross the lock gates and go left to walk over the weir stream on the high concrete bridge.

Turn right along a woodland footpath which follows a fence. At a stile the path enters the Beltring Hop Farm nature reserve. After a footbridge, the path passes between a lake and a stream before entering a large field. Turn half right to walk parallel to the stream to find a three-arm signpost by a footbridge. Cross the stream and turn immediately right across a second bridge. Follow the path ahead, which turns left past a wood to a point near the far corner of the field. A wooden waymark post indicates the approach to a bridge flanked by stiles leading on to Bullen Island in the Medway. Keep to the right on the island to cross the next bridge, which spans the main navigation channel.

On the mainland the path follows the River Bourne to a stile. Turn left over a footbridge and go immediately right to follow the Bourne upstream. Cross the water again on reaching another footbridge by

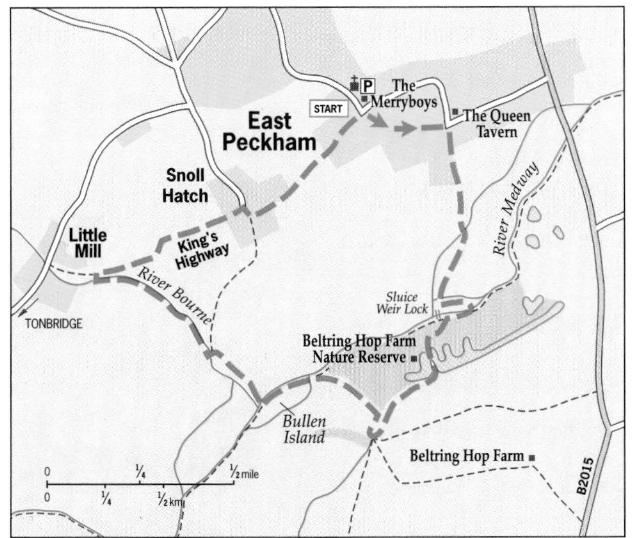

In Beltring Hop Farm's nature reserve

Millstream Cottages.
Turn right on to a footpath which follows a fence. After a double bend the path, known as the King's Highway, widens to run below two banks. Cross a stile to enter Snoll Hatch and turn right to follow the main street past the former post office and round the corner. A pavement follows the road into the centre of East Peckham.

East Peckham
There is no old church in this village because the community has drifted south to the river, leaving its 14th-century church isolated two miles away. On its present site the village has three pubs surviving from the days when hop pickers from London thronged the area every autumn.

Whitbread Hop Farm
The hop farm, where hops were handpicked until as recently as 1969, has the largest group of Victorian oast houses and galleried barns in the world, now housing two award-winning museums. Of the many events and attractions here, the greatest must be the magnificent shire horses that pull the Lord Mayor of London's golden coach, making the two hour journey to the City each November in their specially built horse box.

King's Highway
The east-west footpath linking Little Mill with Snoll Hatch was part of the original Tonbridge-to-Maidstone main road until replaced by a 'new' road in 1763.

What to look out for

Kingfishers frequent the River Medway and cuckoos can be heard in spring. On Bullen Island purple loosestrife, thistles and cow parsley grow among the many meadow plants. Along the River Bourne, several species of dragonfly can be found resting among the reeds.

Common rockrose

Outwood Mill

WALK 27
SURREY
TQ327456

Following a pleasant walk through woodland and across Outwood Common, this is a walk that can be muddy underfoot.

Information

The walk is three miles long
Level walking, can be very muddy
Several stiles – one very high
Pub with a garden just beyond Outwood Common
No refreshment *en route*

START
Outwood is best approached from the A23 south of Reigate, crossing the M23 on a minor road. There is parking on Outwood Common, opposite the windmill, for about ten cars.

DIRECTIONS
Take the path through gate into the woods, passing the cricket ground on the right. At the back of the pavilion, take the path leading diagonally into woods on the left.

In about 250yds, just before the stream at the bottom, bear right, and keep on the right bank of the stream. At junction turn right and almost immediately cross a stream over a plank. Follow the path up to the left for about 100yds to a more substantial bridge and cross the stream again. At the top of the bank turn right. Follow the path for about ¼ mile, keeping to the left where it forks at the edge of the woods. At the next junction, after about ¼ mile, turn right through the wooden barrier. Keep forward, past the cottages on the right. (To visit the parish church of St John the Baptist, turn left by the cottages.)
Continue along track past cottages, maintaining the same direction for approximately ½ mile between field edges, heading towards farm buildings, to a lane. Turn immediately right over a stile on to a public footpath. From now on keep forward in a straight line through fields, over four stiles and across tracks for about a mile, until eventually returning to the common.

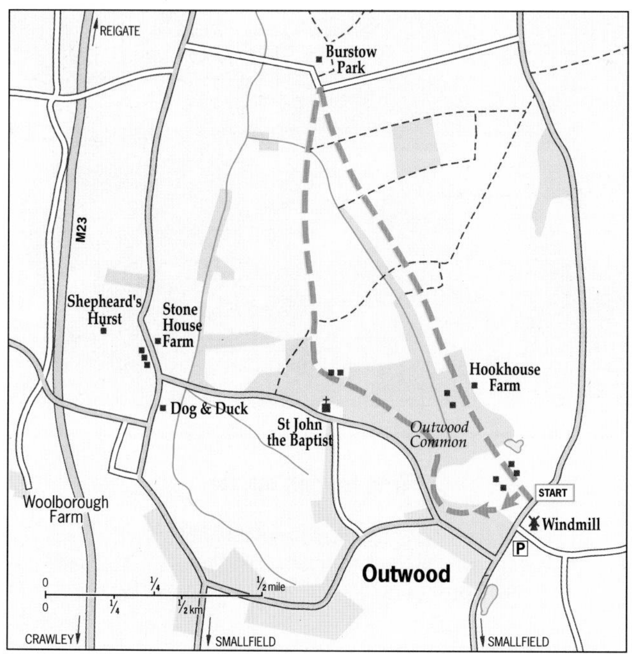

Outwood Windmill
This is claimed as England's oldest working post mill. Built in 1665, it originally had a companion which has long since disappeared. The mill is open to visitors on Sunday afternoons (closed in winter); there is also a small museum, a collection of old coaches, a shop and a picnic area on the site.

Visiting Outwood's 17th-century wooden windmill

Outwood Common

Part of the scenic Harewood Estate which belongs to the National Trust, the common is freely available to the public.

What to look out for

Jays inhabit the woods and there are lots of blackberry bushes, providing an autumn feast for many bird species. Listen out for the tapping of the great spotted woodpecker.

Frimley Green

WALK 28
SURREY
SU891563

From Frimley Lodge Park the walk goes along the canal then through woodland of pine and silver birch on sandy paths.

START
Frimley Green is three and a half miles south of Camberley on the A321. The walk starts from Frimley Lodge Park, next to the church. For the parking area, drive into the park, bear right and follow the signs 'Canal South & Trim Trail'; the parking area is by a miniature railway.

DIRECTIONS
From car park walk a few yards up the track to the canal. Turn right onto towpath and continue for about ¼ mile to the road bridge. Go up the steps and turn left across the bridge. Opposite Potters pub, turn left along a track and bear right along the signposted bridleway. Almost

Information

The walk is one and a half miles long
Level, easy walking, with one short flight of fairly steep wooden steps
No stiles
Seats along the canal
Dogs prohibited on the play areas in the park
The King's Head pub has a garden and play area
Frimley Lodge Park, at the start of the walk, provides lots of attractions and facilities

The Basingstoke Canal at Frimley Lodge Park

immediately bear left off the main path along a narrow footpath.

Continue through the pine woods at the back of a school, keeping to the left wherever there is a choice. On reaching the marked bridleway turn left and keep left at the next signpost. Remain on this path for about ¾ mile and eventually emerge onto Windmill Lane.

Continue ahead to the road, turn left and after a few yards cross the narrow bridge over the canal (with care – there is no pavement). A few yards ahead is the King's Head pub. Take the path to the left, immediately after the bridge, leading back down to the canal towpath. Turn right and return along the canal to the car park.

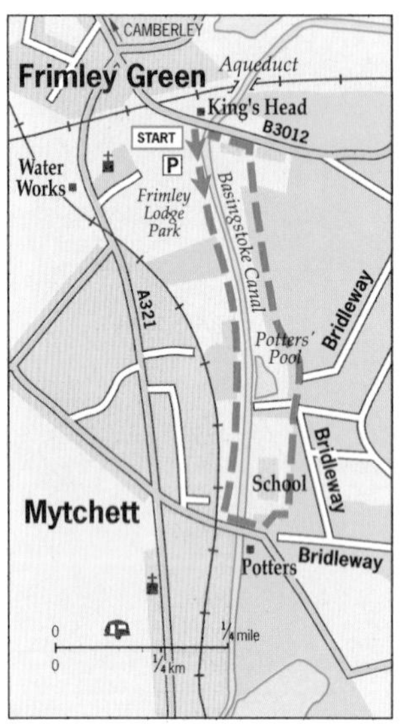

Frimley Lodge Park

Covering nearly 70 acres of meadowland and mature woodland, Frimley Lodge Park includes formal play areas, picnic sites with barbecue facilities, a trim trail, a miniature railway (which operates on selected Sunday afternoons), a pitch and putt course and a pavilion with a cafeteria.

The Canal

Built between 1789 and 1794, the Basingstoke Canal was once busy with barges carrying timber for ship- and house-building, grain, malt and other produce from north Hampshire to London, returning with cargoes of coal and manufactured goods. It was formally re-opened in 1991 by HRH The Duke of Kent after a long programme of restoration begun in 1974.

The canal is stocked with fish, and day fishing tickets can be purchased at all local tackle shops. They must be obtained in advance.

Grey squirrel

The miniature railway at Frimley Lodge Park

What to look out for

Grey squirrels and woodland birds can be seen among the pine trees throughout the year; fungi, such as the colourful but poisonous fly agaric, abound in autumn. There are pike in the canal, where moorhens can usually be seen.

The Castle at Donnington

WALK 29
BERKSHIRE
SU462691

The combination of castle ruins and nature reserve with a clear chalkland river, make this walk interesting and enjoyable for all ages.

Information

The walk is three and a half miles long
Gentle, even ground. The nature reserve can be very boggy
Very little road walking
A few stiles
Pub in Bagnor; Watermill Theatre restaurant in Bagnor serves lunches on weekdays and matinée Saturdays
Grassy area for picnics around the castle
Dogs will need to be on leads through golf course

START
Donnington is on the outskirts of Newbury just north of the A4. Start the walk at Donnington Castle which is west of the village on a minor road off the B4494 (signposted 'Donnington Castle'). There is a free car park.

DIRECTIONS
Facing the castle on the car park side, turn left and take the path down a slope into Castle Wood. (If you don't wish to visit the castle first, you can leave the car park by the path in the top left-hand corner.)
The path from the castle joins the path from the car park at a wooden gate. Continue through the wood with the golf course to your left until you reach a stile and gap in the fence. Go through the gap and turn left, watching out for motorised golf carts crossing, and proceed down the path between a hedge and a fence, signed 'Footpath'.
Continue over the meadow, following sign 'Lambourn Valley Way' to the gate. Go through the gate and turn right along a gravel drive into Bagnor.
Continue through Bagnor past the Blackbird pub, ignoring a signed footpath to the right. Turn left along the road signed to the Watermill Theatre. Turn left again along the signposted by-way across the Winterbourne stream into Rack Marsh Nature Reserve.
Cross the River Lambourn, go over the stile (it can be really boggy just here) and bear half right away from the river.
Cross the stile and follow the path with a new fence on your right.
Where you see two five-bar gates on opposite sides of the path, go through the gate on the left and keep left along the edge of the field. Cross the stile into the next field – this stile is fenced at the bottom and dogs might need lifting over.
Continue to the road at Bagnor Bridge.
Turn left back to the 'Blackbird' and retrace your steps along the gravel lane, past the houses, through the gate and across the meadow to the 'Lambourn Valley Way' sign.
Turn right, continuing along the edge of the golf course, passing Donnington Grove, a

What to look out for

Downland flowers such as cranesbills, burnet saxifrage, salad burnet and small scabious grow here in profusion, while the hedges provide rich pickings during the autumn. Look out for kingfishers and herons near the river. Rack Marsh Nature Reserve, comprising rare and ancient, undrained riverside meadows, protects such plants as bogbean, ragged robin and marsh orchids. Sedge and reed warblers inhabit the reed beds alongside the chalkland streams.

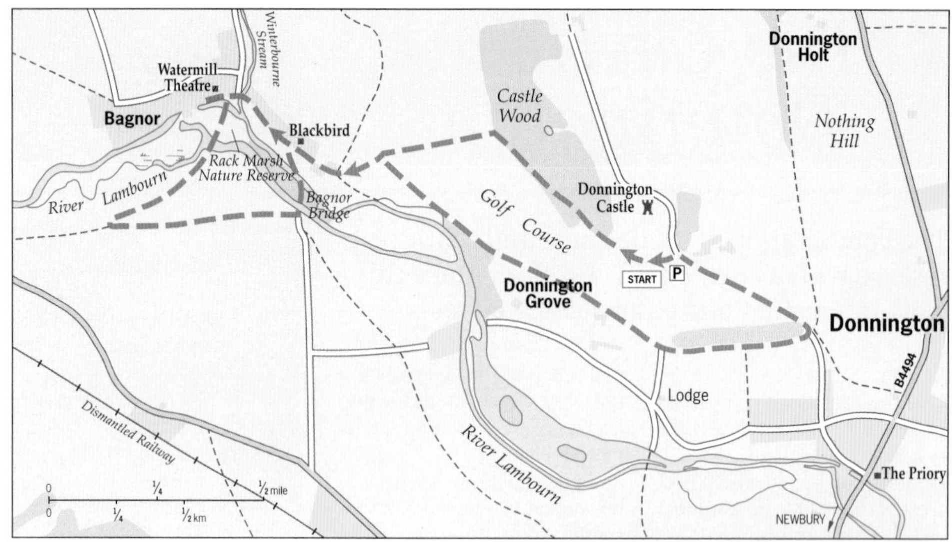

castellated house, on the right. Continue past a large farm complex on the right and at the end of its walled garden, just before the tarmac drive turns sharp right, turn half left along a path through the trees and proceed to the road. Turn left up the approach road to Donnington Castle to return to the car park.

Donnington Castle

An information board at this ruined castle gives a brief history. During the Civil War Sir John Boys, Governor of the Castle, held it for the Royalists through two sieges. In 1643, after the first battle of Newbury the parliamentary General declared that he would leave no stone of the castle standing unless Sir John surrendered, but Boys continued to stand fast, even when much of the castle was in ruins, and at last the enemy withdrew.

The remains of Donnington Castle

The River Windrush at Minster Lovell

This walk is in the lovely valley of the River Windrush, with meadows, bridges, the ruins of an old mansion and abundant wildlife.

WALK 30
OXFORDSHIRE
SP324115

Information

The walk is three miles long
Mostly level, even ground, but can be rather muddy
Virtually no roadwalking
A lot of stiles to cross
Pub in Crawley with a children's play area; restaurant in Minster Lovell serves afternoon tea
Picnic places in the meadows
Dogs will need to be on leads

START

Minster Lovell is about two miles west of Witney just off the B4047 between Witney and Burford.
Start from the parking area at the top of the lane to the Hall and church.

DIRECTIONS

Turn right out of the parking area and proceed for about 100yds along the road. Turn right over the stile just past Manor Farm and go across the meadow, bearing left towards the chimney of Crawley Mill. The River Windrush and the ruins of Minster Lovell Hall are on your right.

After 1½ miles, cross the stile and go along the edge of the fields, crossing two more stiles to reach a track. Walk up the tree-lined track for about 600yds, turn right at junction by a house and descend into Crawley. Turn right with care (Lamb Inn on left) and continue along the pavement to cross the River Windrush. Beyond the bridge ignore the first farm gate, cross the road and take the path on your left through the narrow gate opposite the mill complex. Follow the track round to the right for about ¼ mile. Go through the gate and turn right at another gate a few feet ahead, then go up the edge of the field to the road. Cross the road and go over the waymarked stile. Cross the narrow field to the stile and go downhill through the woodland, over stile and through a meadow. Continue forward, crossing two waymarked stiles. After second stile bear right to cross another stile (by a gate) into a meadow. Continue along meadows, with river on right, and eventually cross stile and follow path through pine woods. At end of trees turn right over plank bridge. Cross another stile and head for Minster Lovell Hall, going through the gate to the

The ruins of the great house of Minster Lovell

stately ruins. Walk through the grounds, past the church and back to the starting point.

Minster Lovell Hall

This romantic ruin is now managed by English Heritage. It was built in the 15th century by William Lovell on the site of a Priory which had been in his family since the time of King John. William's grandson, Francis, cuts something of a sinister figure in history as confidante and favourite of Richard III. When Richard lost his throne to Henry VII at Bosworth Field, Lovell fled the country, but returned and was last seen at the Battle of Stoke. It is said that he returned to his home and hid in a secret vault, tended by one faithful servant, who alone knew of his whereabouts. She died, taking her secret to the grave and leaving the last of the Lovells walled up alive. In 1708 workmen discovered an underground vault containing the skeleton of a man, sitting at a table. Even as they looked the whole crumbled to dust!

Rabbit

What to look out for

Hazelnuts, sloes, elderberries and blackberries growing in the hedge in autumn prove a great attraction for birds and small mammals.

Wet meadow flowers grow in profusion and colourful damselflies can be seen in May and June.

WALK 31
OXFORDSHIRE
SP418398

The Moated Castle at Broughton

Information

The walk is just over two and a half miles long
Level, easy ground
Very little road walking
Several stiles to cross
Pub in North Newington with children's play area
Grassy areas for picnics along the walk
Dogs will need to be kept on leads

Fox

This is a gentle walk across parkland, meadow and field, in an area that is richly steeped in Civil War history.

START
Broughton is about two miles south-west of Banbury on the B4035. The start is in North Newington, a short distance north of Broughton. There is plenty of parking in the main street.

DIRECTIONS
Go down Park Lane at the east end of North Newington. Turn along a grassy path with a wall on the right and a fence on the left. Cross the stile and traverse the meadow, then go through the gate, over the road and cross the stile opposite. Head across the middle of the field towards the church spire. Cross the road and turn slightly right to go over the stile. Bear right to head diagonally across the field, still keeping the spire ahead. Enter the next field via two stiles on either side of a track, proceeding diagonally across this field, heading slightly to the right of the spire. On your left is the Sor Brook lined with pollarded willows.

Broughton Castle's sturdy gatehouse

Go over stile and cross the road to the gatehouse of Broughton Castle. Turn right past the gatehouse and then left over the stone stile into the park, with the moated

What to look out for

Wildlife is abundant in this area; brown hares are often seen in the open, while spotted flycatchers prefer the woods. Along the hedgerow listen out for songbirds such as yellowhammers and lesser whitethroats. In the meadow by Park Farm at the start of the walk are defensive earthworks dating from the Civil War. There is also a fine 17th century dovecot.

castle and church on the left. Walk straight up the hill, past the woodland and cross stile to leave the park. Cross the field to the barn and turn right onto the fieldside track to the road.

Go through the gate and cross the road to the waymarked route. Cross the stile and continue along the edge of the field with the hedge on your right. Go through the wooden gate in the corner of the field and along the edge of the next field. Turn right over the stile and go diagonally downhill, continuing on the track to return to North Newington.

Broughton Castle

For the last 600 years Broughton Castle has been

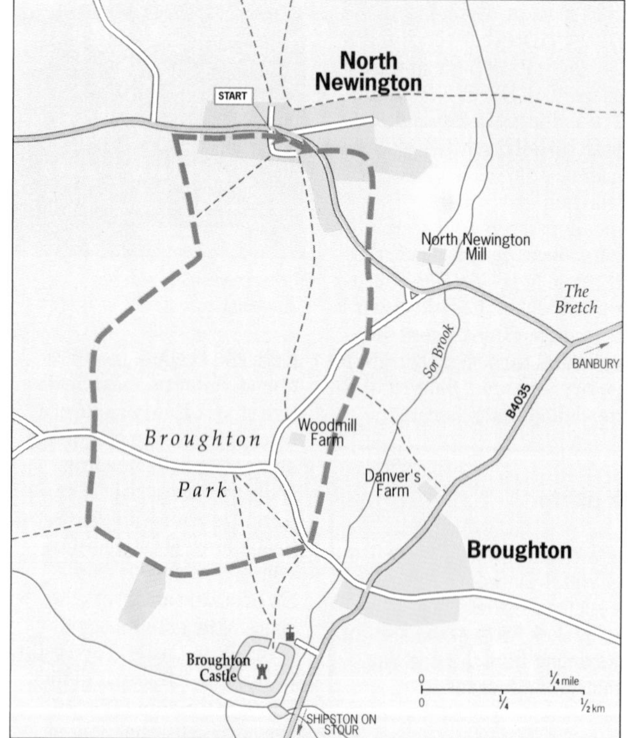

The lovely gardens of Broughton Castle

the home of the Fiennes family. Here, in the tense weeks before the outbreak of the Civil War, eminent Parliamentarians like Hampden and Pym met with William Fiennes, Lord Saye and Sele ('Old Subtlety' to his contemporaries). During that war the castle suffered little damage, and at the Restoration 'Old Subtlety' tactfully installed a painting of Charles II embarking for England, placing above it the inscription (in Latin) 'There is no pleasure in the memory of the past'.

The Castle is open to the public on the afternoons of Bank Holiday Sundays and Mondays (including Easter), on summer Wednesdays and Sundays; Thursdays too in July and August.

The Thame Valley at Cuddington

WALK 32
BUCKINGHAMSHIRE
SP737112

With bridges over the River Thame, abundant wildlife and historical interest, this pleasant walk has universal appeal.

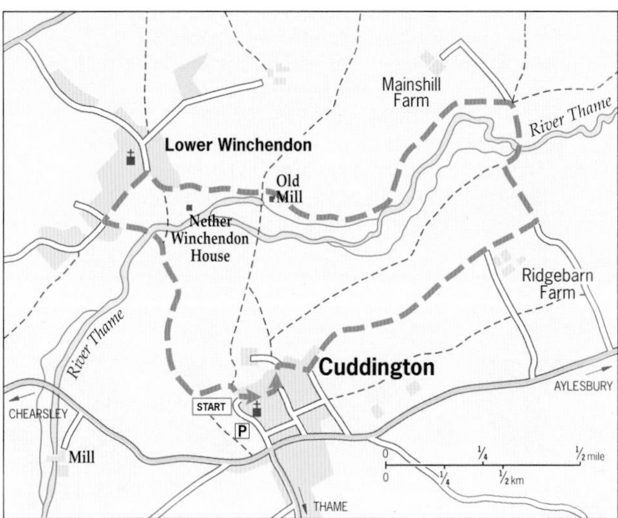

Information

The walk is three and a half miles long
Level, easy ground
Several stiles to cross
Very little roadwalking
Pub in Cuddington
Grassy meadows suitable for picnics

START
Cuddington is just off the A418 between Thame and Aylesbury. The start is near the church, where there is room to park.

DIRECTIONS
Turn right behind the church and walk down the street past Tibby's Lane and turn right into Frog Lane. Turn left down the bridleway at the junction of Frog Lane and Spicketts Lane. Follow this green lane for ½ mile, passing Ridgebarn Farm on the right. Where the lane turns right, cross the waymarked stile on the left. Follow the side of the meadow and turn right in the corner of the field to the old pollarded aspen (don't cross the stile). Turn left here to cross over the River Thame. Continue straight ahead with a line of pollarded willows on your right. Cross over the stile and turn left over the next stile. Continue along the edge of the meadow and at the second stile head diagonally across the meadow to a track with an overgrown enclosure on the left.
Bear left with the track and cross the stile. Turn right to follow the waymarked route across the water meadow to the Old Mill at Nether (or Lower) Winchendon. Bear round to the right and cross the stile by the barn. Turn left along the track into the village passing, on your left, a wild boar enclosure and Nether Winchendon House. At the junction by the church turn left, and in 300yds, opposite the telephone box, turn left again onto the footpath past 'Langlands'. Cross the wooden slat bridge over the River Thame and continue up the causeway. Turn left along the grassy path with bungalows and a duck pond on your right. Turn right to go up Tibby's Lane into Cuddington.

Lettice Knollys and Nether Winchendon House
The 16th-century manor house in Nether Winchendon, with its glorious twisted brick chimneys and great gateway, was the birthplace of Lettice Knollys, friend of Elizabeth I.

She was married three times, first to the Earl of Essex, then to Elizabeth's favourite, the Earl of Leicester, and lastly to Sir Christopher Blount. Lettice lived to the enormous age of 95, and at 92 could 'yet walk a mile in the morning'.

Wild Boar

Wild boar are bred at Nether Winchendon. These animals became extinct in England during the 17th century, the last record of them in the wild being in 1683. Boars are larger than domestic pigs and are brownish-black in colour. The young are brownish yellow with dark stripes. They are forest animals and in olden times the hunting of them was deemed a lordly sport.

What to look out for

There are large numbers of pollarded willows in the meadows by the river, and this ancient form of woodcraft still provides local farmers with stakes and posts. In the hedges are hazelnuts, blackberries, sloes and elderberries, while reeds, rushes and marsh marigolds line the fast-flowing river.

There is a small area of wilderness where such plants as brambles and hogweed grow amid hawthorn, ash and horse chestnut trees, providing varied habitats for the rich wildlife. Look out for lesser spotted woodpeckers, willow warblers, moorhens and herons as well as rabbits and kestrels.

There is an early (1772) single-handed clock in the tower of Nether Winchendon church. Inside the church its loud ticking and the swinging of the 14ft pendulum and 60lb bob give an eerie sense of the passing of time.

The lovely old 13th-century church at Cuddington

Burnham's Magnificent Beeches

Here is a woodland walk with a difference – and one that cannot fail to impress. Woodland, dells, clearings, ponds and pathways seem designed to entrance and captivate.

WALK 33
BUCKINGHAMSHIRE
SU957851

Autumn in Burnham Beeches

START
Burnham Beeches is just north of Slough by Farnham Common, off the A355. Start at East Burnham Common car park. There is plenty of room to park. Note: East Burnham Common is not near East Burnham village.

DIRECTIONS
Turn left from the car park and walk up the road to the crossroads signed 'Victory Cross'. Continue straight on. After 150yds turn down the first path on your left to Upper Pond.
Go over the dam to the right of the pond and carry on up the path beneath the pine trees. After 50yds turn right along a small path into the pine trees (just before a fork in the main path) and right again at the next well-defined crossroads of paths. After about 150yds pass an enormous old beech bowl and reach Middle Pond.

Cross the dam with the pond on your right and bear left. After 150yds reach a clearing and keep on the main path. The 'Druid's Oak' is on your right.
Cross the road by the shelter and in 20yds, where the paths join, bear right to cross 'Seven Ways Plain'. After 200yds bear right at a junction of three paths, and continue for about ½ mile

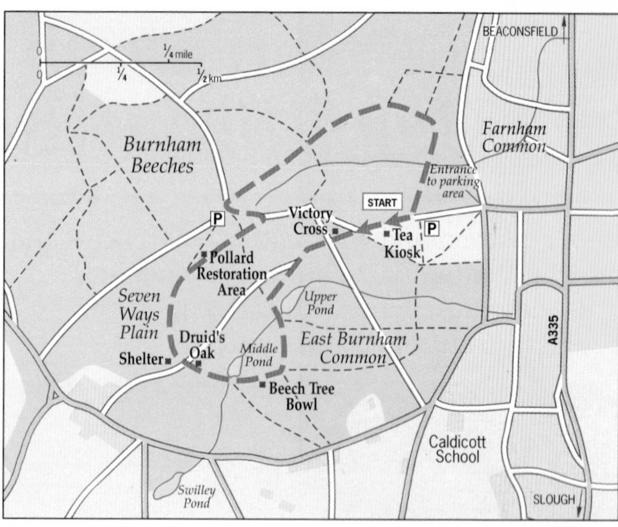

through an Ancient Pollard Restoration Area.

On reaching the road, turn left for about 250yds then right, opposite a parking area, along the path marked by a barrier in the bottom of the hollow.

Where five paths meet go half right ahead. Follow the path till it forks at the summit of a short, steep incline, then bear left. The main path bears to the right where another path crosses diagonally. Keep to the main path and after about 100yds turn right and descend to the stream 100yds ahead. Cross the stream and carry on back up to the road 50yds ahead and East Burnham Common.

Burnham Beeches

This lovely area of mixed beech wood was purchased by the Corporation of the City of London in 1880. Still owned and managed by that body, it is a permanent public open space, and an official guide can be bought at The Glade café.

Pollarded Beech and Oak Trees

The ancient craft of pollarding involves periodically lopping trees at between eight and 12ft above the ground so that they provide successive crops of new wood on an established trunk. It also increases the lifespan of the tree by slowing down the rate of growth, and the average age of the ancient pollards of Burnham is 350 years. With about 700 of them, this is the largest stand of such trees in the world.

Sadly, since pollarding ceased in the 1820s the trees are now ageing rapidly, but Burnham Beeches has several 'Ancient Pollard Restoration' sites, where old trees have been pollarded anew in an effort to save them.

Information

The walk is two miles long
Level, easy walking with a few gentle slopes and just one short section that is a bit steeper
No stiles
Ice cream on sale at East Burnham Common
Café at East Burnham Common
Plenty of places to picnic

What to look out for

The 450-year-old Druid's Oak is the largest oak tree growing here, with a circumference of 30ft!
Upper Pond and Middle Pond were created artificially in 1800. Now naturalised with reeds and water lilies, they offer a home to wildlife including dragonflies, moorhens and mallards.
Seven Ways Plain is the site of an Iron-Age fort, possibly associated with the 7th-century British chieftain, Caedwalla. Today its banks and ditches are not easily distinguished.
Among the birds that frequent the beeches look out for nuthatches, great spotted woodpeckers and treecreepers – and in summer you might be lucky enough to hear a nightingale.

Ampthill Park and Woodlands

WALK 34
BEDFORDSHIRE
TL037382

This is a scenic walk with spectacular views over open countryside. It includes wide open grassland, water and woodland areas and is adjacent to the attractive small town of Ampthill which has an interesting Georgian centre and lots of antique shops.

START
Ampthill is seven miles south of Bedford and just north of junction 12 of the M1. Start from St Andrew's Church on the road to Maulden. There is ample parking in the town.

DIRECTIONS
Follow the clearly marked footpath to the left of the church down Rectory Lane into Holly Walk. Keep left along the edge of the graveyard and follow the yellow signposts for the Greensands Ridge Walk, through the holly tunnel and over Church Hill until you meet the road (can sometimes be busy). Cross over and go through the kissing-gate to the right. Follow the path into the woods and take the right-hand path down a sunken tree-lined avenue to Ampthill Park House. The path here can be muddy. Keep to the track by the western edge of the house, and at the far corner go over a stile onto the footpath running south-west past Park Farm and up the hill. Cross the stile into the park and keep forward past the reservoir (on the left) and up on to the ridge. At the top, turn left. On the right-hand side of this path is Katherine's Cross. Keep following the central path, going eastwards towards the lodge, skirting the left-hand side of the lodge. Continue through the kissing-gate and alongside some allotments before coming out on to Park Hill. Go down Chapel Lane to return to the town.

Ampthill Castle and Katherine's Cross
Ampthill Park is the site of old Ampthill Castle, where Henry VIII imprisoned Katherine of Aragon for some years during and after the trial and subsequent divorce. This site is now marked by Katherine's Cross, carved with rather sad verses. It also offers panoramic views over the Bedfordshire countryside, and well-placed seats and picnic tables enjoy the same views. The parkland is the remnants of an ancient deer park which once surrounded the castle and was landscaped by 'Capability' Brown in the 18th century.

Blackberry

What to look out for

The walk starts along the appropriately named Holly Path, its trees covered in berries during the winter – food for mistle thrushes. Blackberries too abound during late summer and early autumn. Look out for pochards and tufted ducks on the reservoir, especially in winter, and the many types of dragonfly and damselfly that hover over the water on sunny summer's days.

Information

The walk is about two and a half miles long
Minimal road walking
One short, fairly steep section
A few stiles
Several seats
Some picnic tables along route; grassy area on the site of the old castle for picnics
Two pubs in Ampthill, both serving food; the Tudor Arms has a garden and also serves afternoon teas

The view across Ampthill Park

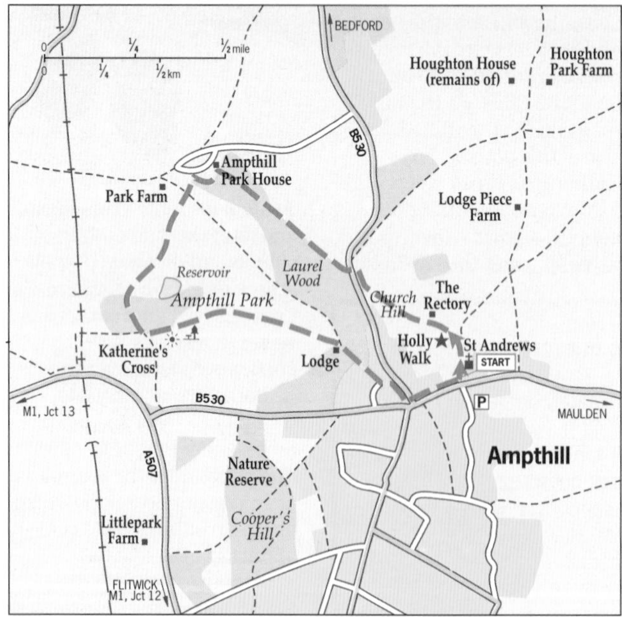

Holly Walk

This sunken track, bounded on both sides by a thick holly hedge, forms a natural tunnel of trees. It once formed part of the area known as the Warrens which, as the name suggests, were used to breed rabbits for the supper tables of the medieval inhabitants of Ampthill. In 1800 the Ampthill Enclosure Award meant that the Warrens largely disappeared and the land was given over to agricultural or forestry use.

Houghton House

Lying just half a mile north of Holly Walk, the ruins of Houghton House perhaps deserve a detour. This Jacobean country house is thought to have been John Bunyan's 'House Beautiful' and the hill outside Ampthill his 'Hill Difficulty' from *The Pilgrims' Progress*. Houghton House is now in the care of English Heritage.

WALK 35
ESSEX
TL663143

The Castle at Pleshey

Information

The walk is one and three quarter miles long
Level ground
Very little roadwalking
No stiles
Pub in Pleshey with garden
Grassy area for picnics overlooking the moat
Dogs should be kept on leads

This is an easy and very interesting walk, with fascinating ancient earthworks, a water-filled moat inhabited by ducks and other wildfowl, and some lovely wide green lanes.

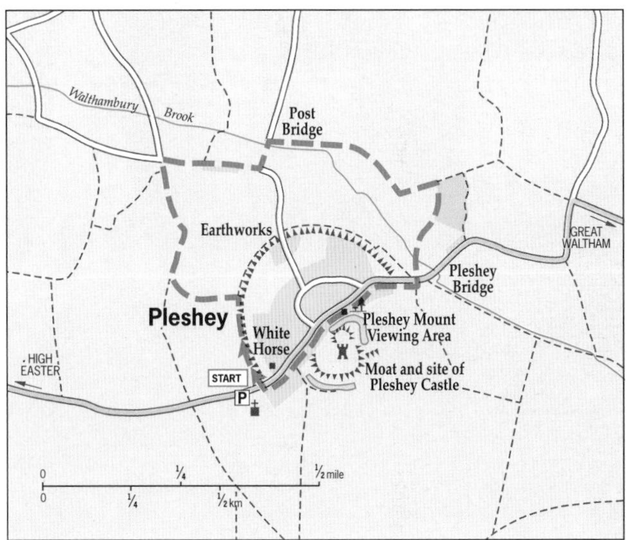

START
Pleshey is just north of Chelmsford, west of the A130, near Great Waltham. Start the walk outside the White Horse pub at the western end of the village, opposite the church. Be sure to park carefully and considerately by the church.

DIRECTIONS
Take the public footpath to the left of the White Horse pub. On the right, between the path and the pub, is part of a deep, defensive ditch, a mile in circumference, which is probably pre-Roman.
At the field boundary turn left and, keeping the hedge on your right, walk along the edge of the field. Go through the gap in the hedge at the corner of the field and turn right onto a very pleasant and open green lane.
At the road turn right, past some houses, to the T-junction. Turn left across the bridge over Walthambury Brook and right along the bridleway beside the stream (can get rather muddy). The bridleway soon becomes a green lane, along which you continue as it bears

What to look out for

The defensive ditch seen on the first part of the walk is part of the evidence that Pleshey was inhabited before the Romans came.
Bushes of sloe, hawthorn and elder line the green lanes, while the stream is overhung by willows, and growing with sedges and reeds. Both harbour a rich wildlife: look out for willow warblers, lesser whitethroats and yellowhammers.

The delightful village of Pleshey

round to the left. Turn right opposite the electricity transmission pole along the footpath (signed) past some newly-planted trees.

At the field boundary cross the wooden bridge over Walthambury Brook, and bear left along the footpath to cross a field of young willow trees and reach the road. Turn right onto the pavement to Pleshey Mount viewing area, which is off the road on your left, opposite the telephone box. Complete the walk along the main street through Pleshey.

Pleshey Castle

Ancient Britons, Romans and Saxons were all here, but it was the Normans who built a sturdy castle on the Saxon mount, and Richard II who caused its demise.

In September 1397 Richard came to Pleshey to visit his uncle Thomas, Duke of Gloucester, and invited him to ride to London, apparently to 'discuss matters of state'. His real purpose was to have his uncle kidnapped and murdered.

Pleshey Castle was subsequently allowed to fall down, and all that remains today is a brick arch. It is privately owned, but arrangements to visit can be made via Strutt and Parker, Chelmsford (tel: 258201; an admission charge is made). There is an information board at Pleshey Mount Viewing Area, which has well-kept grass and seats overlooking the moat.

The Roman Fort at Bradwell-on-Sea

This is an interesting and exciting walk, with views across the wide Blackwater estuary and over the North Sea, dotted with skimming sails. It includes a beach, a nature reserve, and a Saxon chapel, which was founded on the walls of a Roman fort.

WALK 36
ESSEX
TM023078

Information

The walk is two and a quarter miles long
Flat, easy walking
No road walking
No stiles
Dogs should be kept on leads
Grassy area for picnics within the Roman fort

START

Bradwell-on-Sea is about nine and a half miles east of Maldon, on the estuary of the River Blackwater. Start at Eastlands, just over two miles east of Bradwell-on-Sea along the East End road. There is space here for parking, but use it carefully and considerately.

DIRECTIONS

Set out along the causeway towards St Peter's Chapel, following what was the old Roman road and later the pilgrim's route. At the chapel bear left past the modern bird look-out tower which stands on or near the site of the northern wall of the Roman fort. Go through the gap into scrub land on your left, and follow the path onto the sea wall towards the headland (Sales Point) and the beach. At Sales Point, where the sea wall turns left, there is a magnificent panorama of the Blackwater estuary and the North Sea.
You can descend to the beach here, where the sandy ridge on the seaward side has locked itself firmly onto the sea wall. Retrace your steps to return to the starting point.

What to look out for

Bradwell Cockle Spit Nature Reserve is an area of salt marsh which harbours a rich population of marine life, on which flocks of waders such as dunlin, curlew and redshank come to feed at low tide.
The shell sand of the beach contains whole shells, including mussels, periwinkles, sand gapers, razor shells and the American slipper limpet.
The walk is dominated by the presence of the gaunt Saxon chapel, founded by St Cedd in AD653 and now re-consecrated after years of neglect and use as a barn.

Othona Roman Fort and St Peter's Chapel

The Roman fort was built on a little island at the mouth of the Blackwater in the 3rd century AD. From these walls the Roman legionaries, auxiliaries from North Africa, scanned the North Sea for German pirates.
Later, in AD653, Bishop Cedd built his chapel across the Roman wall, utilising the wall's firm foundations, as well as taking bricks and tiles from the fortress itself.

Thames Sailing Barges

These beautiful flat-bottomed cargo vessels, many of them built nearby at Maldon, at the head of the Blackwater estuary, were formerly used

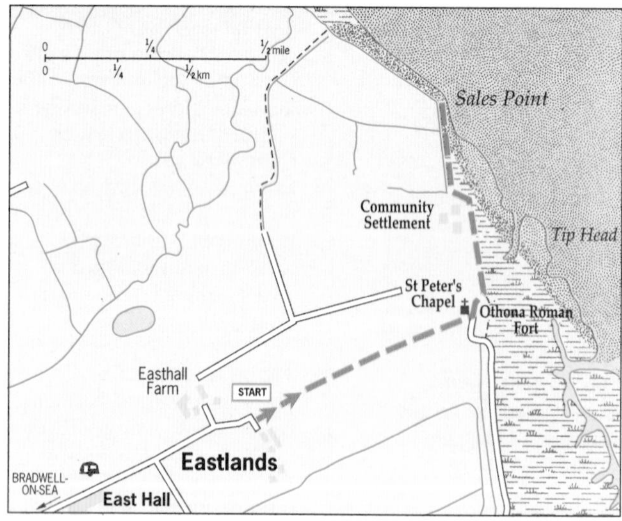

Sales Point, the destination of this walk, overlooks the Blackwater estuary and the North Sea

to ferry cargo up river and round the coast and were specially designed to sit securely on the mud at low tide. They are powered by a great mainsail and prevented from drifting with the wind by the use of lee-boards.

There was always an annual race downriver – a great event in which these vessels competed against each other – and in recent years there has been a revival of interest in the craft.

Framlingham

WALK 37
SUFFOLK
TM286636

This walk starts in an interesting town which is full of character and has a splendid castle. The route then heads out into the countryside, with panoramic views across rolling farmland.

Information

The walk is three and three quarter miles long; the shorter option is just under three miles
Mostly easy tracks
There are several pubs in Framlingham, including The Castle Inn at the start
Framlingham Green, next to the castle, is suitable for picnics
Toilets in Framlingham

START
Framlingham is about seven miles west of Saxmundham on the B1119. Park on the corner near the church and castle, or in the car park for the castle itself if you intend to visit.

DIRECTIONS
Set off along the one-way road (with the flow) until you come to a crossroads. Go straight on down the B1119 for Saxmundham, passing the Fire Station on your right. Where the road bends left, take the track forking off to the right, signposted 'Public Bridleway North Green'. Keep straight ahead on this main track for about ¾ mile and pass through a gate.
(If following the shorter route, go right here towards New Barn and resume directions at * below.)
Head for the left hand end of a clump of trees. Here, before the trees, the path turns 90 degrees to the left along a hedge, then right at the end. Go right on to a bridleway heading towards more trees. The track passes a plantation, and then turns 90 degrees left and then right at more mature trees (signpost). The track passes a wood on the left, and where the main track bends left towards Home Farm, go straight on, then after 50yds turn right at a public footpath sign. The path goes up a gentle incline to join a gravelled track.
*Pass through Edwards Farm, where the track becomes surfaced. Follow this to the road, turn right and in 50yds turn right down a signposted footpath across the field. On reaching the houses, continue straight on around the back of them on a small footpath. Where this emerges on to a small housing estate, go left and then right on to the road leading into

The church tower

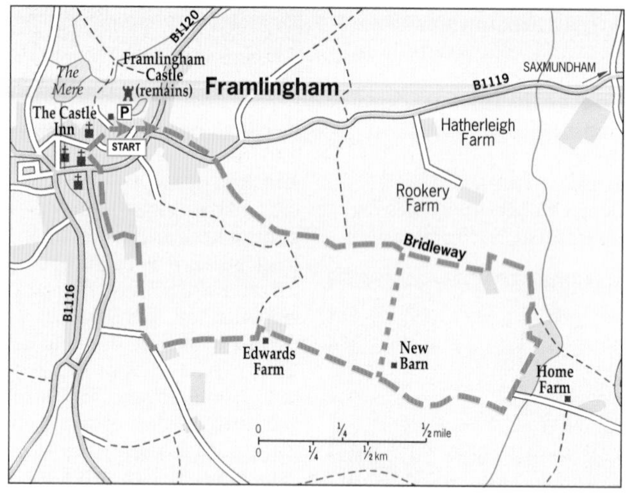

Framlingham Castle

Framlingham. Go straight on at the cross roads, then join road with the church opposite. Turn right to return to the castle and start point.

Framlingham Castle
Built in 1190 by the notorious Bigod family, Framlingham was one of the first castles not to include a keep, having instead 13 separate towers, linked by a curtain wall – a Saracen idea brought back by returning Crusaders. While all but one of the internal buildings are now gone, the walls and towers are well preserved, and it is possible to walk right around the top, from where there are magnificent views. It was at Framlingham in 1553 that Mary Tudor organised her army of supporters to march on Lady Jane Grey, and here that she later proclaimed herself Queen.

Saxtead Green
Not far from Framlingham, Saxtead Green is well known for its 18th-century post mill, so called because it was built on a single pivot post which was balanced by wheels running around a circular track. The mill has two pairs of stones, and a fantail which keeps the mill into the wind, and worked until 1947.

What to look out for

The rolling farmland here offsets a magnificent Suffolk skyscape. The land is drained by many streams and ditches. Look out for birds in the hedgerows in summer and listen for skylarks above.

Heath and Coastal Marsh at Walberswick

Walberswick stands amidst marshes and heath, flanked by a broad shingle beach – a sleepy village with neat houses and beautifully trim gardens. Part of the walk goes through a National Nature Reserve.

WALK 38
SUFFOLK
TM500749

Information

The walk is four and a half miles long
Level, easy terrain
A few stiles/gates
Virtually no road walking
Pub and tea room
Ice cream van usually on car park in summer

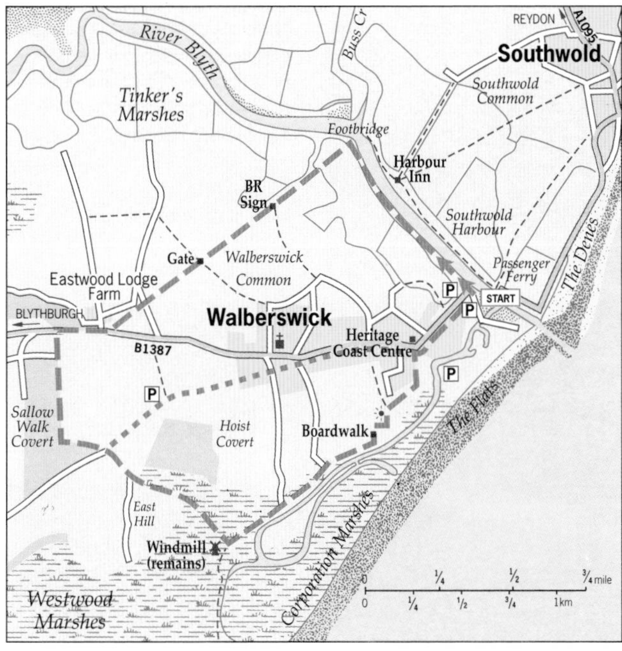

START

Walberswick lies at the end of the B1387, to the east of the A12 between Saxmundham and Lowestoft. Start the walk from the free car park opposite Southwold Harbour.

DIRECTIONS

From the car park follow the river wall inland to the footbridge. Turn left, on to the tarmac cycle track, and follow its path through bracken and gorse bushes. Where the tarmac track bends left, at sign 'BR', the walk veers right down a bridle path marked with yellow-topped posts. Continue straight on, ignoring track on left, and eventually the gorse gives way to heath. Go through a gate and after ¼ mile the track emerges on the busy B1387. Turn right here, and about 250yds down the road, take the bridleway on the left, keeping to the left of a small wood.

Shortly after the path bears left, it crosses a minor road (offering the option of returning directly to the village). After crossing the road, the signed route goes right, then left beside the gate at the entrance to conservation land. After 100yds the open marshes appear and you should head for the brick tower of a ruined windmill. To the right, in the distance, is the unmistakable bulk of the nuclear power station at Sizewell, 7 miles south. Turn left at the windmill to cross a stile on a wooden bridge, and follow the path beside the dyke. Keep to the left bank for

The River Blyth

nearly ¾ mile and, where a large footbridge crosses the dyke to the right, take a small footbridge left onto a path parallel to the dyke.

Soon after, turn left onto a boardwalk which crosses the area of marsh grasses. The path dodges through a thicket, then goes right to a field corner; close by are two World War II pill boxes, the second with a wooden seat in front. It is worth pausing here to enjoy the excellent view across marshes and coast. Turn sharp right just past here, and where the path goes over a small rise, bear left, back onto the road. There is a green with a play area here, as well as the Heritage Coast Centre and refreshments.

Heritage Coast Centre

The Suffolk Heritage Coast is an Area of Outstanding Natural Beauty and the small centre in Walberswick is one of several which provide displays to help visitors appreciate the area.

Southwold

Only a mile north, and accessible on foot either by footbridge or ferry across the river, Southwold is an interesting small town with lots of green open spaces – the legacy of a disastrous fire in 1659. Wherever you stand in this little town, you can see a white lighthouse looming above the houses and the roof-tops. Not far away is a Mecca for beer drinkers – Adnam's Brewery.

Southwold's famous lighthouse

What to look out for

This area has always been outstanding for birds. In winter it's one of the most likely spots to see a great grey shrike, and in summer the scrubby heath is home to nightjars, stonechats, lesser whitethroats and nightingales. The reed beds hold breeding marsh harriers, bitterns and bearded tits, and sometimes a rarity such as the purple heron or a spoonbill. Adders, common lizards and slow worms are quite common.

The King's Forest at West Stow

WALK 39
SUFFOLK
TL815715

The walk follows a marked trail, taking in a pleasant mix of wide tracks and tiny paths through the conifer plantations, broad-leaved trees and clearings of The King's Forest.

The path through The King's Forest

START
West Stow is just north of the A1101 between Bury St Edmunds and Mildenhall. Follow signs 'West Stow', turning left just before the village with signs 'Forest Lodge'. Park at the Forest Lodge car park.

DIRECTIONS
From the car park, walk along the main track just past the lodge to reach a sign on the left indicating the start of the King's Forest Trail. Go down this path, following the yellow-topped posts. In about 50yds the path turns right to go through a dense plantation of trees (yellow markers are on the tree trunks here). After crossing a narrow track, the path bears sharp right and in about 150yds crosses a wider track. The path winds for 250yds through well-spaced trees with some undergrowth. Where it comes to a junction with a track, turn left and continue, to emerge onto a clearing. Follow the path down the left-hand side of the clearing, continuing with a younger section of forest on the right, and arrive at a junction in another large clearing. Here turn left along the side of the clearing, and at the bottom turn right onto the track following the lower edge, past a short block of

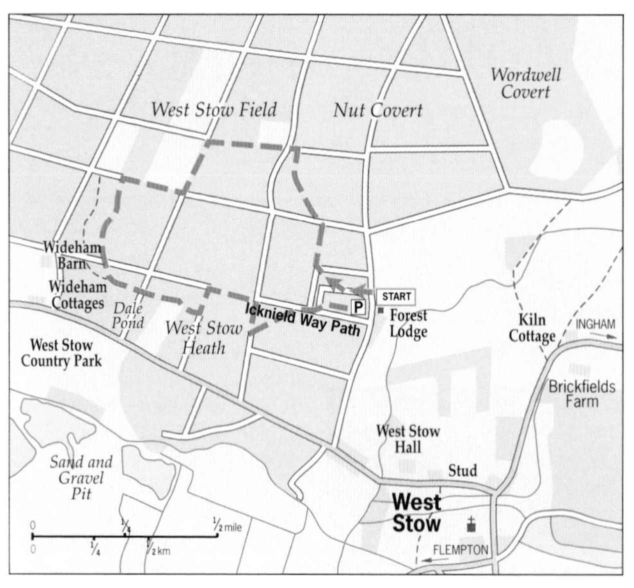

Information

The walk is two and a quarter miles long
Level, easy ground
Dogs should be kept on leads
Pubs at West Stow and Icklingham
Picnic area at car park

continuing into mature, well-spaced pines. The path goes right at the next junction and after 100yds, just after a slightly wider track, bears left through a plantation of younger trees before trees on the right, then on to another clearing on the right-hand side.

Look for a yellow-topped post where a small path goes off to the left into the wood, and follow it, weaving through conifers and deciduous trees. Continue across a bridleway which runs roughly parallel for the first 50yds or so. Continue, following yellow markers, through a plantation of mature conifers with little ground cover.

What to look out for

Thetford Forest, of which The King's Forest is a part, is one of the last strongholds of the red squirrel in England. It is also home to four species of deer – fallow, red, muntjac and roe. The latter are most common, and the only species not introduced here. Although they exist in large numbers, they are timid and not easy to see, keeping to small groups rather than large herds.

The muntjac are the descendants of escapees from Woburn Park in Bedfordshire at the end of the last century.

Muntjac

The path crosses a track and after 100yds enters a section of deciduous trees, then winds on, emerging at a junction with mature conifers ahead. Turn left onto the track for about 100yds and at the next junction turn right onto a bridleway. At the next crossing of paths, go right and soon take the small path going left by a yellow marker into deciduous trees, emerging briefly on the right-hand side of a very small clearing. Continue straight on, back to the car park.

West Stow Country Park
Within this area of heath and grassland is the famous reconstruction of West Stow Anglo-Saxon village, open daily during the summer, with an excellent visitor centre. The original village was preserved after being buried in a sandstorm.

Burnham Thorpe

WALK 40
NORFOLK
TF852418

Information

The walk is about four miles long
Level easy ground
About half a mile of road walking
A few stiles to cross
Dogs should be kept on leads on the road; under control everywhere else
Pub in Burnham Overy Staithe with bar meals and garden
Ice cream van often on staithe in summer
The sea wall at Burnham Overy Staithe is suitable for picnics

This pleasant walk follows in the footsteps of the young Horatio Nelson, who was born in the village, through pastures and along tracks down to the salt marshes and creeks of the North Norfolk coast.

START

Burnham Thorpe lies about four miles west of Wells-next-the-Sea and about a mile inland. Turn off the main coast road (A149) on to the B1155 then take minor road south to the village. Start the walk from Burnham Thorpe church, just to the north of the village centre. Park in front of the church's main gate.

DIRECTIONS

From the main gate of the church, walk away from the church across the grass and on to a track. Bear right and almost immediately take the signposted footpath on the left, crossing over stile and keeping hedge on the right. Go through a gateway into a

Low tide at Burnham Overy Staithe

large meadow with a number of ponds. Keep the hedge on the right until reaching a grove of trees, then bear left keeping trees to the right. As the trees come to an end bear right to a footpath sign and stile. Cross stile and climb the bank of a disused railway, then go left and after about 100yds turn right down the bank. Follow the path up a gentle hill with a hedge on the right, cross into next field and continue in the same direction until reaching a road by a cottage. Turn right and after about 200yds, where the houses end, turn

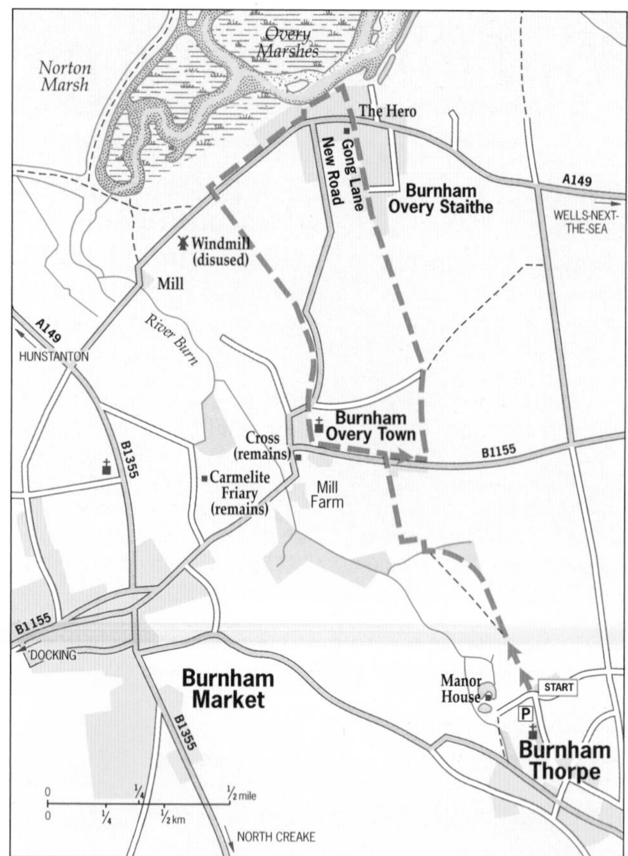

What to look out for

The meadows near Burnham Thorpe church can be good for wild duck, especially in winter. Many common butterflies are found along the hedgerows during summer. In winter look out for brent geese, especially on the coastal sections. Both churches on the walk are worth a visit.

left down a track. Keep straight on. Eventually sea, dunes and salt marsh come into view. Continue until the track becomes metalled and the outskirts of Burnham Overy Staithe are reached. At the main road cross over by The Hero pub and follow the narrow lane (East Harbour Way) down to the staithe. (A path to the right runs along the sea wall to the beach at Gun Hill.) Follow the road around to the left. The road then turns inland back to the main road. Here turn right, walking along the footpath by the main road until the coast path is signed; this runs parallel with the road but just within the field. Shortly before the tall black windmill turn left, crossing the road and proceeding up a wide track. Eventually reach a minor road and turn right. Follow this road until it bends to the right, just before Burnham Overy Town church. Go straight ahead through the churchyard then turn left along the road for about ¼ a mile. Turn right by the cottage and telephone box to meet the outward route, and retrace your steps to the start point.

Burnham Thorpe Church
Horatio Nelson's father was rector here from 1755–1802 and the great naval hero was born in Burnham Thorpe in 1758. The rectory where he was raised was later demolished. The church has a small exhibition on Nelson's life, including a cross made of timbers from HMS *Victory*.

Castle Acre

WALK 41
NORFOLK
TF816150

A fascinating walk through water meadows and along tracks and lanes linking the ruins of a castle and a priory.

Information

The shorter walk is about three miles, the longer about four and a half miles
Mostly level easy ground though there are some gentle hills
About a mile of road walking, mostly along a wide (sometimes rough) verge
Several stiles
Pubs and a café in the village
Suitable picnic sites at the castle and by the ford
Toilets at entrance to Priory

START
Castle Acre is about four miles north of Swaffham just off the A1065. Turn off the main road at the hamlet of Newton. There is room for parking in the village, but take care not to cause inconvenience. The walk starts from the church, towards the western end of the village.

DIRECTIONS
From the main gate of the church walk away from the village, and at the end of the churchyard wall turn left down South Acre Road. Continue down to the River Nar.
Just before the river, turn left over a stile then follow a gravel path by the river towards a bridge. Climb a stile to the left of the bridge onto the road, then turn left. After about 200yds turn right down Cuckstool Lane.
At a break in the hedge on the left, enter the castle remains. Walk up the hill, keeping the boundary hedge on your right, and at the top, just before the road, turn right over a stile. Follow a path into a field keeping the houses on your left.
Cross the next stile and bear left, keeping the houses on the left. Cross another stile by a horse chestnut tree and walk down a gravel path on to the road.
For the shorter walk, cross over at this point and go down North Street, opposite, continuing to St James Green; continue directions at * below.
(For a longer walk turn right and after about 300yds take a track up on the left for about

What to look out for

The castle mound has some interesting plants, native to the chalk which forms the basis of the mound. The tall yellow candelabra-like flower heads of the woolly mullein, a plant largely confined to East Anglia, can be seen in July. There are trout in the River Nar, best spotted from the bridge by the ford.

The lovely ruins of Castle Acre Priory in a rural setting by the river

The River Nar at Castle Acre

At the bottom of the hill bear left. Continue uphill on the track for about ½ mile to join a road, then turn right and follow the road, bearing left by the drive down to the priory. The start point is a short distance further on.

The Castle and the Priory
Castle Acre is a marvellous ruin, standing high above the River Nar. It is also on the line of a Roman road, The Peddars Way.
The castle was built in the 11th century but all that survives are the massive earthworks and the Bailey Gate, which forms an impressive entrance into the centre of the village.
The Priory, also dating from the 11th century, lies in a beautiful setting down by the river at the other end of the village. After the dissolution of the monasteries in 1537 it fell into decay, but despite the subsequent plundering of its stone, it still remains a most spectacular ruin.

¼ mile. Keep right and walk across the common, crossing a small ford and then, after 100yds, take the right-hand track. At the road turn left and walk back towards the village, bearing right at the second road junction to reach St James Green.)
*At the crossroads turn right. At the next junction, turn right by Rose Cottage onto a road with a wide verge. Continue along the verge until the next road junction then turn left.
After just over ½ mile, pass a manor house on the right then turn left down a track.

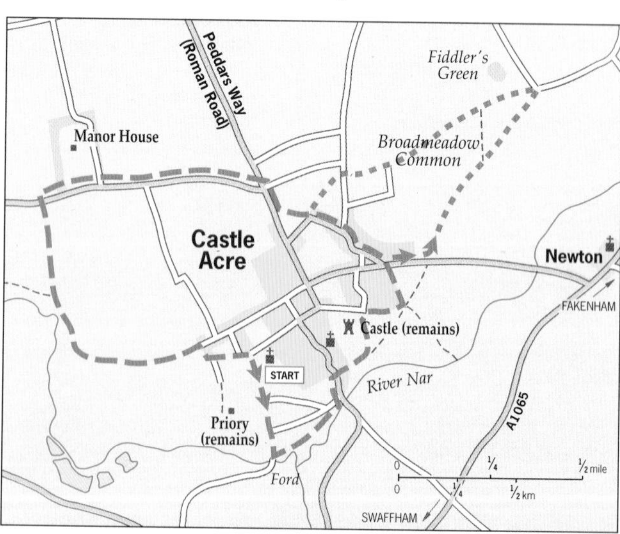

WALK 42
CAMBRIDGESHIRE
TL567662

Reach and the Devil's Dyke

Information

The walk is just under three miles long
Mostly level, easy walking, with one short climb; can be muddy
No stiles
Very little road walking
Pub in Reach serves bar food; no children under 14, but there is a large garden with play area
Pubs in nearby Swaffham Prior and Burwell

Marsh marigold

A pleasant walk through typical flat fenland scenery, with numerous waterways and the occasional windmill. A great attraction is the Devil's Dyke, a huge and ancient earthwork which dominates the landscape.

START
Reach is off the B1102 approximately seven miles north-east of Cambridge and five miles west of Newmarket. It is situated on a minor road between Burwell and Swaffham Prior. Parking is available by the village green.

DIRECTIONS
Walk down The Hythe at the north-west corner of Fair Green to Reach Port. Cross the bridge here, turn left and follow the farm track past the aptly named Water Hall on the left and Rose Cottage on the right, with Spring Hall further down the road. Cross the bridge on the left and turn right on to Barston Drove, a farm track which follows the foot of Church Hill.
Turn left onto a track (once part of the disused railway line), then right over the bridge and left, signed 'Burwell and Devil's Dyke', onto the disused railway track which runs through a nature reserve in a cutting. Take the sloping path up the bank and walk along the edge of the field. A series of fairly steep steps takes you up the embankment, then turn left at the top along the Devil's Dyke. Follow the dyke back from here to Fair Green.

What to look out for

In summer this area is a sea of colour, the yellow fields of oilseed rape are splashed with the bright red of poppies and the white sails of the windmills at Swaffham Prior stand out against a blue sky. A pair of binoculars would be useful.
Hedgerows provide a haven for wildlife, and in late summer and early autumn blackberries, rosehips and sloes are there for picking. Reach Lode supports a variety of water life, and the small nature reserve is home to some unusual plants.

Reach Village and Port
During Roman times, when the fens were wet marshland, Reach was a small port. It continued to thrive well into the 18th century because a navigable canal had been constructed to join it to the River Cam. The port started to decline in the 19th century when the fens were drained, leaving the village surrounded by hundreds of square miles of fertile

farmland, much as it is today. The relatively high chalk hill to the south of the village provided many boatloads of 'clunch', an important building material used to construct local homes, farms and churches. University buildings in Cambridge and the cathedral in Ely were reportedly supplied with Reach clunch.
Reach Fair, started in 1201 by the citizens of Cambridge, has been held annually ever since and the Mayor of Cambridge still performs the opening ceremony. The scene of many gatherings of local farmers and agricultural labourers, it also attracted some 600 fossil diggers, who

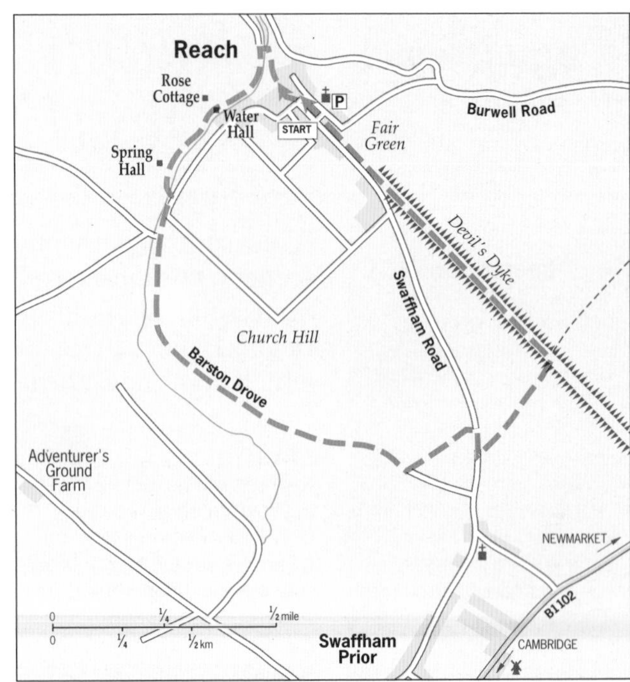

The village of Reach is at the northern end of the Devil's Dyke

worked out in the fens digging and washing fossils which, when ground up, were used as the first artificial fertiliser.

The Devil's Dyke

The Devil's Dyke, or Devil's Ditch as it is sometimes known, is a seven-mile military ditch and embankment constructed between 370–670AD to protect the farmland from invading tribes from across the North Sea. The steep sides and huge ditch, in parts up to 60ft from top to bottom, provided considerable protection.
The Reach end of the ditch was demolished towards the end of the Dark Ages when relative peace led instead to the construction of Fair Green, the village green.

Wimpole Park

WALK 43
CAMBRIDGESHIRE
TL337510

This pleasant circular walk offers views over rolling countryside, unusual for Cambridgeshire, as well as a wide variety of rare livestock, a folly, a lake and the chance to visit Wimpole House and Wimpole Home Farm (National Trust properties).

START
Wimpole Park is seven miles west of Cambridge on the A603 and five miles north of Royston on the A1198 (Ermine Street). Start the walk from the large free car park by the stables.

DIRECTIONS
Walk past St Andrew's Church across the gravel drive to the front of the main hall, and follow the railings west to go through the kissing-gate on the right by the yew tree.
(The walk can be extended by about ½ mile by keeping straight on here and following the path along West Avenue to the plantation, where a right turn will lead you to join the main walk at the Chinese Bridge – see * below.)
The main walk continues straight on to the ha-ha, where you turn right through another kissing-gate into the field. From here follow the red waymarker posts north to the Iron Bridge, with a view of The Folly straight ahead. Cross the stile and follow the

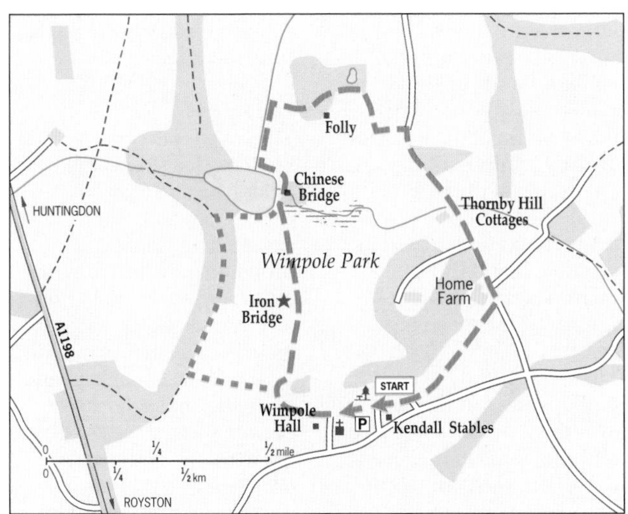

What to look out for

Wimpole's landscape has changed considerably through the centuries and you may be able to see signs of the ridges and furrows which mark the sites of medieval villages. The lake and woodland areas provide a rich habitat for a variety of wildlife and waterfowl, whilst the buildings provide a haven for seven different species of bat.

Information

The walk is approximately two miles long, but can be extended by half a mile
The paths are well maintained, with only a short stretch along a quiet lane; National Trust path closes at dusk
One stile
Dogs must be kept on a lead within the parkland
Restaurant, tea room and National Trust shop at Wimpole Hall
Picnic places within the park; The Folly is particularly suitable
Toilets and baby room at the stables

The magnificent façade of Wimpole Hall

marker posts to the lake and the Chinese Bridge.

*Cross the bridge and turn left round the edge of the field up to The Folly. From here follow the marker posts eastwards to Oddy Doddy Lane, then turn right down the hill past Thornbury Hill Cottages and Home Farm. Shortly after passing Home Farm take the path on the right through another kissing-gate. This will lead across the fields back to the car park.

Bat

Wimpole Hall

Wimpole Hall was built by Sir Thomas Chicheley in the mid 17th century and has been altered and extended by successive generations of owners. It only achieved something approaching its present form in the late 18th century whilst in the ownership of the Earls of Hardwicke. The house was left to the National Trust by its last owner, Mrs Elsie Bambridge, the daughter of Rudyard Kipling, on her death in 1976.

The grounds too have undergone great changes over the years, assuming their 'natural' looks in the second half of the 18th century at the hands of such famous landscape artists as Robert Greening, 'Capability' Brown and William Eames. Books and leaflets giving a more detailed history are available from the shop.

The Folly

The Folly is perhaps the most imposing feature on the landscape and provides the perfect spot for a picnic. It was designed by 'Capability' Brown to provide a romantic outlook from the main house, and also served as the head gamekeeper's house until the 1940s. Views from here are dramatic, and a quick examination of the graffiti on the walls will show that people haven't changed greatly over the centuries!

Harlestone Heath

WALK 44
NORTHAMPTONSHIRE
SP711637

This walk through the woods of Harlestone Heath is beautiful at all times of year, and especially in the spring and autumn. There are any number of other paths to explore.

Information

The walk is just under two miles long
Level, easy ground
No stiles
No road walking
The Cottage Tea Rooms (at garden centre by the parking area) serve snacks and light meals
There are many picnic places throughout the woods

START
Harlestone is on the north-west edge of Northampton, just outside the suburb of New Duston on the A428. Park in the lay-by by a garden centre, opposite the main entrance to Harlestone Firs Saw Mill. Start the walk from these gates.

DIRECTIONS
Go through the gates and take the path to the left. The track eventually curves round to the right, with a sawmill straight ahead, and leads to a fenced plantation of young trees in front of the mill. A wide grass verge continues to the right, but take the smaller, sandy track to the left.
Follow this track round to the right through the woods and continue straight over at the crossways, with beech trees to the right, and continue for some distance until turning right in the dip. Just after a track joins from the left, reach a crossways and go straight on. Turn right at the next junction, distinguished by four large beech trees, and walk down the fine, wide avenue. Just past a clearing on the right by the mill, a road joins from the right, returning to the start point.

The entrance gate to Harlestone Heath

Great spotted woodpecker

The Spencer Family
Harlestone Heath, or Firs, is owned by Lord Spencer, as is much of the land in this area, but he is happy to allow public access to the rides. Nearby Church Brampton and Chapel Brampton are also part of Lord Spencer's estate,

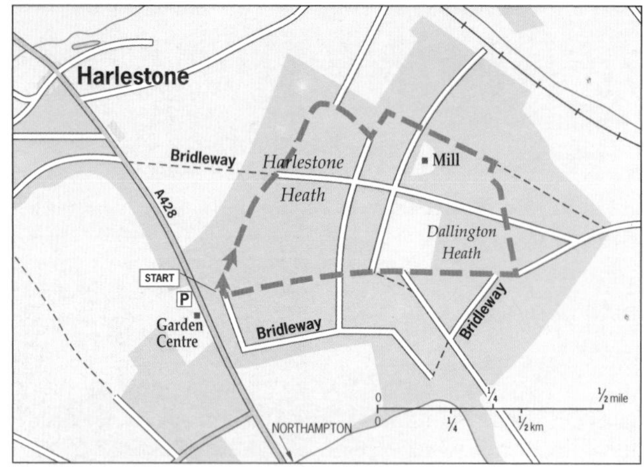

as is the village of Harlestone. The church at Lower Harlestone, built in the 14th century of orange-brown stone, is well worth a visit. The Spencer seat is at nearby Althorp House. Before 1500 the Spencers were modest farmers in Warwickshire, but then the acquisitive and shrewd Sir John Spencer began amassing lands. The family was awarded a barony in 1603 and an earldom in 1765 and has advanced its status over the centuries with a series of beneficial marriages. Like all great families its members have dabbled at times in politics and affairs of state, but farming and the running of their estates has always been their first priority.

On the edge of the wood

What to look out for

Despite the extensive planting of conifers, Harlestone still has many beautiful deciduous and broad-leaved trees – it is worth taking a field guide to identify the species. Great spotted woodpeckers may be heard in the woods.

WALK 45
NORTHAMPTONSHIRE
SP747769

The Woods at Maidwell

This is a most attractive walk which is particularly lovely in the spring and autumn, though it provides a great deal of wildlife and wildflower interest at most times of the year.

Information

The walk is about three miles long
Some ups and downs, with one short but fairly steep descent
A few stiles
No road walking
Dogs should be kept on leads
Pub in Maidwell village serves food
There are several picnic places along the route

START
Maidwell is some ten miles north of Northampton on the A508.
Park either in the village, or at the top of the lane leading to Hall Farm, taking care not to cause an obstruction.

DIRECTIONS
Follow the lane down past Hall Farm, where the outline of a medieval fish pond can still be discerned, then up and down past Dale Farm Conservation Area. Take the right hand fork after the stream at the bottom and go up the track to Dale Farm, branching right down a small track by the barn.
(For a much shorter walk, go down the lane to the bridge at the bottom. Here take the footpath to the right up through the woods and over the footbridge and stile by the yellow-tipped post and so back to the start point across the fields.)
The main track, which is waymarked, passes more farm buildings on the right. Follow the fence round to the left and keep straight on at the end of the wooden fence. Turn right at the end of the field, keeping the hedge on your left. Keep straight on through two fields, then turn to the right towards the woods and at the corner go into the trees and descend the bank. Cross a stream and climb up through the woods to meet a track.
Turn right here and walk up and along the edge of the wood for quite a long way. Shortly before the end of a field, reach a yellow-tipped post on your right which signals a stile and footbridge back through the woods. Do not follow this sign, but turn left along the footpath across the field. Climb a stile into the next field and then another. Then aim for the left of the house ahead, cross another stile and so re-enter the village at the start point.

Creeping speedwell

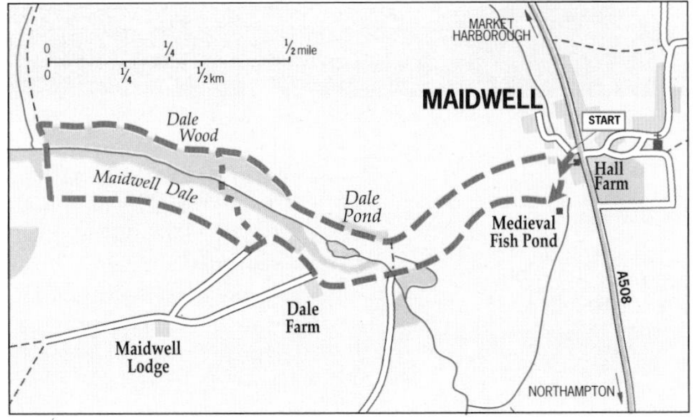

Medieval Fish Ponds
The site of medieval fish ponds can be clearly seen in

The track leads through Maidwell Dale farmland

What to look out for

This walk offers an excellent variety of flowers, trees, birds and animals in their natural surroundings. Maidwell Dale and Wood are untypical of much of Northamptonshire, reminiscent instead of a corner of the Peak District.

the field on the left of the bend in the lane, shortly after the start of the walk. Before the comparatively recent invention of refrigeration and fast transport, fish ponds were used to supply fresh fish to the tables of mansions and monasteries.

Stratford's Shire Horse Centre

WALK 46
WARWICKSHIRE
SP205549

This is a pleasant, easy walk from Stratford-upon-Avon, visiting the Shire Horse Centre and Farm Park and the lovely village of Clifford Chambers, and crossing the River Avon to the church where Shakespeare lies buried.

Information

The walk is just under four miles long
Level, easy ground
Several stiles
Some road walking along a surfaced footpath
Dogs should be kept on leads at the Shire Horse Centre and through neighbouring pastures
Refreshments, including meals, at the Shire Horse Centre. Pub at Clifford Chambers for bar meals; no children's room
Grassy areas suitable for picnics at the Shire Horse Centre and by the River Avon

START

The walk starts from the centre of Stratford-upon-Avon, but can be started from Clifford Chambers (ample roadside parking), or from the Shire Horse Centre (parking free for visitors). The Centre is one and a half miles south of the town, off the B4632.

DIRECTIONS

From the Gower Memorial to Shakespeare, walk towards Clopton Bridge. Turn through gates to the Old Tramway and follow it for a mile, passing the new bypass, Severn Meadow Road (A4390) to the junction of the A3400 and the B4632. Turn right along the B4632 (footpath) for about 200yds. Opposite Cross o' th' Hill Farm climb a stile and go diagonally right to a waymark post left of Springfield House. Bear right along the field-edge, passing the house, to the gateway ahead and follow a track across the next field to the Shire Horse Centre.

If not visiting the Centre, turn left along the byway for about 100yds to the waymarked gateway on the right and take the public footpath to a stile into a meadow. Turn left and, towards the end of the meadow, veer right to a stile. Cross the next field to a kissing-gate, and make for a railed bridge over the little River Stour. Beyond the bridge, a fenced path skirts a fish farm and passes Old Mill to the end of Clifford Chambers' main street, with

Stratford's Trinity Church across the waters of the River Avon

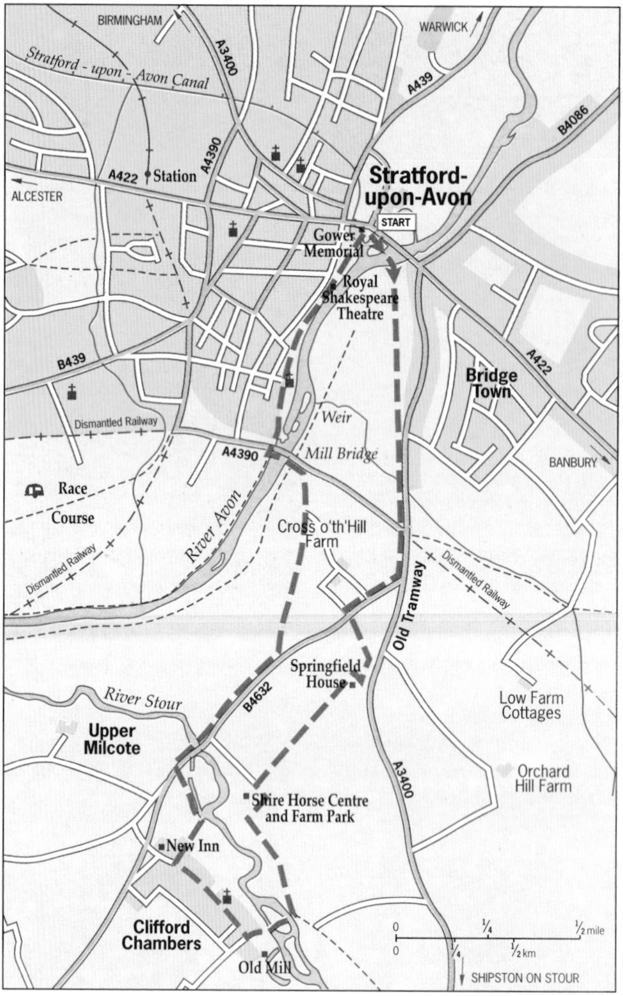

the Manor House to the left. Turn along the village street, and about 100yds before the New Inn a public footpath, signed to the right, passes between bungalows. After it curves left, a weir on the Stour can be viewed by diverting along a short path to the right. Return to the original path and continue to a metal gate, then between railings and the river to stile. Bear right along a field-edge to the B4632.

Turning right on its footpath for nearly ½ mile, climb a stile on the left and cross a field to a fence bordering a drive. Follow the fence to a gate and descend a surfaced path to a stile below the bypass embankment. Turn left to a kissing gate by the Avon and go under the bypass. (As an alternative to the main route, follow the riverside path into Stratford.)
Beyond the bypass, cross Mill Bridge and turn to follow Mill Lane to Holy Trinity Church, where Shakespeare lies buried. Go through the churchyard and out by the main gate. Turn right for a few yards, enter the Avonbank Gardens and walk through them, past the theatre, back to the Gower Memorial.

What to look out for

On leaving Stratford via the Old Tramway, you will pass one of its wagons and a notice giving the history of the line. At the Shire Horse Centre there are a dozen great heavy horses and several rare breeds of farm animals. The famous swans of the River Avon can still be seen.

Clifford Chambers
Though close to busy Stratford, this charming village can be enjoyed without the distraction of through traffic. There is a gem of a half-timbered rectory and an interesting church.

Carrion crow

Thor's Cave

WALK 47
STAFFORDSHIRE
SK109552

A lovely walk from the village of Wetton, which rises to the spectacular entrance of Thor's Cave, named after the Norse god of thunder, before descending into the beautiful Manifold valley.

START
Wetton village is on a minor road one mile west of Alstonefield and about six miles north of Ashbourne. The National Park car park lies on the southern edge of the village.

DIRECTIONS
From the car park turn right, walking away from the village centre towards Grindon. Take the first turning right, signposted 'Wetton Mill', then in 200yds turn left at sign 'Wetton Mill/Manifold Valley'. After about 30yds, turn off the road to the left, following a walled green lane, signposted 'Concessionary path to Thor's Cave', for ¼ mile.
After crossing a stile by a gate, continue along a track for another 50yds, then turn right over a stone stile and follow the waymarked path down the field, to the right of the hill. At the end of the second field cross a fence stile and descend on a sometimes slippery path to the cave, which is prominent in the limestone crag above (take particular care with children here). After visiting the cave (superb views), descend via the steep flight of steps (slippery after rain) to the valley.
Cross the footbridge, turn left and follow the 'Manifold Track' (not signed) along the winding, wooded course of the river, which is to your left for about ¾ mile to Weag's Bridge. Turn immediately left over the bridge and follow the minor road which

0 ¼ ½ mile
0 ¼ ½ km
334 Ossoms Hill
The Manifold Track
Foot Bridge
Wetton
The Olde Royal Oak
P
START
ALSTONEFIELD
Thor's Cave
River Manifold
322 Wetton Low
The Manifold Track
Car Park & Picnic Site
GRINDON
Weag's Bridge
Cattle Grid
Cattle Grid
Beeston Tor
Caves
Bridleway
Bridleway

Information

The walk is three miles long
Varied terrain, with one steep descent and ascent and an easy, level section on a former railway track
A few stiles
Some road walking on quiet lanes
Dogs should be kept on leads
The Olde Royal Oak in Wetton has a family room
Picnic site at Weag's Bridge
Toilets at car park

Bird's-foot trefoil

shortly climbs steeply uphill for about ½ mile. After crossing a cattle grid, turn left over a stone stile and ascend across a field, keeping the wall to your left.
At the top of the field turn left onto a lane, which will bring you back to the start point in about ½ mile.

Thor's Cave
Set 300ft above the Manifold Valley in a huge limestone cliff, Thor's Cave was inhabited by prehistoric man and evidence found here suggests that the cave was occupied more or less continuously until Romano-British times.

The Manifold Track
This leisure route uses the line of the former Leek and Manifold Light Railway, which ran on a narrow gauge track up the valleys of the Rivers Hamps and Manifold for 30 years from 1904. It catered mainly for local traffic, particularly taking milk from the Staffordshire hills to the Potteries, and featured delightful primrose yellow carriages and unique tank engines, originally designed for use in India.

The mouth of the spectacular Thor's Cave

What to look out for

The River Manifold disappears into underground channels during the summer months, reappearing at Ilam, several miles downstream. This is a common feature of rivers running across the limestone rock in this part of the Peak District, which is known as the White Peak because of the predominant colour of the rock. If you look carefully at the rocks in the many dry stone walls which cross-cross the landscape, you will find the fossils of sea lilies and shells, laid down in a shallow, tropical sea some 300 million years ago.
Early purple orchids and meadow cranesbill will be found in summer by the path into the valley from Wetton, and in May and June listen for blackcaps and willow warblers.

Creswell Crags

WALK 48
DERBYSHIRE
SK538743

In the seemingly unpromising location of the Derbyshire-Nottinghamshire coalfield, this walk takes in one of the most famous British prehistoric sites, and has the added bonus of some fascinating wildlife and an excellent visitor centre.

Information

The walk is about one and a half miles long
Clear, level field paths
Little road walking
A few gates and some steps
Dogs must be kept on leads
Pubs and restaurants in Creswell village
Toilets, information and picnic area at Creswell Crags Visitor Centre

START

The Creswell Crags Visitor Centre is one mile east of Creswell village, on the B6042 road, between the A616 and A60 on the Derbyshire-Nottinghamshire border. The car park closes at 5pm.

DIRECTIONS

From the Visitor Centre car park, walk east past the picnic area along the track through the trees for about 100yds to a gate. Turn left here, along the waymarked bridleway and follow the well-defined farm track towards Hennymoor Farm. Just before reaching the first hedge, turn left again and follow a grassy track, keeping the hedge to your right. Shortly, a small gate leads onto Crags Road (B6042). Turn left here and in about 30yds, turn right on to another bridleway via a barred metal gate. Keep on this bridleway for about ½ mile, with a shelter belt of trees on your right, passing Bank House farm on the right.

Reach the A616 on the outskirts of Creswell village and turn left, and after 100yds turn left again back on to Crags Road (B6042), signed 'Creswell Crags Visitor Centre'. On reaching the traffic lights, turn right on to the path which runs around Crags Pond, passing in turn Church Hole Cave and Boat House Cave on the south bank, and Mother Grundy's Parlour, Robin Hood's Cave and Pin Hole Cave on the north bank by the road.

At the eastern end of the lake keep left and, just before reaching the road, go down the steps on the right, with

What to look out for

The spectacular magnesian limestone gorge of Creswell Crags is a Site of Special Scientific Interest (SSSI) because of its geologic importance and natural history. The series of caves which mark its sides are the home of long-eared and other bats, and the valley floor is rich in wild flowers such as great willowherb, yellow archangel and common comfrey. Introduced species such as the bright yellow monkeyflower have made their home here.

Crags Lake was created in the mid-19th century by damming the stream, but soon became colonised with moorhen, little grebe and water vole. The stream supports water crowfoot, water starwort with water figwort. Look out for the jackdaws, spotted flycatchers and pied wagtails which nest in the rock crevices.

The dramatic scenery of Cresswell Crags

the stream to your right, and return to the Visitor Centre and car park.

The Creswell Caves

One of the world's earliest works of art was found by archaeologists investigating the caves of Creswell. The engraved image of a horse was found on a fragment of rib bone from Robin Hood's Cave, and other examples were found in the cave known as Mother Grundy's Parlour. They are thought to have been the work of a wandering tribe, known as Creswellian man, which settled in the gorge as the Ice Age glaciers retreated about 13,000 years ago. But the occupation of the Creswell caves began long before that. The bones of Ice Age mammals such as hyena, bear, reindeer, bison and woolly rhinoceros have been found, and the first evidence of man is the crudely-fashioned stone axes and scrapers dating from about 43,000BC and used by the Neanderthal people. Occupation of the caves continued more or less continuously through Roman and medieval times.

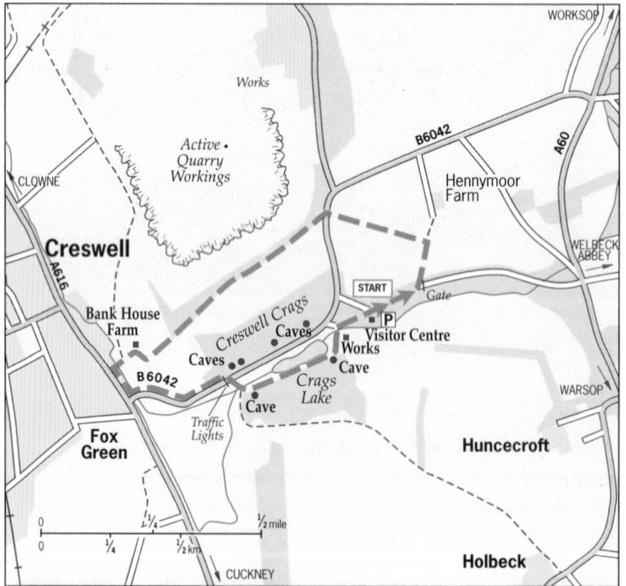

The Welbeck Estate

The crags and pond at Creswell were part of the estate of nearby Welbeck Abbey. The pond was created by the Duke of Portland for duck shooting, and Boat House Cave was where he moored his boats. Originally founded by monks of the Order of the White Canons, the present Abbey dates from the 18th century and now occupied by Welbeck College.

Cromford Canal

Explore Derbyshire's industrial heritage, from the site of Richard Arkwright's first cotton mill, along a beautifully-restored canal, and back through delightful woodland.

WALK 49
DERBYSHIRE
SK302569

START
Cromford Wharf and Meadows are just off the A6, 18 miles north of Derby and three miles south of Matlock Bath. There is plentiful parking on Cromford Meadows and at the High Peak Junction.

DIRECTIONS
From Cromford Wharf, set out south along the towpath, signed 'High Peak Junction', with the canal on your right. Follow the towpath for just over a mile to reach High Peak Junction. There is a choice of routes here.
(The shorter alternative is to cross the Derwent at High Peak Junction by the footbridge, signed 'Holloway', and walk up the lane towards Lea Bridge, where you meet the longer route at * below.) The main walk continues for about ¼ mile to the Leawood

Arkwright's Cromford Mill, built in 1771

What to look out for

The Cromford Canal is a haven for wildlife, with a profusion of wild flowers including blue water-speedwell, water mint, forget-me-nots and marsh marigolds. Birds include mallard, coot, moorhen and, if you are lucky, the occasional kingfisher, while small mammals which may be seen include water shrews and water voles.

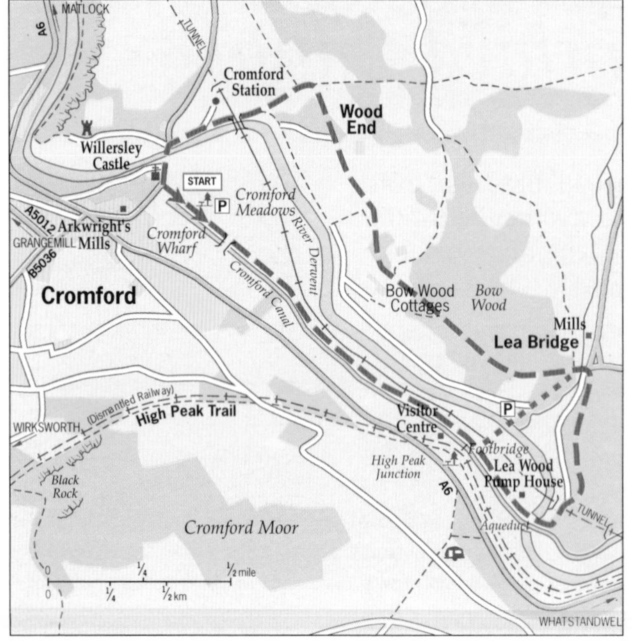

Pump House, crossing the Derwent by an aqueduct and then turning left over the railway tunnel entrance on the path through Lea Wood to reach Lea Bridge*. At the road turn left and cross bridge, then branch right through squeeze-stile into a wood. Follow the main path, bearing left through this pleasant mixed woodland.

Eventually emerge onto a green lane and at fork, keep right on a well-defined path. Continue across four fields and through wood. At the far end continue to a crossways and turn left to descend to the road, joining it under the railway bridge. Pass Cromford Station and the entrance to Willersley Castle (private). Carefully cross Cromford Bridge to return to the car park.

Cromford Canal

Built to serve Richard Arkwright's Cromford Mill (the first water-powered cotton mill in the world), the Cromford Canal was opened in 1793. It was heavily used for the transportation of cotton and other goods until the coming of the railway in the 1860s. The five and a half mile stretch between Cromford and Ambergate has been restored.

Lea Wood Pump House

This distinctive building, with its classically-shaped chimney, was built in 1840 to pump water from the nearby River Derwent into the canal. The original steam-powered beam engine is still inside, and is currently under restoration by enthusiasts. It is occasionally open to the public at summer weekends.

Sir Richard Arkwright and Cromford

Richard Arkwright transformed textile manufacturing from a cottage industry to a factory operation, and his first mill, the fortress-like Upper Mill near the start of the walk, was built in 1771. It now includes a visitor centre. At the height of its production the mill employed 500 workers, many of whom lived in Arkwright's model village of Cromford, and many of his cottages still survive. He amassed a great personal fortune, but he died in 1792, just before the completion of his stately country house, Willersley Castle (private), near the end of the walk.

Shrew

Information

The walk is about three and a half miles long
The first part, along the canal towpath, is easy; the return is more strenuous
Several squeeze-stiles
Dogs should be kept on leads, except in Cromford Meadows
Picnic area in Cromford Meadows, near the start; also at High Peak Junction
Pubs and cafés in Cromford
Toilets at Cromford Meadows

The Reservoir at Denton

This is a very enjoyable and interesting walk from the village of Denton, which goes across an old railway track, round the reservoir and back across the fields via the Grantham Canal.

WALK 50
LINCOLNSHIRE
SK869324

START
Denton is three miles south-west of Grantham, just off the A607. Park carefully and considerately in the village. The walk starts at the telephone box, behind a tree in Main Street.

DIRECTIONS
Take the signed footpath opposite the telephone box. Go through a gate and follow the path under horse chestnut trees and through a kissing-gate. Turn right along the road for a few yards, then turn left at the footpath sign. Go through two kissing-gates to reach the road in front of the church. Turn right and follow the road round past the Welby Arms. Keep straight on at the junction with the main road and go left at the next junction. Walk down to the bridge over the stream and turn right through a gate along the signed footpath. Cross two stiles, then the old railway line, then another stile and carry on alongside the stream. Do not cross the stile and bridge on your right, but continue over the stile by the white gate, leading to Denton Reservoir. Walk about three quarters of the way round the reservoir, then look out for a footpath sign on the left, directing you down some wooden steps and across a footbridge.
This path leads through the fields and over two stiles. At the end of the second large field, where you meet the Grantham Canal, pass through the gap in the hedge, turn right over a stile by a five-barred gate, going away from the canal. Follow the path which leads along the edge of two fields and then comes out through a nine-barred gate on a track leading away from a farm to the road. Cross over the road and walk down Rectory Lane, turning right at the bend into West End, on the edge of the village of Harlaxton. Continue down the track ahead and keep straight on to cross a stile. The footpath now bears half-right over the field, aiming to the right of the trees where a stile is set into the hedge bordering the road. Go over this stile, cross the road and take the footpath through a gate opposite, leading across the field back towards Denton. There are two stiles to cross on either side of the old railway line, then a footbridge.

Teal

Information

The walk is about three and a half miles long
Easy walking, with a few gentle inclines
A lot of stiles
Pubs in Denton and Harlaxton serve food; children welcome
Reservoir banks ideal for picnics

What to look out for

The reservoir is popular with anglers who come to fish for roach, perch, bream and pike. It is also a favourite spot for birds, including mallard, teal, grey heron, great crested grebe, moorhen and coot, especially in winter.

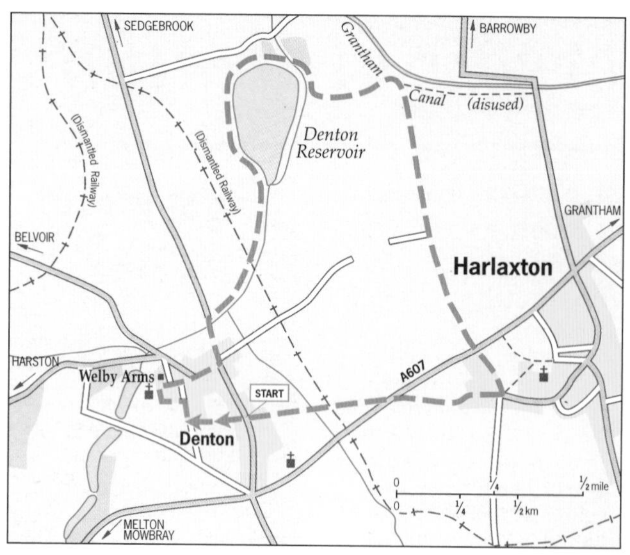

Walk up to a stile in the far right-hand corner of the next field and return to the start.

Denton Reservoir and the Grantham Canal

Originally built as a feeder for the Grantham Canal, the Denton Reservoir can hold up to 61 million gallons of water. The canal dates from the 1790s and runs from Grantham to West Bridgford, where it links with the River Trent. It fell into a decline in the middle of the 19th century, losing the battle with the railways, and finally closed in 1936.

The village of Denton

WALK 51
LINCOLNSHIRE
TF366914

The Mill and Two Churches

This is a pleasant and interesting walk, with a working mill, a canal, two churches in one churchyard and the site of a medieval priory.

START
Alvingham is three miles north-east of Louth. Start the walk at the west end of the village, from a parking area signed 'Two Churches', which is to be found near the mill in Church Lane.

Information

The walk is three miles long
Level, easy ground
A few stiles
No pub in village, but plenty in Louth nearby
The towpath of the canal is suitable for picnics

The open track near Alvingham

What to look out for

Alvingham is a delightful village with much to see, including a pottery, a working blacksmith's forge and even village stocks. Along Grange Lane, extensive vistas open out across the desolate marshland, where lapwings display in spring.

DIRECTIONS
Walk over the road bridge past the mill, through the farmyard and through the gate into the churchyard. Turning right, follow the hedgeline and cross the first two of three bridges leading over the canal. Turn left and walk along the towpath, crossing a stile after ½ mile. After about ¼ mile the canal curves to the left. Cross the stile and turn right onto the lane by the bridge, then after the bend turn right over another bridge, passing through a gateway, signed 'bridleway'. This track passes to the left of a cottage and windpump and then crosses the dry bed of the River Lud. It then follows the line of a dyke, round a couple of bends, until it comes to a lane. Turn right here past Grange Farm, and proceed along Grange Lane for about ¾ mile. At a junction go straight on then after a right-hand bend turn left up a track, following a footpath sign. Keep straight on along the edge of a lawn,

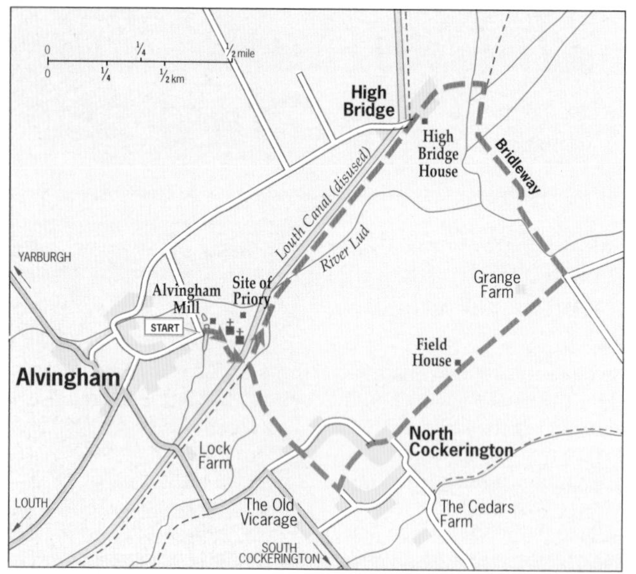

over a stile and across the field, keeping the fence to your left. Climb another stile, go down the path and turn right at the junction of paths. Go straight across the road, following the footpath sign, and so return to the start point.

Alvingham Mill

There has been a watermill in Alvingham since the time of the Domesday Book. The present mill, which may well be on the site of the original, was built in the 17th century. The mill is open on Bank Holidays and some summer afternoons.

Alvingham Mill

A Maze in the Wye Valley

WALK 52
HEREFORD & WORCESTER
SO554174

This walk is in the beautiful Lower Wye Valley. Following the river bank downstream, it crosses the Wye via two ferries and returns from the foot of Symonds Yat Rock along a quiet lane, rising gently to give fine views.

Information

The walk is two and a half miles long
Easy, mainly level ground, but a long, steep climb to Symond's Yat Rock
Virtually no road walking
Dogs are not allowed in the Jubilee Park
No stiles
Cafés and kiosks at the Jubilee Park and the Wye Valley Leisure Park; pubs *en route*
Grassy area suitable for picnics by river

START
Whitchurch is on the B4164, five miles south-west of Ross-on-Wye, just off the A40. Park at the Jubilee Park beside the B4164 (parking free at time of going to press, but a charge may be introduced in the near future), or in the car park (charge) of the neighbouring Wye Valley Leisure Park.

DIRECTIONS
Cross the bridge leading to the Maze in the Jubilee Park and turn left along a tarmac track to the Church of St Dubricius. The riverside path can be reached by going through the churchyard, or alternatively by following the footpath to the right at the end of the wall through the kissing-gate, from which a narrow flagged path leads to the river.

The River Wye below Symond's Yat Rock

Turn right, to go downstream past the Wye Valley Leisure Park, then pass through a kissing-gate to a large riverside meadow. Beyond the meadow the path ends at Ye Olde Ferrie Inne. A chain ferry is operated by the inn (but not in adverse weather conditions, nor when the river is in flood. If the ferry is not operating, or if you wish to shorten the walk, continue the route at * below).

Take the ferry to the far bank, where there is a pleasant walk downstream to the Ancient Hand ferry at the Saracen's Head Hotel. Re-cross the river there and turn right along the

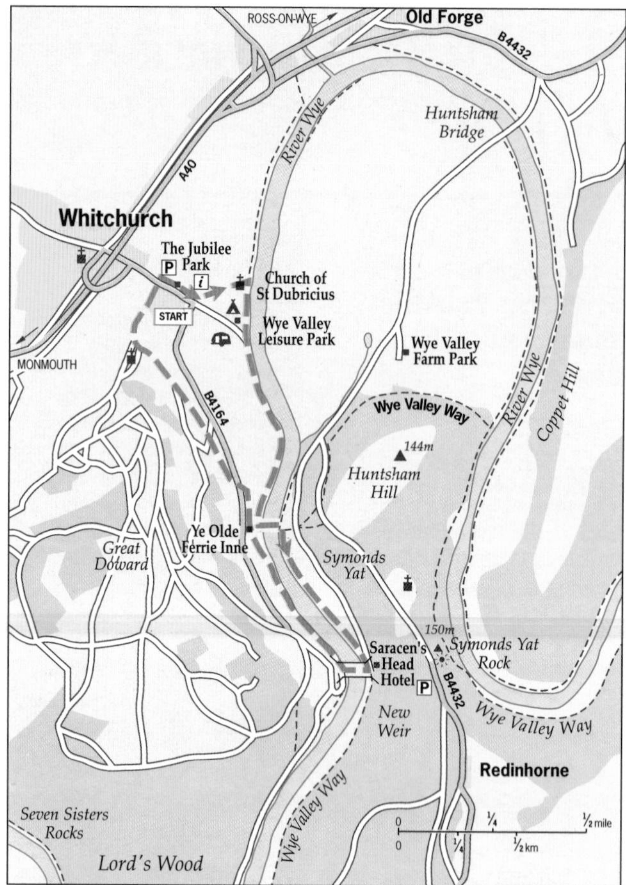

track, which runs past the rear of Ye Olde Ferrie Inne * to the B4164.

Follow the road ahead, past a telephone box, and fork left up a lane.

Shortly, at a junction, keep straight ahead between two white cottages, then pass to the left of another white cottage ('Crossways'), to where the track bends left, below a United Reformed Church. Continue straight ahead through a kissing-gate to a field and follow the right-hand hedge down to a second kissing-gate on the B4164. Turn right here for the Jubilee Park, and to return to the starting point.

The Jubilee Park
The Park's attractions include the Jubilee Maze – a hedge maze constructed in 1977 to commemorate the Queen's Silver Jubilee – with lovely gardens and countryside walks, the Museum of Mazes, the Amazing Puzzle Shop, the World of Butterflies, a garden centre and a restaurant. There is also a Tourist Information Centre here. The park is closed from Christmas to the end of January.

The Parish Church of St Dubricius
Dubricius was a 6th-century bishop, teacher and founder of churches.
According to legend, when Peipiau, the King of Erging, discovered that his daughter was pregnant, he ordered her to be put in a sack and drowned in the Wye, but the girl was washed ashore alive. The king then tried to burn her to death, but next morning she was found nursing her child, Dubricius, whose Welsh name, Dyfrig, means water baby.
The church, on a site dating from Saxon times, is mainly 12th century.

What to look out for

Symond's Yat Rock is a splendid viewpoint, and the best point for viewing the famous peregrine falcons which have an eyrie here. Buzzards are a common sight, circling above the valley. There is usually plenty of activity to watch along the River Wye, which is popular with canoeists and pleasure boats.
In the churchyard there is an old preaching cross, with a 15th-century shaft and modern head, an unusual open vault (of the Gwillim family) and a large tulip tree.

WALK 53
HEREFORD & WORCESTER
SO452656

Croft Castle and Croft Ambrey

This an easy figure-of-eight hill walk on National Trust land, linking the late-medieval Croft Castle with the even older fortification of Croft Ambrey, a mile away and 400ft higher.

START
Croft Castle is seven miles south-west of Ludlow, off the B4362. Start from the free car park (small charge if you are not visiting the castle). There is a map of the estate, which is always open to the public without charge.

DIRECTIONS
From the car park, walk back along the drive and cross a cattle-grid. Turn immediately left, down a path through woods to the Fishpool Valley. Ascend the valley track to the left, passing a stone-built Gothic pumphouse and a pool. At the track junction on the left, just before the next pool, turn left by the remains of a lime kiln, go along the side-track for about 10yds, then leave it for a path on the right. Fork right and climb to Ambrey Cottage, there meeting a broader path, and turn left through a gate. (To shorten the route, avoiding the climb to Croft Ambrey, continue the walk at * below). Bear right to a gate leading into Croft Wood, climb the path and cross a track to reach the top of a rise (splendid view). Go through a gate and bear to the left of a wire fence to a path (another magnificent view). From a stile on the right climb a path bearing left. It swings through the ramparts of the hillfort and over the high ground in the centre. Beyond the hillfort descend a path through ferns, and fork left. There is a view east to the distant Malvern Hills, before the path bears left and drops to a stile. Turn right along the path beyond and right again through a small wooden gate. Descend between trees and go right along the track at the bottom. Ignore a major track (after about 70yds) bearing left and continue to a fork, where a lesser track

Mole

descending to the left leads back to Ambrey Cottage. *Pass through the gate used before and bear left of a covered reservoir to descend open grassland. Follow the path through a line of old, twisted chestnut trees, down a meadow and under more trees to a gate, from which a track leads back to the car park.

What to look out for

A wide variety of trees can be seen, including many unusual non-native species. Look under the overhangs of the Castle towers for house martins' nests and watch for buzzards soaring over the hillfort. Fallow deer, badgers and polecats are among the creatures who inhabit the area. The chain of five pools in the Fishpool Valley is a lovely example of late 18th-century 'picturesque' landscaping; the remains of a lime kiln can be seen near the Gothic pumphouse.

Croft Castle
The stone walls of the castle date from the 14th and 15th

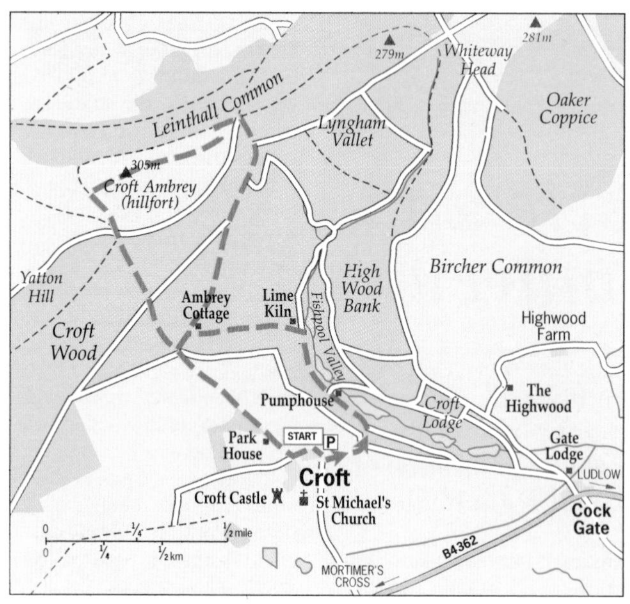

Information

The walk is three miles long
Long, gradual climb to Croft Ambrey
No road walking
Dogs should be kept on leads
A few stiles to cross
Grassy area suitable for picnics at Croft Castle car park

centuries, but the interior was thoroughly 'modernised' in the 18th. The Croft family lived here until 1746, and returned after buying back the castle in 1923. Although it remains the family home, it now belongs to the National Trust and is open at weekends and on selected days from Easter to October.

Croft Ambrey

The 1,000ft-high hillfort, covering 38 acres, was occupied from the 4th century BC until the Roman invasion of Britain. Today it provides some of the loveliest views of the Welsh Border country.

The church in the grounds of Croft Castle

WALK 54
HEREFORD & WORCESTER
SO995759

The Lickey Hills

This walk explores part of the lovely 524-acre Lickey Hills Country Park, with its varied scenery of pools, woods, open grassland and a golf course – and there are magnificent views from Beacon Hill.

START
The Lickey Hills rise at Rednal, on the south-western outskirts of Birmingham. Leave the M42 at junction 1 and take the B4096. This leads directly to the free public car park behind the Old Rose & Crown, off Rose Hill.

DIRECTIONS
From the car park pass left of the café to a large pool and skirt it to the right. Follow a chain of small ornamental pools uphill and pass between two of them to join a broad track. Opposite a green bank with picnic tables branch right, climbing very steeply and soon forking left. At the top of the track turn left, climbing again and forking right by a seat. Cross a diagonal path and continue through blackberry bushes, then bear left along a path beside Scots pines. At the cross-path turn right through the pines and veer left, between toilet blocks, to the open plateau of Beacon Hill. Cross to the battlemented toposcope (sadly vandalised) at 987ft above sea level and enjoy the views, before descending right towards Birmingham. Walk along well worn grass paths, passing a North Worcester Path marker post, and on your right an Ordnance Survey Trig point, then descend through woods. After 200yds descend log steps and at the bottom turn left, soon crossing (carefully) the municipal golf course. In 300yds, on the far side of the course, the path runs right beside a line of trees and reaches a cross-path. Turn right along a heavily wooded bridleway for about 200yds, then bear right along the edge of the golf course. Finally turn right through an attractive

Kite-flying on Beacon Hill

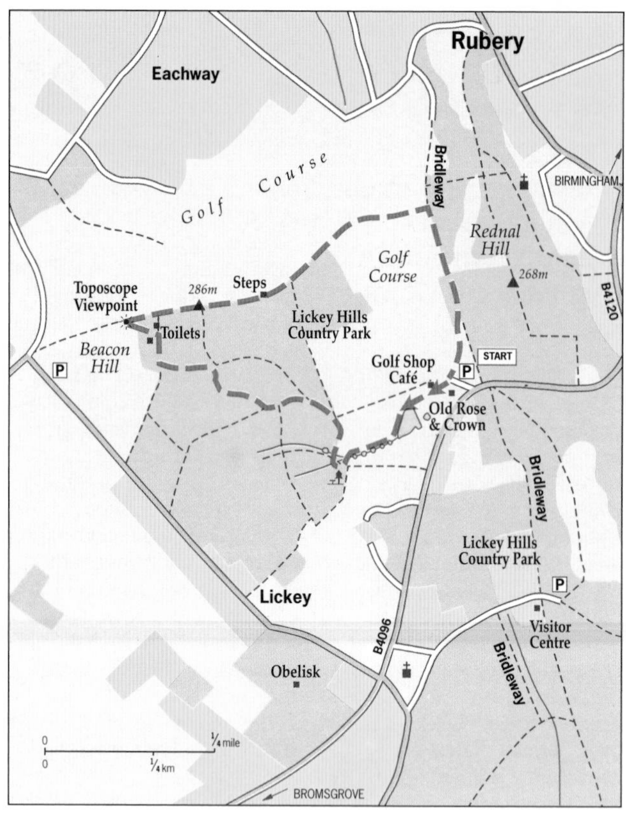

from the Silver Jubilee of George V in 1935. It once bore a plaque recording the gift of 34 acres of hillside to the citizens of Birmingham by the Cadbury family in 1907.

The Lickey Hills Visitor Centre

Information about the country park can be obtained at the visitor centre, which stands half a mile south of the B4096, along a path starting from a footbridge east of the Old Rose & Crown. Cars can reach it by turning right from the car park and left along Warren Lane, just before the church.

The North Worcestershire Path

During the walk you will see waymark posts with the initials 'NWP'. These indicate the route of the North Worcestershire Path, a 21-mile walking route from Forhill Picnic Site, on the Roman Ryknid Street, to Kinver Edge.

What to look out for

The pool at the start of the walk is home to a variety of wildfowl, and in summer there are yellow flag irises at its edge and an array of wild flowers on the bank beside the path. In the woods you may hear the drumming of a great spotted woodpecker; look out for the wood warbler and redstart, both summer visitors to the area. You may see squirrels, but the little muntjac deer are much more timid.

Information

The walk is one and a half miles long
Hilly ground; well-defined paths
No road walking
Dogs should be kept on leads when crossing golf course
No stiles
Light refreshments at café near start of walk and at Lickey Hills Visitor Centre
The plateau of Beacon Hill and the grassy area by the car park are suitable for picnics
Toilets at Beacon Hill

beech avenue to return to the car park.

Beacon Hill

As its name suggests, the hilltop provided a link in the chain of burning beacons that once covered the country to warn the population of danger, such as the Spanish Armada in 1588, or to celebrate victories and anniversaries, as it did at the Queen's Silver Jubilee in 1977. The stone fountain below the toposcope dates

On Wenlock Edge

WALK 55
SHROPSHIRE
SO613997

Information

The walk is three and a half miles long
Mainly gentle hills, but some steep descents in woods
No road walking
Dogs should be on leads through fields at end of walk
One stile
Refreshments (seasonal) *en route* at Stokes Barn; pubs and cafés at Much Wenlock
Grassy area suitable for picnics at car park

This is mainly a woodland walk on National Trust land at the northern end of the 15-mile long Wenlock Edge. Beginning with Blakeway Hollow, now a rough, sunken lane but once the main road from Much Wenlock to Shrewsbury, it passes the viewpoint of Major's Leap.

The path to Blakeway Hollow

START
The A458 Shrewsbury–Bridgnorth road crosses the northern end of Wenlock Edge at Much Wenlock. Start the walk from the National Trust's free car park, which is signed a quarter of a mile along the B4371. There are also car parks in Much Wenlock, including one for visitors to the Priory.

DIRECTIONS
At the car park, cross the grass to a gate, climb steps and turn left into a hedged, unmetalled lane (Blakeway Hollow), following sign 'Blakeway Coppice' for about ½ mile to reach a signpost at the edge of the wood.
(Two miles can be cut from the walk by following the Harley Bank arrow to the right and continuing the route at * below.)
Follow the 'Blakeway Coppice' sign and fork left to a gate. After about 50yds take a stepped path on the left, signed 'Major's Leap'. The narrow path follows the wooded crest of the ridge for about ½ mile until a short path to the right leads to the Major's Leap viewpoint.
Return to the edge of the escarpment, where a path outside the trees, high above a limestone quarry, is followed to the right (Shropshire's highest point, 1,792ft Brown Clee Hill, to the left).
After about ½ mile, before the end of the quarry and above the quarry buildings, an old track angles back and steeply down to the right. Descend it to join the main track bearing right through the woods.
After about 250yds bear right to return to the entrance gate.
Follow the signposted Harley Bank path to the left, * soon descending steeply through Harley Wood. After about 300yds, take a path forking

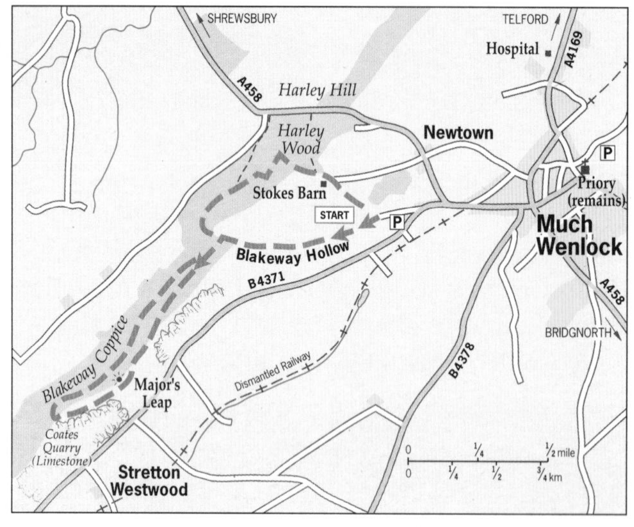

Major's Leap

The Royalist Major Smallman of Wilderhope Manor is said to have survived a leap on horseback from the limestone crag when escaping from Roundhead troops during the Civil War.
From the Leap there is a fine outlook across Ape Dale, with a distant view of the Berwyns in North Wales.

Honeysuckle

up to the right and after another 300yds bear right again up a stepped path at a signpost. At the top turn left and continue for about 150yds to a horse barrier and an old milestone.
Turn right through a gate and keep ahead to the stone buildings at Stokes Barn. Go through a gate and bear right by the barn entrance and signpost 'Much Wenlock'. Another signpost points the way down to a small wooden gate, from which the path descends through fields to a stile on Blakeway Hollow, with the car park to the left.

Much Wenlock

This lovely and interesting little town lies below the northern tip of Wenlock Edge. The ruins of its Cluniac Priory (English Heritage) date from the 12th and 13th centuries. Features of the town include the half-timbered Guildhall of 1540, a local museum, a magnificent church and many other fine buildings.

A pretty timbered cottage in Much Wenlock

What to look out for

Fossils can be found in the pale limestone of Wenlock Edge, which also nurtures many flowering plants, including orchids, not found in other soils. It is possible to look down into one of the limestone quarries, and in Harley Wood there is an old milestone.

Shropshire's Lake District

This is an easy, level walk round Cole Mere and along the Shropshire Union Canal to Blake Mere, thus visiting two of the nine meres, or lakes, in this geologically unique area known as 'the Shropshire Lake District'.

WALK 56
SHROPSHIRE
SJ435328

Information

The walk is about three and a half miles long
Level, easy ground
No road walking
Dogs should be kept on leads
No stiles
Nearest pubs and cafés are at Ellesmere
Grassy area beside car park suitable for picnics
No bathing or paddling in meres
Toilets at Cole Mere

Beautiful 'lakeland' scenery

START

Colemere Country Park is two and a half miles south-east of Ellesmere, between the A528 and the B5063, and immediately north of the hamlet of Colemere. Start the walk from the free car park beside the lake.

DIRECTIONS

From the car park set off clockwise round Cole Mere by joining the path along its western shore. At the far end of the mere, ignore a right fork and continue to a lane. Turn right, past a lovely thatched, black and white cottage, to the Shropshire Union Canal, and follow its towpath to the left until another large lake (Blake Mere) appears on your right. (The walk can be extended by 2 miles here by following the canal past Blake Mere and through a short tunnel. After about ¾ mile cross a bridge over a spur of the canal and turn right into the small town of Ellesmere. Walk through the town and return along the A528 (footpath), passing the Mere, the Cremorne Gardens and the Boat House Restaurant. Regain the canal at the road junction with the A495.)

The main route, after viewing Blake Mere, returns along the towpath and passes under the lane to the next bridge, about 700yds farther on. Cross the bridge, then follow the path to the left through Yell Wood. Bearing right, the path goes down the east side of Cole Mere and returns to the open grassy area near the car park.

What to look out for

Cole Mere is a lake of great interest for its bird life and the activities of its sailing club. Great crested grebes are common in winter, woodpeckers drum on old trees, and bats fly over the water at dawn and dusk. It is the only place in England where the rare least yellow water-lily can be found. Beyond Blake Mere is a short canal tunnel, and many holiday narrow boats pass along the Shropshire Union Canal in summer.

The Meres

The nine meres in the Ellesmere area are relics of the Ice Age glaciers that covered Britain 25,000 years ago, extending south of Shrewsbury. The withdrawal of the ice left a thick coating of glacier debris, or moraine, but pockets of ice survived in hollows and when they melted, meres were formed. They could be described simply as enormous puddles, mostly without streams flowing in or out, which are sustained by rainfall or the water table. The largest of the lakes, The Mere at Ellesmere, covers 116 acres and has a visitors' centre.

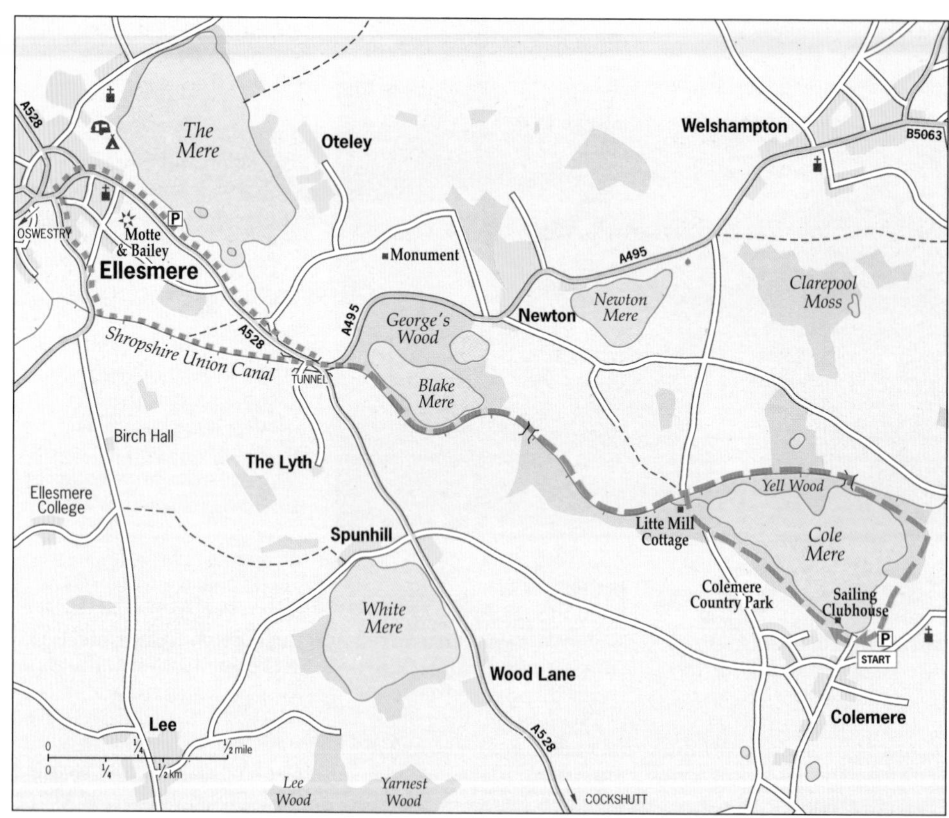

To the Summit of Twmbarlwm

WALK 57
GWENT
ST237929

Information

The walk is two and a half miles long
Two steep sections
Several stiles
Dogs should be kept on leads
Pub near the entrance to the Forest Drive in Cwmcarn
Toilets at the Visitor Centre

A hill walk which may be combined with the Cwmcarn Forest Drive (Easter to the end of October only). The views from the summit are just rewards for the effort involved, not to mention the sense of achievement.

START
Leave the M4 motorway at junction 28 and take the A467. Signs for the Cwmcarn Forest Drive will be seen after about seven miles. The walk starts from the car park (Pegwn-y-bwlch) on the Cwmcarn Forest Drive; when the Forest Drive is closed (November to Easter) park at the Visitor Centre and walk up the footpath on the right hand side of the centre. After passing a small lake, take the path to the right over a stile signposted 'Pegwyn-y-Bwlch'. Continue up this path, crossing three tarmac roads to reach the car park.

DIRECTIONS
Go over a stile signposted 'Castle Mound' and climb the well worn path. The gradient relents and the walk then crosses the fortification ditch of an Iron Age hill fort. Continue across the summit plateau to reach the 'trig' point. Directly ahead now is a large mound, known locally as the 'Twmbarlwm Pimple'. After taking in the view, follow a broad track down to a stile and then, keeping a

The way up to the summit

forestry plantation on your right, head down to a road. Follow the road for about ½ mile then take a track on the right leading down beside a fence. Cross a rutted track, bear right along fence and head for a stile, signed 'Darren', in the corner of the field. Go over the stile and continue with the fence on your left. Shortly turn left by a public footpath sign and proceed along the bottom of the field to reach a stile in the corner.
Continue beside the fence to later emerge from the trees. The track now descends with a line of pylons on the left.

Cross a stile and head down towards some old farm buildings. Turn right and follow a track leading to a gate and then downhill through the edge of a larch plantation and through a gate into a narrow secluded valley. Turn right at the T-junction, cross a stile and ascend a broad track up the side of the valley. At a crossing with a new forest road, keep forward to the top of the pass and the return to the car park.

Cwmcarn Forest Drive
The seven-mile Cwmcarn Forest Drive was the first of its kind to be developed in Britain. It is open from Easter to October and provides breathtaking views, picnic sites, barbecues and play areas. At the entrance to the drive is a visitor centre providing local information, souvenirs, maps and guides.

Twmbarlwm Mound
According to legend, this

large mound covers the grave of a great Welsh chieftain who died fighting the Romans some time back in the first century AD. Archaeologists, however, disagree, claiming that it is a Norman motte, upon which a watch tower once stood.

The mound is certainly a prominent landmark, visible from many parts of Gwent, and from its summit the panoramic view extends over Newport, the Severn Estuary, the Quantock Hills and, on a clear day, as far as the Brecon Beacons.

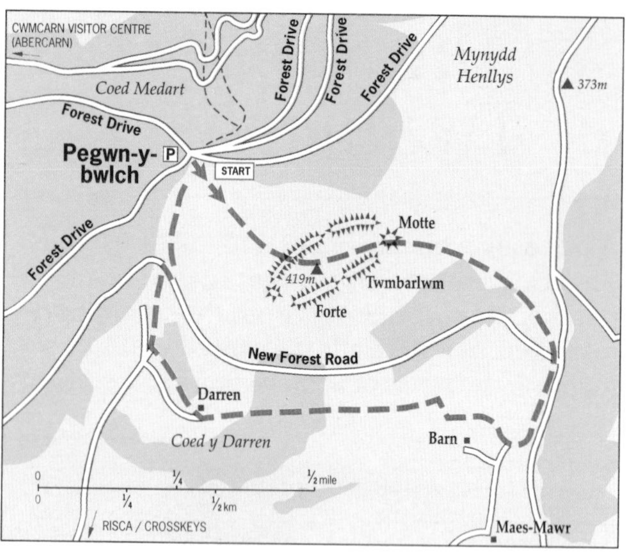

The view from the top

What to look out for

Ebbw Forest is a large area of coniferous woodland including Japanese larch, sitka spruce and Scots pine. Coal tits and goldcrests forage among the foliage and are easiest to spot in winter.

Wood sorrel

Along the Glamorgan Canal

WALK 58
SOUTH GLAMORGAN
ST143804

A pleasant and peaceful walk along a section of a historic canal with so much natural history that it has been turned into a nature reserve.

Information

This walk is one and a half miles long
Mostly level and easy going with just one short ascent
No stiles
Pubs and toilets in Whitchurch

START
Take the A470 from Cardiff and then follow the A4054 through Whitchurch. Turn down Velindre Road. Go past the hospital and turn down Forest Farm Road. Park in the small parking area on the right, opposite a pylon; an old millstone set in the ground marks the entrance to the Glamorganshire Canal Local Nature Reserve.

DIRECTIONS
Go through the gate, follow the left-hand track and soon cross an iron bridge. Continue along the canal towpath for about ¾ mile, passing between the Melingriffith feeder stream and the old Glamorganshire canal, then pass an old lock, before reaching the remains of a second lock. Here the canal, as such, comes to an end and the water disappears into a concrete pipe.
Turn right and ascend a flight of steps up a bank. At the top, turn right along a shady path that follows a narrow ridge above a wooded slope known as Long Wood – an interesting contrast to the outward journey, with a variety of trees and wildlife. After about 50yds there is a log seat and the course of the now dismantled railway can be seen to the left.
At a junction of paths just below a house, keep to the right and follow a wider track which leads on beside a stone wall and back to the starting point.

Broad-leaved dock

An old – and once well-used – lock on the canal

The shady path that leads through the Long Wood, dappled with sunlight through the leaves

Melingriffith Feeder
This old industrial waterway once supplied water to the Melingriffith Iron Works.

Glamorgan Canal
Completed in 1794 this canal was built to transport iron ore, coal and limestone on a 25-mile journey from Cyfartha, near Merthyr Tydfil, to the mouth of the River Taff in Cardiff. It fell into rapid decline when the Taff Vale Railway was constructed.

What to look out for

The grey heron may be seen fishing in the canal, which is home not only to the fish, but also to a number of marginal and waterside flowering plants including Himalayan balsam with its pink flowers, marsh marigold, purple loosestrife and arrowhead, to name but a few. Long Wood is an interesting stretch of mixed woodland containing beech, ash, elm, alder, oak, holly, sycamore and hazel. In spring the ground may be carpeted with primroses, ramsons and bluebells. Among the trees you may see squirrels and perhaps a great spotted woodpecker.

Around Rhossili

WALK 59
WEST GLAMORGAN
SS414881

A coastal walk on the western side of the Gower Peninsula, providing wonderful vistas out to sea, with the serpent-like promontory of Worms Head a prominant feature.

START
Follow the A4118 from Swansea and about one and a half miles north of Port Einon turn right along the B4247. The road ends at Rhossili where there is a large car park opposite the Worms Head Cottage Hotel.

DIRECTIONS
Leave the car park to follow a tarmac path down to a gate and continue along a broad track beside a stone wall. The ditch and rampart of an Iron Age fort can be seen on the right. At a point where the wall bends around to the left, keep straight on across the grass towards the coastguard station, which doubles as the Gower Coast Reserves Centre. Continue around the headland to the left, keeping well back from the edge of the cliffs. The

Information

The walk is three miles long
A level route with just one brief ascent. Care needed on cliff edges. Check at information centre for crossing times (two and a half hours either side of low water) if you wish to cross the causeway to Worms Head; it is a very rocky route which needs to be taken seriously
A few stiles
Café, hotel and information centre at start
Toilets at start

The curving sands of Rhossili Bay, with the downs behind

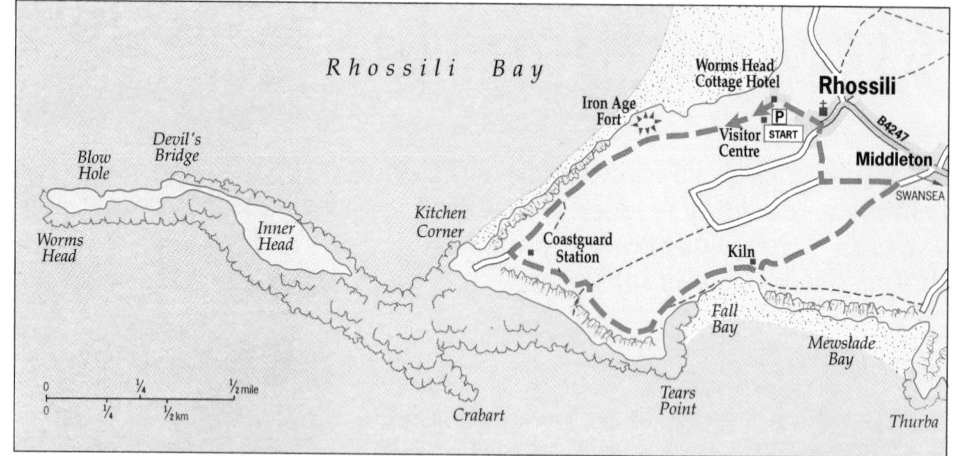

path leads on through the gorse and soon rejoins the stone wall. In due course the path drops down to Mewslade Bay. Where the path divides keep straight on to follow the gently ascending higher route. Continue along the top of the headland for about a mile. On reaching the remains of a lime kiln at the head of a little inlet, follow a track up to the left and climb an iron ladder over a stone wall.

Turn right and follow the path around the edge of a field to reach a stile. Continue, crossing three more stiles, then look out for an easily-missed track on the left, between hedges. This takes you through a tunnel of trees to a stile. Cross this and the stile opposite to continue along an avenue of trees. At the end cross another stile and keep forward across the field to another stile. Continue along a broad rutted track to reach a T-junction. Turn right here and follow a cart track back to Rhossili. On joining a road turn left and make your way back to the start, passing Rhossili church on the right.

Rhossili Bay

Said to be one of the finest unspoilt beaches in Britain, this three-mile stretch of golden sands is half a mile wide at low tide. The *Helvetia* was wrecked in a storm on Monday 31 October 1887 and remains of its timbers can be seen embedded in the sand.

Worms Head

Known as the 'Land's End of Gower', this fascinating promontory is a mile long and it takes its name from the Scandinavian word *Orme* which means serpent. Connecting the inner and outer headlands is a natural rock arch known as the Devil's Bridge. The outer headland is a bird sanctuary where kittiwakes, fulmars, guillemots and razorbills may be seen in the summer. A stepped path leads down from the coast-guard station to a causeway.

Rhossili Church

The foundations of this church date back to the 6th century but the present building is of Norman construction. Inside is a white marble tablet commemorating Petty Officer Evans, a local man who died in 1912 with Captain Scott on his ill-fated expedition to the South Pole.

What to look out for

The outer extremity of Worms Head is a bird sanctuary and several species of seabirds can be spotted all along the route – herring gulls, guillemots, kittiwakes and fulmars are summer visitors to the cliffs; oystercatchers favour the rocky shore, and gannets may be seen offshore. Local flora includes thyme, thrift and salad burnet. Hang gliders may often be seen taking off from Rhossili Downs.

Manorbier Castle

WALK 60
DYFED
SS064977

An easy walk taking in a section of the Pembrokeshire coast path with exhilarating views across the sea. Special features include a prehistoric burial chamber, and Manorbier church and castle.

Information

The walk is one and a half miles long
Few stiles
The paths are easy to follow but take care when crossing the top of a deep fissure
Pub in village
Toilets at car park

START

Manorbier is about six miles west of Tenby, turning left off the A4139 onto the B4585 to reach the village. The walk starts from a large car park just below the castle.

DIRECTIONS

On the seaward side of the car park follow a path to the right to reach the beach. Walk across the beach to the left hand corner and go up a flight of concrete steps and cross a stile.

The path then gently ascends with pleasant views across the bay, but take very great care where the path goes around the top of a deep fissure – there is a steep drop below.

Soon reach the King's Quoit, the remains of a prehistoric burial chamber, and follow the path to the left of the burial chamber and ascend through the ferns, dipping in and out of hollows, heading back towards Manorbier.

The path follows the edge of a field with a good view of the castle.

In due course reach a gate, continue through the churchyard to the road and turn left. Descend, passing Manorbier church (well worth a visit) on the right. On rounding a corner, go left over a stile into the car park.

To visit the castle, climb some steps in the trees on the right and on reaching a pavement, turn right. Cross the road with care and go through a metal gate in a wall to the castle.

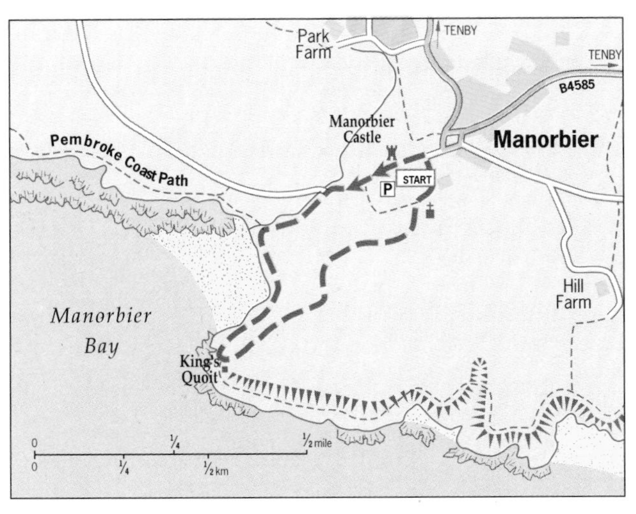

Guillemot

King's Quoit

This is one of many neolithic burial chambers to be found in Wales. The capstone

The sturdy defensive walls of Manorbier still stand in the leafy valley

measures 16ft 9in long, 8ft 6in wide and is up to 2ft thick.

Manorbier Church
Dedicated to St James the Great Apostle and Martyr, this church has a tall, square, fortress-like tower and is perched on the hillside opposite the castle. These tall-towered churches were intended as lookouts and refuges. The nave predates the castle and in the chancel is a 13th-century effigy of a member of the de Barri family, who built the castle. The 14th-century oak loft leading into the tower is one of the few remaining examples of medieval church woodwork in the county.

Manorbier Castle
Constructed of quarried limestone this picturesque castle was established by Odo de Barri, a follower of Gerald de Windsor. His famous grandson was Giraldus Cambrensis, otherwise known as Gerald of Wales. In 1188 Gerald, who was then Archdeacon of Brecon, travelled through Wales with Baldwin, the Archbishop of Canterbury. Afterwards Gerald recorded their travels in a fascinating book *Itinerary Through Wales*. He described his birthplace, Manorbier, as 'the pleasantest spot in Wales'. His greatest wish was to became Bishop of St David's, but King John refused to grant his wish and he died a disappointed man in 1216. He is buried at St David's Cathedral.
The castle is open daily from May to September and for a week at Easter.

What to look out for

There are lots of interesting shells on the beach, and look out for fulmars, herring and great black-backed gulls, guillemots and razorbills.
An assortment of wild flowers includes thrift or sea pink, hemp agrimony, English stonecrop, red valerian and ox-eye daisy.

WALK 61
DYFED
SM734272

St David's (Penmaen Dewi)

Information

The walk is three and three quarter miles long
Craggy slopes to ascend on return route; can be avoided by returning from the headland along outward route.
A few stiles
The nearest pubs are in St David's
Good picnic spots along the walk
Toilets in the car park at Whitesands Bay

This is a very strenuous, but interesting walk on a headland at the extreme west of Wales. It passes a secluded beach and takes in the remains of a promontory fort and a prehistoric burial chamber.

START
To reach Whitesand Bay follow the B4583 for two miles on the north-west side of St David's. Normally you have to pay a small fee for parking here.

DIRECTIONS
From the car park cross the road and go over a stile in a wall to the right of a telephone kiosk. Follow the coastal path beside a fence, keeping to the right as it wanders around through the gorse. As you come over a rise the bay of Porth Melgan is seen below. Keep straight on ignoring two paths to the right. (A detour can be made at this point down to this secluded beach.)
Follow the path on a gentle

The sandy bay at Porth Melgan is well worth the short detour

ascent around St David's headland. The path goes through a rampart of piled up stones, the remains of an Iron Age promontory fortress, which is known as the Warrior's Dyke. Turn right. Further on you will pass a cliff on the left where rock climbers may be seen in action (but not during the nesting season). Detour right here to visit Coetan Arthur, a prehistoric burial chamber, then return to the path.

Go over the next hump and on through the heather and rocks with Carn Llidi silhouetted against the sky on the right. Descend to a junction of paths and follow the broad track to your right down into the shallow valley above Porth Melgan.

Continue go up the other side (the longest uphill stretch on the walk), passing through a kissing-gate on the way. On reaching a junction with a concrete path, you may like to continue to the summit of Carn Llidi (at 600ft altitude, this is a good vantage point – the west coast of Ireland can be seen on a clear day), but otherwise turn right and follow the surfaced path downhill to join a track beside a wall.

Cross a stile beside a gate and pass through Danyardig farmyard. Then follow a metalled lane which brings you down to the Whitesands Road. Turn right and make your way back to the car park.

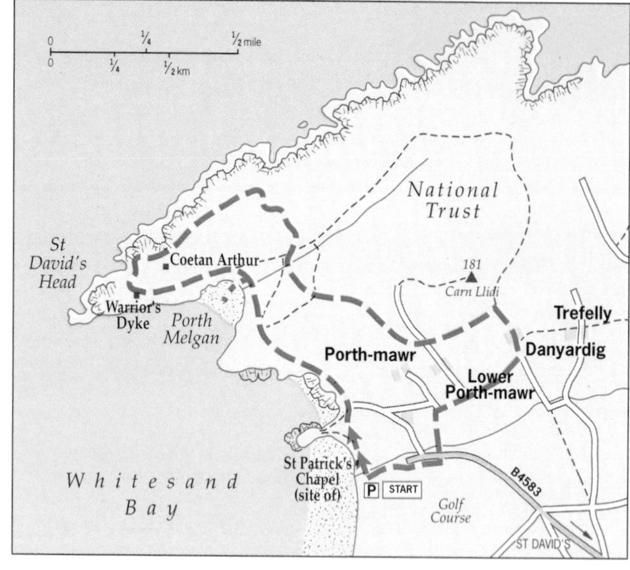

St Patrick's Chapel

A stone tablet near the start marks the site of a chapel dedicated to St Patrick. He is reputed to have sailed from here to Ireland in the early part of the 5th century.

Arthur's Quoit (Coetan Arthur)

This is a prehistoric dolmen with a capstone 12ft long and 1ft thick. Legend has it that it was thrown here by King Arthur from the summit of Moelfre Hill.

St David's Head

The view from here is particularly fine. To the south is Ramsey Island and westward lie the smaller islands called the Bishop and Clerks. On a very clear day you can look north across Cardigan Bay and see Snowdon, nearly 100 miles away.

What to look out for

Look for interesting shells on the beach.
Atlantic grey seals may sometimes be seen basking and fishing off this coast. Sea birds may include razorbills, guillemots, kittiwakes, fulmars and gulls.
The wild flowers are particularly beautiful in spring and early summer.

Razorbill

Above Llangrannog

WALK 62
DYFED
SN311542

A very pleasant walk providing stunning views from a fine stretch of coastline that is owned by the National Trust. It is easy to follow and the paths are well maintained. It may be enjoyed at any time of the year providing it is not too windy.

START
Llangrannog is reached by turning off the A487 at Brynhoffnant to follow the B4334. Drive down through the narrow streets of the village to reach a car park overlooking the beach.

DIRECTIONS
At the right-hand corner of the small beach, ascend a flight of concrete steps to a path which gradually ascends, soon giving views down over Llangrannog. Shortly reach a picnic table

Information

The walk is one and three quarter miles long
Several stiles
Tea rooms and two pubs in Llangrannog
Picnic places with tables along early part of walk
Toilets in Llangrannog

The bay at Llangrannog

tucked away in a corner on the right.

Further on, look down on the top of Carreg Bica, the strange rock that can be seen from the beach. Around the next corner is a flat area with a picnic table and a superb view out to sea.

Ignore the stile on the right and continue along the cliff-top path. After about 20yds a stepped path on the left leads down to a charming hidden cove.

Continue along the cliff-top path beside a fence. Cross a stile and the path begins to rise again. Go over another stile and turn left along a broad track. (A detour track leads out to the headland from here.)

Continue around the headland, with new views appearing all the time.

On reaching a junction of paths, keep to the right, directed by an erosion control notice. Follow a path up to the col above, and then go over a stile beside a gate. (From here you can follow a concrete road up to the coastguard station on top of the hill of Pendinas Lochtyn, returning the same way and turning right at the gate.)

Follow the coastguard road, then cross a stile beside a gate and head straight down to two more stiles in succession to rejoin your outward route by the picnic table on the platform overlooking the sea.

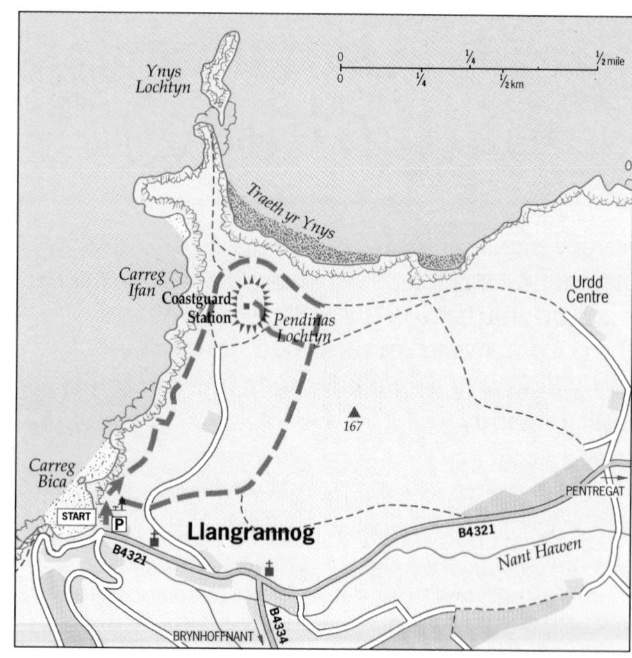

Llangrannog

Set in a steep green valley, this is a pretty village that is very popular during the tourist season, when car parking can sometimes be rather a problem.

What to look out for

Colourful cliff-top flowers are at their best in May and June; look out for thrift, sea campion, common scurvy-grass and sea carrot in particular. Stonechats and linnets are present in the area for much of the year, and seasonal summer visitors include the whitethroat.

Carreg Bica

This strange looking crag is 50ft high and dominates the sandy beach. According to local legend, it is actually a tooth that was troubling the Devil. Unable to bear the agony any longer, he yanked it from his jaw, threw it over his shoulder and this is where it landed.

Ynys Lochtyn

It was on this headland that the composer Edward Elgar found inspiration for his *Introduction and Allegro for Strings*. He wrote in his diary:

> 'On the cliff between blue sea and blue sky, thinking out my theme, there came to me the sound of singing. The songs were too far away to reach me distinctly, but fitting the need of the moment I made the little tune which appears in the introduction.'

The Artists' Valley

WALK 63
DYFED
SN685952

Much of this walk is well shaded by trees making it a particularly enjoyable excursion on a hot day. Stunning views and pleasant riverside paths are features of this walk which you will find particularly memorable.

Information

The walk is two and a quarter miles long
There is some ascent involved but it is fairly easy going
One stile
Pub in Talybont further along A487
Toilet in car park

START
This walk starts from the small village of Furnace which is on the A487 about ten miles south-west of Machynlleth. Park in Ynys Hir car park (RSPB), open from 9am to 9pm (or dusk if earlier).

DIRECTIONS
From the car park follow the entrance drive up to the main road. Directly opposite is the Dyfi Furnace. Turn right along the narrow pavement and by the Hen Efail craft shop, cross the road to follow the road up Cwm Einion – 'The Artists' Valley'.
After about 400yds leave the road at a bend by a footpath sign and continue up a rocky track beside a stone wall, bearing right with the wall. On reaching a junction turn left then follow the track

Crossing the shady Furnace

beside a fence and on through the trees. On joining a lane keep straight on, but shortly leave it to follow a signposted track leading down through the trees to the left.

Ignore a track to the right and stay on the main route. Go through a small gate and cross a bridge over the river, then head up to a stile. Do not go over it, but follow the path to the left passing beneath a little yellow cottage.

Go through a gate and turn left along a lane. On reaching another lane turn left and shortly follow a signposted path on the right which leads around the hillside of Foel Fawr.

Continue along the wide track through the ferns, cross a little stream and then descend to a farm in the valley below. On joining the farm drive, turn left.

Pass a memorial to Major General Pugh, then leave the road at a cattle grid and turn left along a signposted path to follow a stone wall on your right.

At the end of the wall go over a stile and turn right along a metalled lane. This rises for a short way and then drops down to the A487.

Turn left and follow the road back to Furnace.

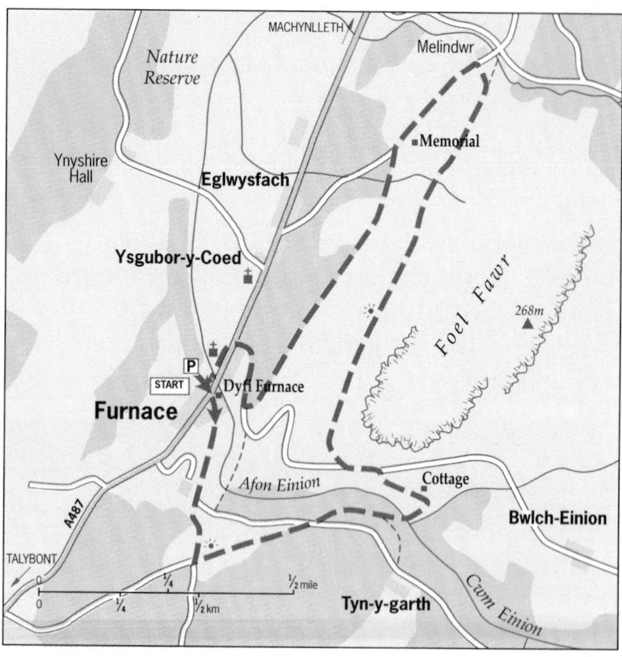

Trailing St John's-wort

Dyfi Furnace

This is the best preserved example of an 18th-century charcoal-burning blast furnace in Britain. It was set up in about 1755 and was in use for about 50 years. It later became a saw mill and the waterwheel which can be seen on the side of the building was installed at this time. This hamlet is known as Furnace but its correct name is Eglwysfach or Ysgubor-y-Coed.

Foel Fawr

The viewpoint on Foel Fawr offers a panoramic vista across the Dyfi estuary, taking in the mountains of southern Snowdonia. There is a legend that King Arthur once leapt across this estuary and his horse left its hoof print on a rock which can still be seen.

What to look out for

The 900-acre Ynys Hir Reserve is home to many breeding birds including redstarts, pied flycatchers and all three species of woodpecker.

Butterflies to be seen include pearl-bordered and marsh fritillaries, and the plantlife includes ling, bog pimpernel and trailing St John's-wort.

The Flooded Village

WALK 64
POWYS
SN928646

This is a varied walk in the beautiful Elan Valley – an area often referred to as the 'Lake District of Wales'. It is a particularly scenic walk, with wonderful views from the top of the pass.

Information

The walk is four miles long
A few stiles
One ascent to top of mountain pass
Refreshments in the visitor centre
Several suitable picnic places on the walk
Toilets in visitor centre and in Elan Village

START
The Elan Valley Visitor Centre is about three miles south-west of Rhyader on the B4518. The walk starts from the car park.

DIRECTIONS
From the car park walk up the road to pass through the entrance gates and turn right across a Bailey bridge which spans the River Elan beside a now disused suspension bridge. Turn right then left to pass through a gate and follow a broad stony path beside a fence, ascending gradually through the trees, with views down to the river.
On reaching a junction turn left and shortly right to follow an old railway track above the Visitor Centre. The track rises gently, soon becoming level with the top of the dam, then passes a quarry on the right which provided stone for the construction of the dam. Beyond the quarry, the track soon becomes a narrow stony path following the edge of the reservoir.
On reaching a stream on the left, the main ascent of the walk begins beside a conifer plantation. After a few yards, when the track divides, keep left and at the end of the plantation keep straight on, ignoring the track to the right.
Less steep now, the broad grass track passes a ruined farm house and leads pleasantly to the top of a col.

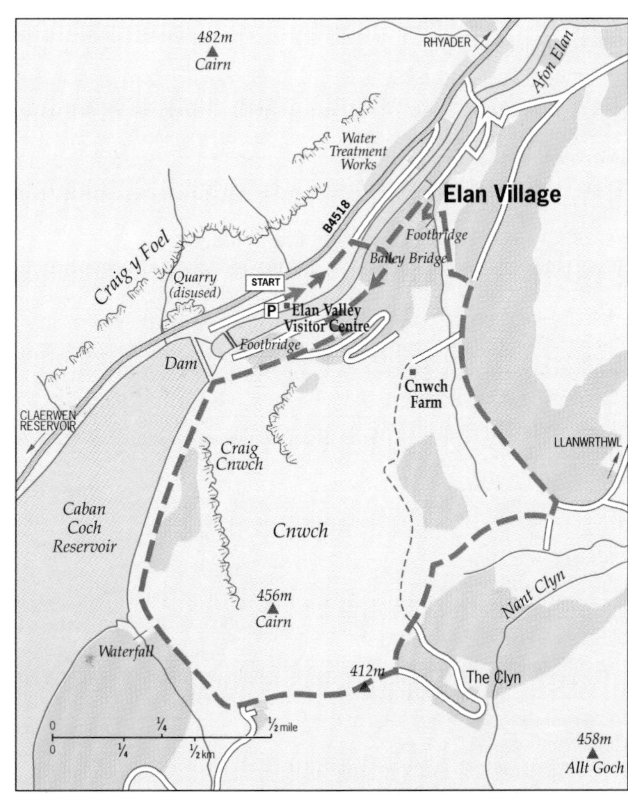

The bridge across the Caban Coch Reservoir, in the drowned Elan Valley

Continue, to reach a gate and join a surfaced lane. On reaching a T-junction, turn left along a road, passing on the right a wooded slope which is part of the Cnwch and Allt Ddu Nature Reserve (RSPB).

After passing Cnwch Farm, continue round a corner and look out for a green track on the left descending through the ferns. Soon turn left on the track leading down to the village (toilets on the left). Turn right over the Bailey bridge and return to the Visitor Centre car park.

Caban Coch Dam

The Elan Valley Reservoirs were built at the turn of the century to provide water for the City of Birmingham, some 73 miles away. The first dam to be constructed was Caban Coch, opened on 21 July 1904 by King Edward VII and Queen Alexandra, and finally completed in 1906. It stands 122ft high and 610ft long, covers an area of 500 acres and is 800ft above sea level at full capacity.

Elan Village

Built in 1906 to house the reservoir maintenance staff, this attractive village consists of a school, a schoolteacher's house, the Reservoir Superintendent's house, and twelve cottages.

The original Elan village was flooded and beneath the reservoir lie several farms, a Baptist chapel, a church, a schoolhouse and eighteen cottages. Also beneath the water are two large houses – Cwn Elan and Nantgwyllt – which had connections with the poet Shelley. They also inspired Francis Brett Young's novel *The House Under the Water*.

What to look out for

Birds that may be seen on this walk include skylark, meadow pipit, dipper, grey wagtail and pied wagtail. In the woods you may see pied flycatcher, wood warbler and redstart during summer months. Look out for buzzards, peregrines and kestrels – if you are really lucky you may see a red kite with its distinctive forked tail. The visitor centre gives a good insight into the valley and its reservoirs.

Porthyrogof Cave

WALK 65
POWYS
SN918105

This is an exciting walk through wild and romantic scenery, including an impressive waterfall and a limestone cavern that boasts the largest entrance in Wales. Not a walk for wet conditions.

START
West of Brecon, turn south off the A40 at Sennybridge, at Defynnog branch left with the A4215, then turn right onto a minor road to go through Heol Senni and on to Ystradfellte. Continue for about two miles and just beyond a shop on the right and a chapel on the left reach a well-used parking area on the grass verge.

DIRECTIONS
Follow a lane down between fences to go over a stile. At next junction bear right following waymarked path via two footbridges to reach another stile. The path now leads down through trees.

Follow the main path and soon on the right will be seen the Sgwd Clun waterfall. Continue along the path winding through trees to reach a footpath spanning the Afon Mellte. On the other side, turn right and follow a rough, rocky path up a steep slope (note the warning sign), then go right and up again to join a higher path adjoining a fence. Turn left and after about 150yds go right over a stile. Now turn left along a wide track to another stile. Turn left and later reach a stone cottage where an 'advised path' waymark directs you over a stile and on beside a fence, passing through the cottage garden.

Information

The walk is three miles long
Fairly rocky and very steep in places where limestone can be extremely slippery after rain – great care is needed and sensible footwear essential
Virtually no road walking
A lot of stiles
Ice cream shop about 200yds up the road towards Ystradfellte
Pub in village
Area suitable for picnics by 'Blue Pool' towards end of walk
Toilets in Porthyrogof car park

Woundwort

The path joins a lane which is followed between tumbled stone walls for nearly ¼ mile to reach a stile below a white-washed farm.
Soon afterwards the lane meets a road. Turn left, and immediately on the right is the Porthyrogof Cave car park. Go

The Blue Pool picnic area

The entrance to the cave

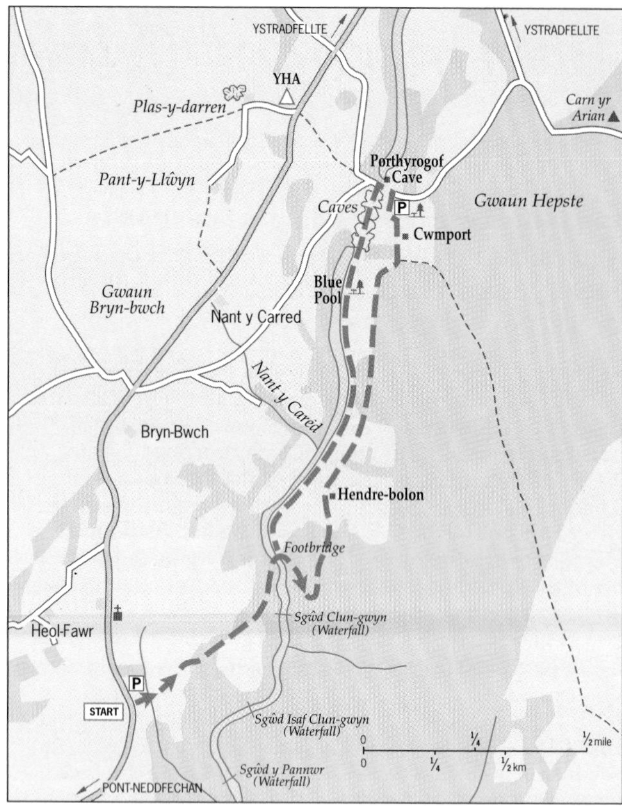

over stile on the left side of the car park and follow a rocky path down into the valley. Turn left beside the river and the large cave entrance soon comes into view.

After visiting the cavern return to the car park and cross the road to follow a footpath (not the bridleway at the same point). Go over a stile and follow a rocky path down the old river bed.

In due course the resurgence of the river is reached. Keep high here and follow the path over rocks. Soon you can descend to the riverside path where a large flat area overlooks the 'Blue Pool'.

At the end of the flat area the track goes up to a stile and continues beside the river, leading on through the trees and over two more stiles back to the footbridge crossed earlier on the walk. From there retrace your steps back to the start.

What to look out for

There is a substantial area of native broad-leaved woodland, including oak, birch, alder, mountain ash and yew. It is also good for ferns, with hart's tongue, brittle bladder fern and green spleenwort much in evidence. Look out in summer for wood warblers and treecreepers, and dippers that bob up and down on boulders in the river searching for food. Kingfishers and grey wagtails may also be seen.

Sgwd Clun-gwyn Fall

This is one of three waterfalls on the River Mellte and its name means 'White Meadow Fall'.

The Cave

Situated at the head of a rocky, wooded gorge, this cave has the largest entrance in Wales at 57ft wide. The River Mellte disappears under a wide arch at the base of a cliff and flows underground for about a quarter of a mile.

A Circuit of the Sugar Loaf

WALK 66
POWYS
SO054713

This short walk, mainly through woods in a quiet and remote corner of Wales, takes in the site of what was once the largest abbey in Wales and the supposed grave of Prince Llewellyn, the last true prince of Wales.

START
Abbeycwmhir is about four miles north of Llandrindod Wells via the A483. Park by the church.

DIRECTIONS
Walk up the road a short way and turn right by a footpath signed 'Owain Glyndwr's Way'. The track passes above the church and then continues through a farmyard.

Cross a stile beside a gate and continue beside a fence. Shortly after this, go through a gate and walk on through the trees.

Passing between two conifer plantations the track gently ascends. Ignore the first turning on the right and bear left at the next junction. When the track joins a forestry road go straight across and continue down through the trees descending into the valley below, still waymarked 'Owain Glyndwr's Way'.

At a track junction turn left and follow a forest track which leads around the base of Sugar Loaf Hill and back to your starting point.

The forest track, south of the Sugar Loaf

Now follow the road uphill for a short way, then go through a gate on the right, opposite an archway in a wall, and continue down a path through a field to reach the ruins of Abbey Cwmhir. After exploring the ruins retrace your steps to the starting point.

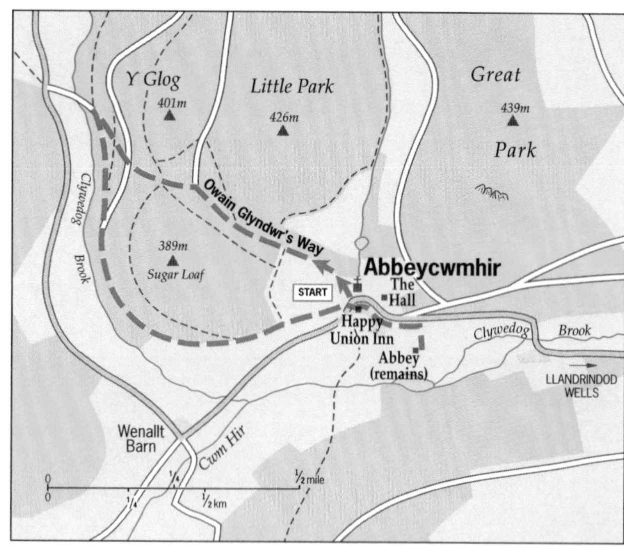

Abbeycwmhir
This isolated hamlet is set among forested hills about five miles east of Rhayader. Opposite the Happy Union Inn is a Victorian church built by the Phillips family. They made their money out of Manchester cotton and lived in the Hall, constructed out of stone from the ruined abbey.

Owain Glyndwr's Way
Linking Knighton with Welshpool, this is a 125-mile waymarked route.
It passes through many locations associated with the Welsh prince Owain Glyndwr, who led a rebellion against the English in the 15th century and became a Welsh national hero.

The Abbey Ruins
Founded in 1143 by a Welsh prince for the Cistercians, Abbey Cwmhir was once the largest abbey in Wales. Its nave, at 242ft long, was only bettered by York, Durham and Winchester cathedrals. The building was badly damaged during Owain Glyndwr's uprising, never to be repaired. It was finally abandoned and its stones plundered for building in the surrounding area.
All that remains to be seen of the abbey today are a few grey stones marking the outer walls, bases of piers, parts of the transepts and the altar steps.

Information

The walk is two miles long
One stile
Pub in village

What to look out for

Mixed flocks of woodland birds can be found during the winter months, comprising species such as marsh tits, great tits and nut-hatches.
During the spring and summer, look out for redstarts and wood warblers, and keep an eye on the skies for buzzards and the occasional red kite.

The Grave of the Last True-born Prince of Wales
Although no original gravestone for the prince has ever been found, and his body has certainly not been unearthed, it is believed that the headless corpse of Prince Llewellyn the Last was carried here for burial after he was killed and beheaded at Cilmeri, near Builth Wells, in 1282. The prince's head was sent to London to be exhibited on Cheapside as a symbol of Edward I's victory and warning to other 'rebels'.
A large slab of slate displaying a carved sword marks the place in front of the high altar where the grave is most likely to have been.

Llangollen Canal and Dinas Bran

Colourful narrowboats and scurrying wildlife enliven this gentle towpath walk, with an option to return via the atmospheric ruins of a hilltop castle.

WALK 67
CLWYD
SJ215423

START
In Llangollen turn off the A5 at traffic lights onto the A539 then turn right after crossing the bridge. Take the first left and soon after crossing the humped-back canal bridge, turn left to car park opposite the school (no weekday parking from September to the end of June between 8am and 6pm; alternative parking by A5/A539 traffic lights).

DIRECTIONS
Return to the humped-back bridge and join the towpath at the wharf café. Pass beneath the bridge to follow the towpath eastwards, soon veering away from the noise of the road below. The canal is bridged by a farm track after about a mile, and by the A539, 500yds or so beyond that. Here the two routes diverge:

(a) For the canal walk, continue along the towpath for another 500yds or so, then cross by a tiny bridge on to the A539 opposite the Sun Trevor Inn. Return along the towpath to the start point.

On the Shropshire Union Canal

(b) For Dinas Bran, pass under the bridge then turn sharp right and cross a stile onto the road. About 25yds after bridging the canal, cross the road and follow a farm track steadily uphill between trees to a surfaced lane known – for good reason – as the Panorama Walk. Turn left to follow the lane, with the hilltop ruins of Castell Dinas Bran soon coming into view. After ½ mile turn left into a narrow lane, then just beyond a cattle grid cross the stile on the right and ascend via a meadow and steeply rising path, over a stile, to the summit.

Descend the far side of the hill by a zig-zag path to gain a green track beyond a grassy hump. Turn left, go through a gate, and descend the track between the trees. Where tracks cross, continue straight ahead and soon pass through a small gate on to a path, which descends steeply at the side of a pasture (seats here). Cross over a narrow lane and follow a surfaced path between fences and finally descend steps to the T-junction of lanes at the start point.

What to look out for

On the canal waterbirds such as moorhens, coots and mallards can be seen, often paddling hard to escape approaching boats. Water voles make their homes among tree roots on the banks. Among the waterside plants look for cuckooflower, marsh marigold and monkeyflower.

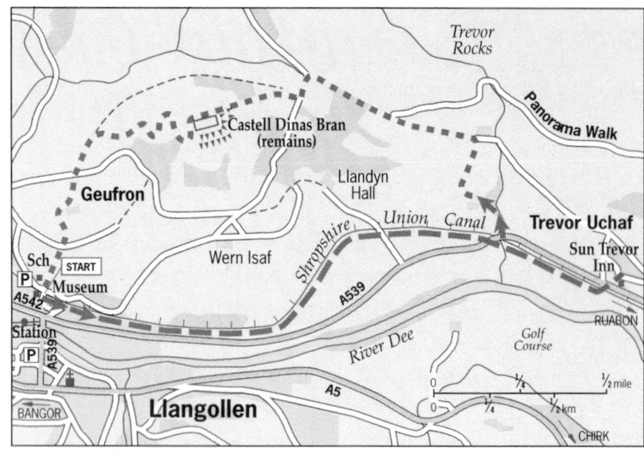

Llangollen Canal

Built by Thomas Telford in 1805, this branch of the Shropshire Union Canal was part of a waterways system linking the Mersey, Dee and Severn rivers.

Four miles east of Llangollen the canal crosses high above the River Dee, on the famous Pontcysyllte aqueduct.

Castell Dinas Bran

The hilltop has been fortified since before the Iron Age, but the castle ruins we see today are the remains of a 13th-century fortification.

Legend has it that the beautiful Myfanwy Fechan lived here. The young bard Hywel ap Einion, deeply in love with the heiress, would toil up the hill each day to sing her praises, only to be spurned for a wealthier suitor. Broken-hearted, Hywel composed his 'Ode to Myfanwy' which was later famously set to music by Joseph Parry and is now a favourite song for male voice choirs.

The view from Castell Dinas Bran

Information

Information
The walk is three and a half miles long by either route
Level towpath on the canal route, but steep paths on Dinas Bran
Half a mile of quiet road walking on the Dinas Bran route
A few stiles on Dinas Bran
Dogs must be kept on leads on Dinas Bran
Pub with restaurant and outside tables for children on the canal walk; café with outside tables at the canal wharf
Ideal picnic places among the castle ruins or alongside the canal

The Precipice Walk

WALK 68
GWYNEDD
SH746212

Despite its name, this superbly situated walk is mostly straightforward. Dramatic views on the 'precipice' section contrast with peaceful lakeside scenery.

Information

The walk is three and a half miles long
Some uneven ground which requires steadiness
Short section of road walking on a quiet lane to start and finish
Several stiles
Dogs must be kept on leads
No pub nearby
Many excellent picnic sites, both on the Precipice Path and by the lake
Toilets at car park

Peregrine

START

The walk overlooks the attractive town of Dolgellau on the A470. Five miles north of Dolgellau on the A470, just south of Ganllwyd, take the minor road signposted to Llanfachreth and Abergeirw. Turn right in Llanfachreth towards Dolgellau. In the corner of the second road junction is a convenient car park.

The start point can also be reached via minor roads from the south, leaving the A494 two miles east of Dollgellau.

DIRECTIONS

From the car park, walk down the minor road of the T-junction for about 100yds then turn left on a track among trees (signposted 'Llwybr Cynwch' and 'Precipice Walk'). Veer right from the track on a good path around a cottage, and cross the wall by a ladder stile. Beyond a second ladder stile is a wonderful view of Llwybr Cynwch, backed by the distant mountain of Cader Idris.

Resist the shore for a little while and instead fork right on a grassy path to begin an anti-clockwise circuit of the little hill above the lake. The path, though narrow and uneven in places, has been well maintained and is perfectly obvious to follow. Information boards at intervals briefly describe the natural history of the area. The so-called 'Precipice' section appears about halfway round the walk, where the path twists across a steep hillside – exhilarating rather than worrying, but

What to look out for

Buzzards and ravens utilise the updraught on the hill for spectacular soaring. Undisturbed by people on the path below, kestrels can often be seen hovering over the hill crest, scanning for some unsuspecting small mammal. Water fowl will be seen or heard bustling among the reeds on the lake shore, and grey squirrels may be seen in the wood.

far distance rise the sinister twin towers of Trawsfynydd nuclear power station, while beneath your feet you can see the scarring evidence of road improvements and, noting derelict cottages, of rural depopulation. What pleases the eye of the visitor may stick like a thorn in the side of the inhabitant.

Yet now that tourism has become an integral part of rural life, natural beauty in this area of the country is being protected not only on aesthetic grounds but, increasingly, as a valuable economic resource.

Evidence of this change of attitudes can be seen on the Precipice Walk, in the tangible form of the more acceptable mixed planting and selective felling methods being used in the forests.

Looking north from Foel Cynwch

keep a tight hold of fearless youngsters.

Five stiles must be crossed before the path eventually circles round to arrive at the southern end of the lake. Follow a good track on the left side of the lake to rejoin the approach path for the return to the car park.

Nature versus Industry

Initial impressions gained from the Precipice Walk are of nature at its most unhurried and unsullied: of rugged mountainsides sweeping down to a glistening river estuary.

Yet the view to the north is dominated by severe blocks of conifers and ugly gaps where felling is taking place. In the

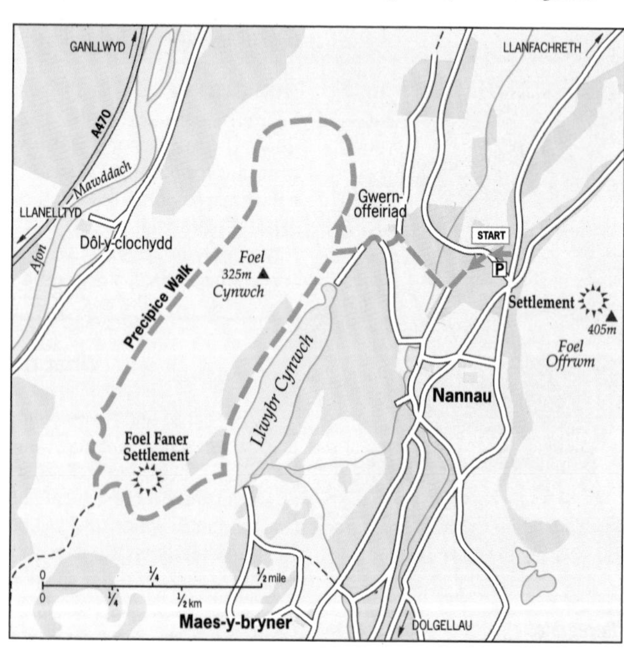

WALK 69
GWYNEDD
SH662720

Aber Falls

An impressive waterfall provides the incentive for this pleasant stroll through pasture and woodland. River bridges and varied wildlife add to the charm of the approach.

Information

The walk is three miles long
Mainly good tracks and paths, but uneven paths near the falls
No road walking
A few stiles on the alternative return path
Dogs must be kept on leads
No pub or toilets
Several good picnic sites on the more open sections of the path

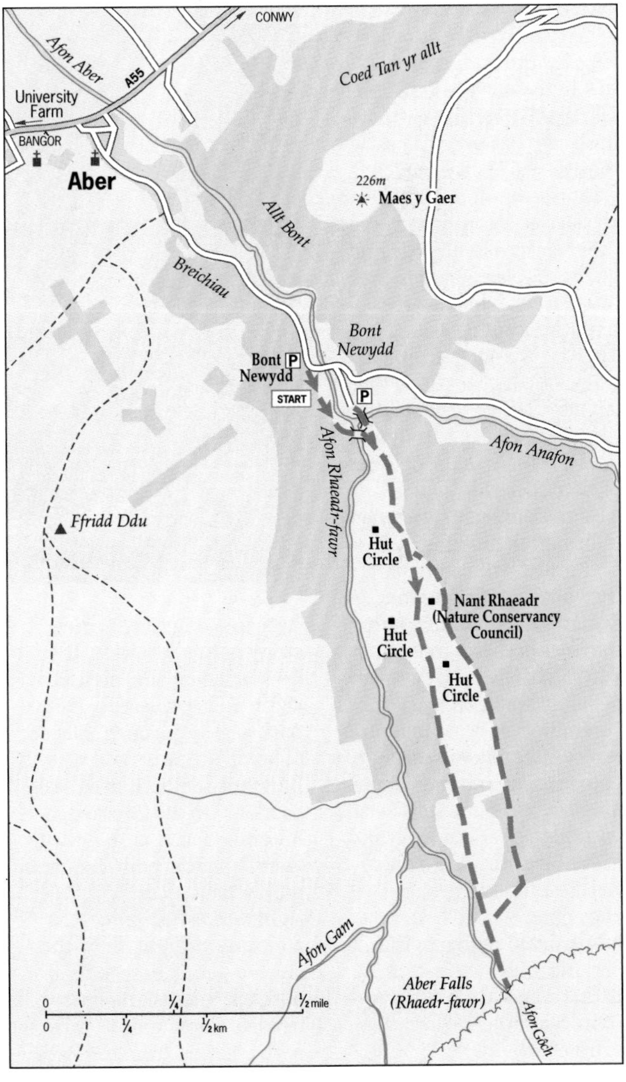

Common mouse-ear

What to look out for

Along the wooded rivers you may see grey wagtails and possibly a dipper. Great spotted woodpeckers, nuthatches, tree creepers and tits also inhabit the valley. The great oak tree just before Nant Rheadr cottage dates to about 1765. Experimental fenced plots nearby contain plants protected from the sheep.

START
The tiny village of Aber lies near the A55 coast road, roughly midway between Bangor and Conwy. From the village, follow the minor road signposted 'Aber Falls' for a little over half a mile to a parking area at Bont Newydd (if necessary, cross the bridge to a second parking area).

DIRECTIONS
Where the road bends sharp left over the bridge, pass through a narrow gate and follow the riverside path upstream (steep slope below to river – take care in wet conditions). After 200yds or so, beyond a confluence, cross the river by a footbridge and go through a gate on to the broad track which arrives from the second parking area. Turn right and, ignoring a track which bears up to the left after 100yds, follow the unsurfaced track through open pastures to the cottage of Nant Rhaeadr, now a Nature Conservancy Council information building. Continue by the main path up the valley, glimpsing the distant falls. Soon the path narrows between trees, and you might hear the thunder of falling water as you walk carefully over protruding tree roots. After passing through a gate the path narrows again and, beyond some steps, leads past huge river boulders into the chilly spray of the falls. Needless to say the path ends here!
It is usual to return to the parking area by the same path, though the following route adds interest for little extra effort:

Return along the narrow, stony path to the gate, then cross a ladder stile on the right. Follow a steeply rising path across the open hillside of boulders, grass and stunted hawthorn (blue-topped stake markers) to the forest edge. Enter the forest at the stile to gain a narrow path. Ignore a path which ascends to the right after 10yds and continue straight on by the level or gently descending path carpeted with pine needles. After about ½ mile the path emerges from the forest at a stile by a gate. Continue in the same line, passing through a gap in a stone enclosure and following the slight path alongside the fence at the forest edge. Enter woodland above the cottage of Nant Rhaeadr, and follow the path by the fence which leads down to the main track of the approach, to return to the parking area.

The Red River tumbling down the rock face is a magnificent sight from far or near

Aber Falls
The Afon Gôch ('Red River') drains a moorland bowl below the high domes of the Carneddau mountains, the second highest range in North Wales. At the falls, where a rare band of hard granophyre rock arrested the eroding action of the stream, the river plunges 120 feet over the cliffs of Creigiau Rhaeadr-fawr in a mesmerising series of chutes and foaming deflections into the swirling pool beneath. The north-facing aspect of the cliffs, their inaccessibility to grazing sheep, and the perpetually misted atmosphere, promote growth of mosses and liverworts.

Barton Clay Pits

WALK 70
HUMBERSIDE
TA026234

Under the shadow of the Humber Bridge, along the south bank of the river, lie a series of fascinating lagoons created by the digging of clay for tiles and bricks. It now forms the focal point of a remarkable riverside conservation area full of interesting things to see.

Information

The walk is around four miles long
Level, easy ground
A few stiles
Dogs are not permitted into the LSHTNC Nature Reserve (alternative route provided) and should be kept on leads elsewhere
Barton Clay Pits Country Park Project Information Centre by the foreshore
Cafés and pubs in Barton; Westfield Lakes Hotel at the foreshore caravan site; light refreshments kiosk weekend and holiday times
Picnic area at the Humber Bridge Viewing Area
Toilets close by

START
Barton is on the south bank of the Humber, alongside the Humber Bridge (A15). The walk starts from the main car park and picnic area of the Barton Clay Pits Country Park.

DIRECTIONS.
Facing away from the river, make your way out of the top right-hand corner of the car park and picnic area.
Pass the ponds along a narrow path which leads parallel with houses and the Humber Bridge to Far Ings Road. Turn right here along the road up to and beyond the Humber Bridge. Immediately beyond the bridge, a narrow gap stile on the left leads into a permissive footpath through an attractive plantation of trees and shrubs.
This emerges at Dam Road, a narrow, traffic-free lane. Turn right, past allotments, as far as the junction. Cross, and almost directly ahead a stile leads down into a field.
Follow the edge of the field straight ahead to a stile by a

The Humber Bridge

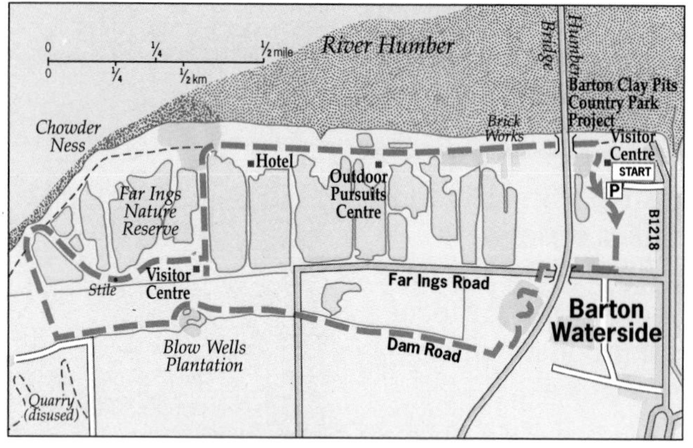

What to look out for

The River Humber is one of Britain's busiest inland waterways and boats of all sizes can be seen, some coming from as far as Southern Europe or the Baltic. Different wildlife habitats, including the Far Ings Nature Reserve, provide a variety of natural history. During the winter brent geese and ducks, gulls and waders occupy the foreshore. The larger lagoons harbour birds such as goosanders in winter; reed-fringed margins are the haunt of reed warblers during summer and water rails in winter. A traditional clay tilemakers yard is passed towards the end of the walk. Special visits are arranged in the summer months to see the pantile makers at work.

footbridge over a stream. Turn left around the edge of the field, having gone past Blow Wells Plantation, then turn right along the hedge.

At the broad gap in the hedge continue in the same direction, keeping the hedge on the left, to a stile in the field corner leading into another narrow lane. Turn right here to the Humber foreshore.

Turn right along the foreshore dyke through a gate, but look for a stile near by on the right, which leads through into the Far Ings Nature Reserve. (No dogs are allowed in here, so if you have a dog with you, you should continue along the foreshore.)

Follow the path past pools and bird hides curving round to the left, ignoring the stile on the right back into Far Ings Road. At a gate on the right leading into a field, cross through two more gates to the Visitor Centre and Information Point opposite. From the Visitor Centre head back along the track which leads to the foreshore, climbing some wooden steps and turning right onto the dyke, and continue past a hotel, a caravan site and a water sports area along the dyke. Keep ahead through gates, back along the foreshore and past brickworks to the car park.

Far Ings Nature Reserve
Old hawthorn hedges and deep reed beds around the clay pit lakes form a wonderful, sheltered natural habitat and area to view waterfowl. The Reserve is owned and managed by the Lincolnshire and South Humberside Trust for Nature Conservation. Please keep to the footpaths in the Nature Reserve.

Common poppy

Sewerby Park & Danes Dyke

WALK 71
HUMBERSIDE
TA197687

This walk includes some superb cliff-top and coastal scenery, woodland and a prehistoric dyke. There is also a lovely country house museum and estate, complete with a small zoo.

START

From the centre of Bridlington, follow Sewerby signs. Just past the railway level crossing, by the model village, turn into the Limekiln Lane car park (pay and display).

DIRECTIONS

From the rear of the car park cross into the overflow field and head towards the sea to pick up the cliff-top path. Turn left along the path, past conveniently placed benches, enjoying the superb views across the Bay.

Where the tarmac ends beyond beach access point, almost opposite Sewerby, continue along the narrow cliff-top path by the edge of fields – keeping well away from the edge. Follow the

Information

The walk is under three miles long
Level throughout, except for steep steps at Danes Dyke, but care needed on cliff-top section
A few stiles and kissing-gates
No dogs in Sewerby Park
Refreshment facilities at Sewerby Park (admission fee) or in Bridlington
Toilets about 200 yards from the start of the walk, and in Sewerby Park

The steep cliffs of Sewerby Rocks

path towards the woods ahead until you reach a steep gorge – part of Danes Dyke.

Follow the path (signed) to the left. Unless you want to go down to the beach, avoid the steep steps on the right, keeping alongside the field until you reach a wooden stile on the left with a wooden signpost indicating Sewerby. (The path directly ahead soon drops down steps and over a footbridge before ascending Danes Dyke and leading to the car park, toilets and start of the Danes Dyke Nature Trail).

Follow the well-used path back to Sewerby which bears slightly left across the field in front of a red pantiled building, the site of a new golf course. Continue to the woods ahead. The path leads between the cricket pitch and the edge of Sewerby Park estate to the entrance to the Park. Continue along the path past the paddocks and back to Limekiln Lane car park.

What to look out for

Small fishing boats as well as pleasure craft are usually active in the bay, and large tankers and container ships can be observed crossing the horizon. There are magnificent views back along the town or up to Flamborough Head with its lighthouse. The chalk cliffs (part of the Flamborough Heritage Coast) are rich in wild flowers and birdlife. Birds to be seen include herring gulls, kittiwakes, shags, razorbills, guillemots, kestrels, and on the return walk, meadow pipits.

The walk passes the paddocks of Sewerby Park which contain deer, ponies and llamas.

Sewerby Hall

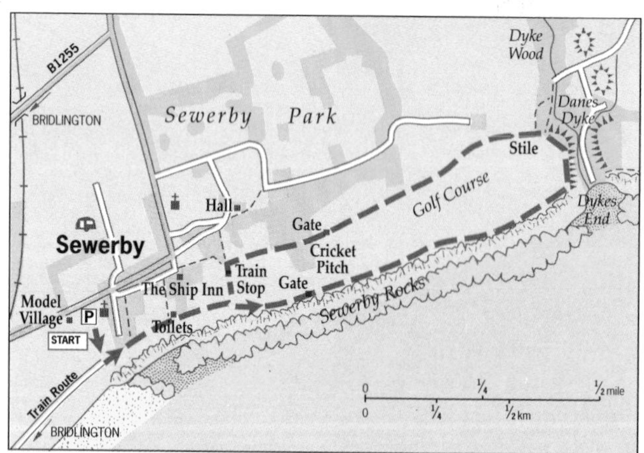

Sewerby Hall, Park and Zoo

The house, built around 1714–20, is now an art gallery and museum, including the Amy Johnson Trophy Room, dedicated to the famous pioneer aviator, who born in Hull. The gardens are full of interest, especially the delightful walled gardens, and there is also a miniature zoo and aviary. The park is open all year, the art gallery and museum from Easter to September.

Robin Hood's Bay

WALK 72
NORTH YORKSHIRE
SE950055

Information

The walk is two miles long
Steep terrain
Several stiles and lots of steps to climb up or down
Choice of cafés, tea shops, pubs, ice cream stalls and fish and chip shops in Robin Hood's Bay village
Picnic site above town, towards end of walk
Toilets at the car park entrance

Dramatic cliff and coastal scenery, a long-lamented clifftop railway line, a foreshore filled with rockpools and a picturesque former smugglers' village of narrow, twisting streets make up this testing walk.

START

Robin Hood's Bay is about five miles south of Whitby. Turn off the A171 onto the B1447 and continue towards the village. Park at the higher coach and car park (charge) at the old station.

DIRECTIONS

From the car park walk past the old station, now the village hall, taking the walkway on the left above the drive down to the Fylingthorpe road. Turn right along the road for 60yds, following the signs 'Railway Path', cross the road and go through a gate on the left onto the old Whitby–Scarborough railway line, now a footpath and cycle trail. Follow the old railway line for a little less than ½ mile until you reach a large, old concrete stile on the left. The path goes in front of the stile along a hedge to another stile. Cross, turning left along the edge of the fields, crossing several stiles. The path bears right above a shallow wooded ravine.

A stile leads into a wood. Keep on the path now descending above the ravine to yet another stile, leaving the wood along a path which curves steeply down onto the road. Turn right to the cobbled slipway and foreshore at Way Foot.

(From Way Foot fork right up

Shag

What to look out for

There are many seabirds along the coast and the foreshore – mainly gulls, but also terns in summer and cormorants in winter.

In the bay and beached by the slipway you will see fishing boats (the traditional North Sea coble is based on a Viking design), nets, and crab and lobster pots.

Life on the foreshore and in the rock pools is abundant, and includes crabs, sea anemones, limpets, periwinkles and small fish such as blennies.

King Street (cul de sac), turning left at the top into Chapel Street to see this lovely, narrow alleyway of shops and houses. Return down King Street.)

Take the opening just above the Dolphin Inn leading to the sea wall. Steps lead down past the viewing area to the sea wall itself. Continue left along the little promenade along the wall, going up the steps behind the town to reach the picnic site.

Follow the path back up to the The Bank (main street), turn right up the steps, and continue along to the roundabout and lower car park; 300 yards beyond this is the Station car park.

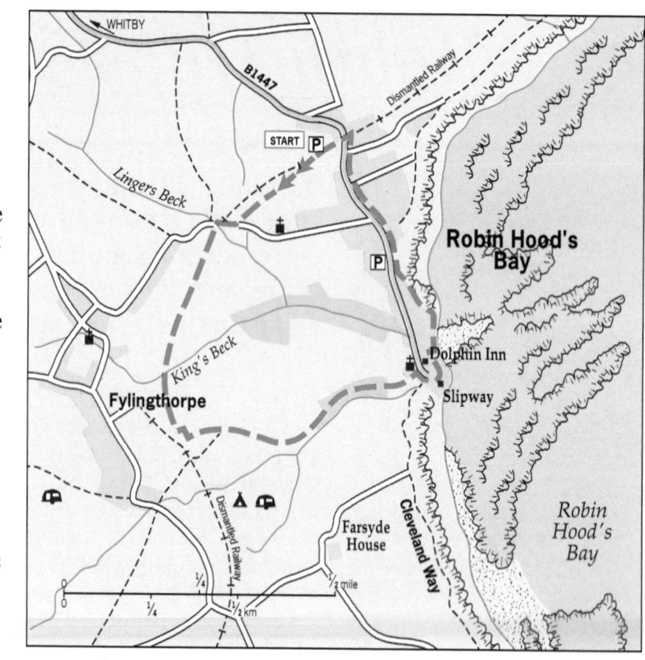

Robin Hood's Bay

Robin Hood's Bay

This is one of the most fascinating fishing and tourist villages along the east coast. With its winding, traffic free streets, narrow houses and old pubs, the village is full of atmosphere. A tunnel carries the Mill Stream, emerging by the slipway, and it was along here that smugglers carried their contraband – brandy, gin, silk, tobacco – at the dead of night, out of sight of the excisemen. The huge sea wall was built in 1975 to protect the town from the erosive power of the sea.

How Stean Gorge and Tom Taylor's Cave

A dramatic walk with splendid views, a streamside section, a footbridge over a gorge and a pathway under a steep overhang. Torches are essential for exploring the cave and can be hired at the café at the start.

WALK 73
NORTH YORKSHIRE
SE092743

What to look out for

The upper gorge has attractive mixed woodland of ash, hazel, thorn and birch trees. Trout can usually be seen lazing in the peat-brown waters of Stean Beck in the first part of the walk. How Stean Gorge offers fantastic water-carved limestone formations, cave systems and elevated walkways. A visit to the cave is the highlight of the walk.

START

How Stean is about seven miles north of Pateley Bridge. At Lofthouse turn left on no-through-road to Stean. Park at small car park (charge) in the quarry on the left.

DIRECTIONS

From the car park walk westwards along the lane to the café which is the entrance point to How Stean Gorge. Ahead across a small field, now used as an additional car park, is Tom Taylor's Cave, which is signposted and is in a small walled enclosure.
From the cave, head for the far left-hand corner of the field to a gate, where orange arrows indicate the way ahead. In the next field keep forward to the barn. Turn left through a gate, then keep ahead across the next two fields, through clearly marked gates. In the next field veer right to reach the 'Nidderdale Way' signpost at the field boundary.
Pass through a stone stile and bear diagonally left across the field to reach a wooden gate in the fence. Descend steps to cross a footbridge then ascend steps to reach a small enclosure with a caravan. Keep right here to reach a lane, passing the caravan on your left. At the lane turn left for the return to the car park.

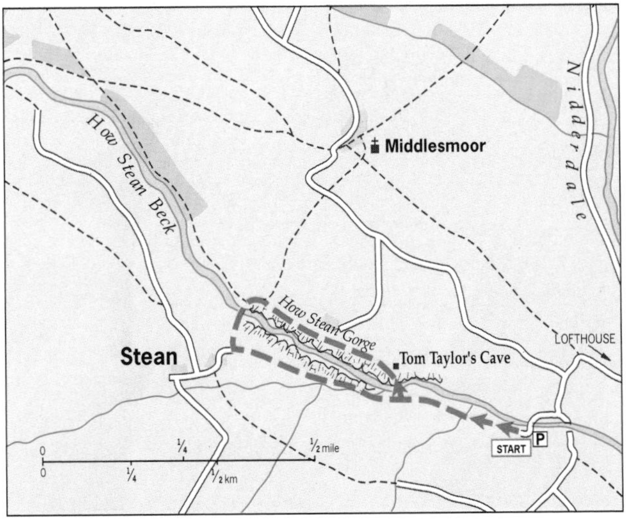

How Stean Gorge

This limestone gorge dates from the Ice Age, the stream carving out a deep ravine. It is 80 feet deep in places, and forms natural rock gardens with mosses, ivy, and a variety wild plants growing out of the crevices. In the

Information

The walk is one and a half miles long
An undulating route, with a steepish climb at the end
Several stiles
Dogs must be kept on leads
Nearest pub in Middlesmoor
Cafeteria, restaurant and ice creams at How Stean Gorge
Toilets at How Stean

The gorge (above), and the path

bottom of the gorge, the stream forms a series of impressive cascades and whirlpools. In dry weather, the really adventurous walker can take the steps down to the limestone bed of the stream at the bottom of the gorge to explore How Stean Tunnel. The tunnel is some 170 feet long and goes under the road – but it is usually very wet.

Tom Taylor's Cave

This beautifully formed cave is reached from the Gorge footpath by a little ladder stile in the entrance. It is 530ft long and reasonably dry, but torches are essential and care must be taken on the uneven ground. It eventually emerges at The Cat Hole, a depression in the ground in the field which is used as a car park and children's play area. The cave is named after Tom Taylor, a notorious local highwayman. In 1868 two boys found 32 Roman coins which had been hidden on a high ledge. They are now displayed in the Yorkshire Museum at York.

WALK 74
NORTH YORKSHIRE
SE012887

Aysgarth Falls

Information

The walk is about two and a half miles long
Slight incline with steps at the start, and more (slippery) steps down to the lower falls
Several stiles
Dogs must be kept on leads
National Park Centre has displays on the geology of the falls and history of the area
Cafeteria and ice creams by the Information Centre
Toilets by the Information Centre

Early purple orchid

A series of creamy white waterfalls formed by the River Ure falling down gigantic steps creates one of the most spectacular natural features in the north of England. But this is also a waterfall that can be enjoyed from close quarters from broad, limestone shelving rocks.

START

Aysgarth is at the heart of Wensleydale on the A684, about seven miles west of Leyburn. There is a car park (charge) at the National Park Centre.

DIRECTIONS

From the centre of the National Park car park, almost opposite the Information Centre café, climb the steps which lead onto the embankment of the former railway. Turn left along the embankment and walk to the end before turning right through a metal kissing-gate. Go up the pasture to a stile, keeping straight ahead to cross another a stile and head for the trees ahead. Bear right just before the trees and continue to a stile in the wall at the corner of the field, emerging onto a lane. Turn right and, taking care with traffic, go down the lane for 120yds. Where the lane bends right, take a narrow pedestrian gate on the left, beside a field gate leading to a track into the woods. Continue for 300yds through the trees, then bear right across a clearing to where the path forks just before the railway cutting. Take the left fork to go over stile next to a gate and turn right alongside the old railway line. The path climbs alongside the top left-hand side of the railway cutting, before descending to a stile by a gate beside a

What to look out for

There is a particularly spectacular sudden view of Bolton Castle across the valley – a magnificent fairy-tale castle (14th century) about half way around the walk. Freeholders' Wood is a fine example of a coppiced woodland, the trees, mainly hazel, being cut to produce long poles for fencing and other purposes. Other trees include ash, rowan, wych elm, sloe and hawthorn, and in spring the woodland floor is covered by wild flowers – wood anemones, primroses, common dog violets, early purple orchids and bluebells. Birds to be seen include nuthatch, chaffinch, warblers and treecreepers, and watch for grey squirrels and the occasional roe deer.

One section of the Aysgarth Falls

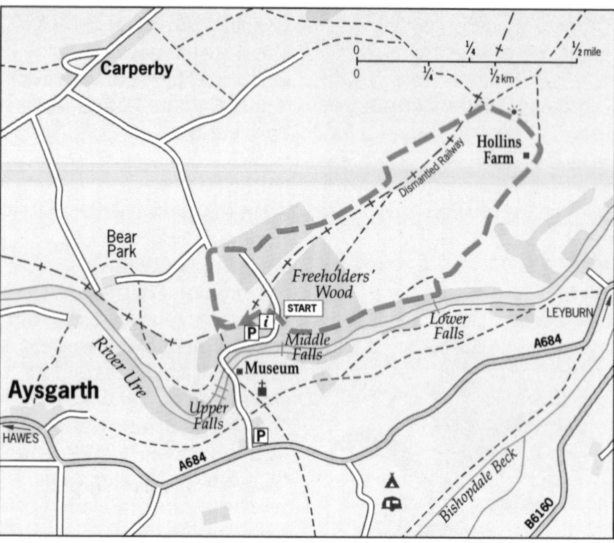

railway bridge and crossing of paths. (Turn right for a short cut back to the Falls.)

Turn left along a track, but as the track bends left, take the signposted footpath right across pasture to a stile. Go over the stile and continue ahead across scrubland until you reach a track. Turn right on the track, cross a cattle grid by the old railway line and continue on the track to Hollins Farm.

Pass in front of the farm, going left through the farmyard (follow the yellow waymarks). Bear left along the path, signposted 'Aysgarth 1 mile'. Continue in the same direction, avoiding Landrover tracks bearing left, passing through any farm gates, and continue straight on to another stile. Cross over and continue for about 50yds, following the path beside the fence.

Directly opposite a wooden footpath sign on the fence marked 'footpath to Castle Bolton', the path bears left towards the waterfalls.

Cross a stile. Directly ahead a narrow, slippery path leads down to the Lower Falls (not suitable for young children). Return to the main path and continue past the Lower Falls viewing area. Follow the 'return path' sign and walk on through the gates into Freeholders' Wood.

Continue on the path past Middle Falls viewing platform to the road. Cross carefully, and take the path opposite back into the car park.

Aysgarth Falls

The total drop over the three sets of waterfalls is about 160ft and the steps have been formed by huge limestone blocks. The viewing platforms give excellent views of the Lower and Middle Falls. The best place to enjoy the Upper Falls is from the far side of Aysgarth bridge, which dates back to Tudor times.

Muncaster

WALK 75
CUMBRIA
SD085964

At the head of Eskdale lie the highest mountains in Lakeland, and at its foot are the dunes and estuary of Ravenglass. This walk incorporates a trip on a miniature railway, a water mill, a castle and a Roman ruin.

Information

After the train ride, the walk is about three miles long
Some steep sections, but not difficult underfoot
Several gates and a stile
Short sections of road walking, one with a pavement, the other on a quiet private road
Refreshment facilities in Ravenglass, including the Ratty Arms next to the railway station
There is a café at Muncaster Castle

START
Ravenglass is just off the A595 about five miles south of Gosforth. Park at the Ravenglass and Eskdale Railway and catch a train. There is an hourly service up the valley (for times and charges, tel. 0229 717171). Alight at the first stop, Muncaster Mill, and the walk starts here.

DIRECTIONS
From Muncaster Mill station go through the mill yard and up the track, past the old wheel machinery and chicken sheds, then turn right along a bridleway, signposted 'Castle' and 'Ravenglass'. Walk along the bridleway for about 20yds.

Two paths lead off to the left. Take the first of these, signposted 'Castle'. Walk up the rather steep path, through woodland, until this levels off and meets a track. Go straight on following a dip between wooded ridges for about ½ mile. At the end of the woodland, go through a gate and turn left.

At the road (A595) go through a gate and straight on, downhill along the pavement, then cross the road with care and go through the gates of Muncaster Castle. Walk down the drive signposted 'Muncaster Church' and 'Footpath to Ravenglass', past the stables, garden centre and café. At the end of the drive, go straight across the lawns, with waterfowl pens to your right, to meet another drive. Cross this and follow a track uphill, signposted 'Ravenglass via Newtown'. At the end of this wooded track, go over the stile and out on to the open hill top.

The route is signposted but the path is not obvious; follow the direction indicated by the signpost, to the right of the hill crest. At isolated gate posts, continue ahead to the plantation with the rooftops of Newtown just beyond. Cross the stile and walk downhill through the plantation to go through a gate and turn along a broad track, passing a house on the left. On reaching a metalled private road, turn right past

What to look out for

The woods of Muncaster Castle contain some very exotic trees. The castle itself is only a century old, built on to fragments of a 14th-century tower house.
Walls Castle has a much better pedigree but is no more than a ruin. In fact it began as a Roman bath-house, associated with the fort of Glannaventa which lies buried on the other side of the track.
From the top of the hill there are fine views, of Ravenglass Dunes (a nature reserve) and the Esk estuary. In the distance to the north is Sellafield Nuclear Power Station.

Roman bathhouse ruins on the right, then continue to the end of the road, passing Walls Caravan Park. Just after the gates is a footpath on the left which leads to Ravenglass station.

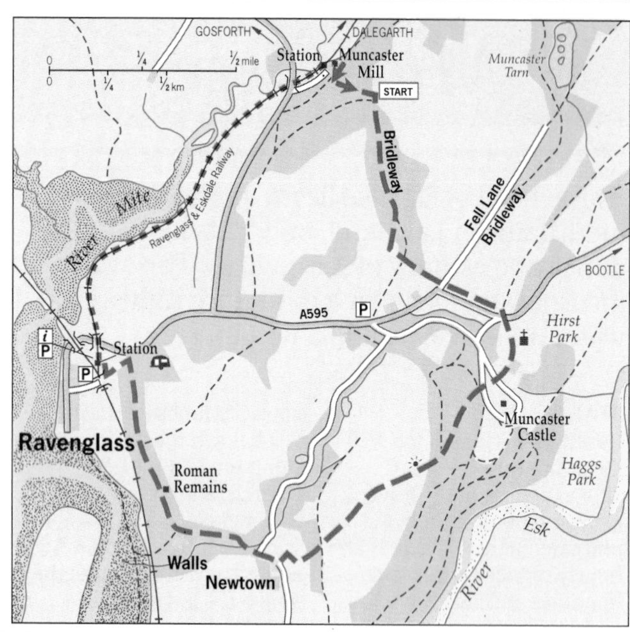

The Ravenglass and Eskdale Railway

The Eskdale narrow gauge railway was opened in 1875 to carry iron ore from Boot to Ravenglass, beginning as a 3ft gauge but converted to 15in gauge in 1915. The railway is now a popular tourist attraction.

Muncaster Castle and Owl Centre

Diverse attractions are offered at this castle, the seat of the Pennington family since the 13th century. Inside is a fine collection of 16th- and 17th-century furnishings and portraits, whilst the lovely grounds include a nature trail and commando course. Muncaster Castle is also the headquarters of the British Owl Breeding and Release Scheme. The garden and Owl Centre is open all year daily; the castle is open April to November, Tuesday to Sunday and Bank Holiday Mondays.

Muncaster Mill

There has been a mill on this site since the late 15th century, and flour and oatmeal are still ground on the premises using water power from the 13ft waterwheel. The mill is open from April to September.

Muncaster, first stop for the train

Gelt Woods

WALK 76
CUMBRIA
NY520592

Towering cliffs of orange sandstone, hanging woodlands, gorges and white-water rapids make this walk exciting. There is also a hint of history – battles were fought here and the Romans took stone for Hadrian's wall from the riverside quarries and left their names engraved in the rock.

Information

The walk is about three and a half miles long
Stepped sections with steep banks and the ground can be slippery
No stiles and only one gate
No road walking
The nearest refreshment and toilet facilities are at Brampton, a mile to the east

START
There is a small parking area on the north side of Low Gelt Bridge, reached by following the A69 a mile south of Brampton (ie avoiding the new by-pass) and turning off at Gelt Side, signposted 'Hayton Town Head'.

DIRECTIONS
Beyond the parking area and RSPB notice, cross the bridge over the Powterneth Beck and go through the fence gap to follow a woodland track.
The track rises up a slope, levels out and then forks. Take the upper track, left, past a seat; the track rises by a series of low steps through beech trees and up some further low steps. Continue to the edge of the woods and then bear right to meet a sunken lane.
Follow this downhill by more shallow steps, either of boulders or branches, and continue past a sandstone cliff on your left. Turn left at a junction and follow the track, with the rushing river down to your right and a high sandstone cliff, behind tall trees, to your left.
Keep on the main path, which rises then bears right and descends via steps to the riverside at a little bridge over

The path through the woods

the Hell Beck. Continue along the track through the woods, with the rushing water of the river still to your right, for about ¾ mile to a gate which leads out to a road at Middle Gelt Bridge.

Follow the same route back, passing the Hell Beck bridge and following the steep path up to avoid the main crook in the river.

After passing the rock faces on your right there is a junction, at which follow the lower path, beside the river, passing the Written Rock of Gelt. The path is made up for a short distance where the natural bank has been eroded. Continue to a junction with the outgoing route, and follow this back to the start.

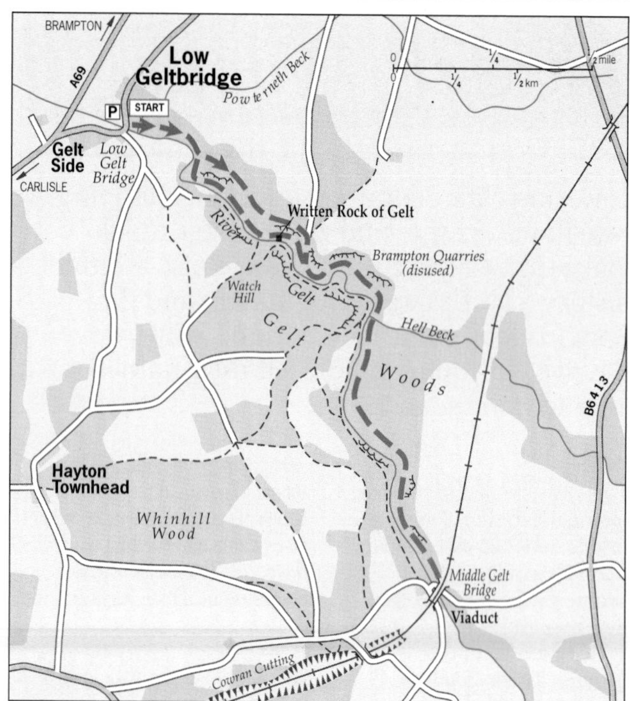

St Bees Sandstone

The rushing waters of the Gelt have sliced through beds of red St Bees sandstone, creating rushes and rapids over harder bands of rock and creating cliffs up to 50 feet high. The beautiful warm colour of the sandstone makes it easy to identify as the building material for local villages. It was quarried here for Hadrian's Wall (there was nothing suitable any closer) and can be seen at its best at nearby Lanercost Priory.

Royal Battles by the Gelt

Historical events in the area include a bloody battle at Hell Beck Bridge in 1570, when 3,000 rebels supporting Mary, Queen of Scots were defeated by Elizabeth's cavalry. Bonnie Prince Charlie also visited the area – he took his army of highlanders over Low Gelt Bridge, marching on his way to Carlisle in 1745.

Long-tailed tit

What to look out for

The woodland is in the care of the RSPB, and bird life includes a special trio of northern birds – pied flycatcher, redstart and wood warbler.

The lofty viaduct above Middle Gelt Bridge was built in 1835 and carries the Newcastle–Carlisle Railway.

The 'Written Rock of Gelt' is a rock face above the river where Romans carved graffiti while they were quarrying stone for Hadrian's Wall. A secret path leads up from the river.

WALK 77
CUMBRIA
NY565325

The Eden Valley

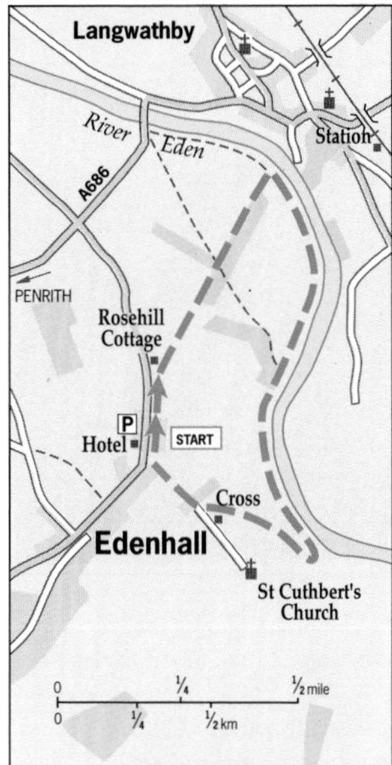

The Eden Valley, between the Lake District and the North Pennines, is one of the most beautiful pastoral landscapes in Britain. The fact that it is often by-passed by visitors helps to maintain its unspoilt quality. This walk is a gentle introduction to the river and one of its most interesting villages.

START

Edenhall lies just off the A686, two miles south of Langwathby. Park either in the village or close to the Edenhall Hotel, from where the walk begins.

DIRECTIONS

Walk out of the village past the children's play area. Just before the red-brick Rosehill Cottage turn right and go through the gate, signposted 'Langwathby and River Eden'. Walk along the track with a fence to your right and sheep pasture to your left. Ahead in the distance is the village of Langwathby. Continue to a wicket gate, between narrow conifer plantations, and keep forward along the path. On reaching the river turn right, signposted 'Edenhall and Church' and walk along the river bank on a raised path to go through a gate. Proceed uphill, past the end of the conifer plantation to your right, then follow a line of beech trees, with a steep slope and the river to your left. Continue along the path (which can be overgrown in summer), passing the high wall of the Edenhall estate deer park on your right, and go down some steps to follow the edge of the park until the river veers away to your left. Go through a wicket gate to join a track, and bear sharp right to follow this over the parkland, past a lone oak and towards the stone Plague Cross. (Here you can detour to the left to see St Cuthbert's Church, retracing your steps to the cross.) Bear right along the metalled track, past the East Lodge and into the village. Turn right on the main road to return to the start.

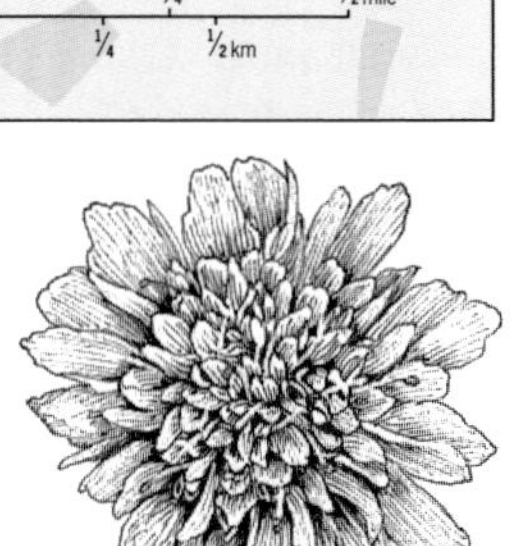

Field scabious

What to look out for

Otters still inhabit the Eden, though they are rarely seen. Most daytime sightings are cases of mistaken identity, usually referring to mink which have become quite common here over the last decade.

Birds of the river include goosander and cormorant during spring and summer; dippers and grey wagtails are residents and kingfishers come and go. In winter, skeins of greylag geese fly up and down the valley, filling the air with their contact calls.

St Cuthbert's Church (above), and the Plague Cross, Edenhall (left)

Edenhall

Edenhall is an estate village, created by the Musgrave and Gibson families. The hall itself no longer exists, but there are some beautiful buildings in soft red sandstone, characteristic of the Eden valley. 'Homefield', close to the tall farmhouse, was a tithe barn and the church tower was once used as a pele, a refuge from raiding Scots at the time of the Border Wars.

The Plague Cross

The stone cross towards the end of the walk is called the Plague Cross and dates back to four hundred years ago, when an epidemic struck the village and killed a quarter of its inhabitants. As no tradesman would risk entering the stricken village or making any kind of contact with its people, villagers paid for their food by placing money in a sink of vinegar beneath the cross.

Information

The walk is about two miles long
Generally very easy underfoot with one short incline
A few gates and no stiles
There is some road walking in Edenhall, a very quiet village with only light traffic
The Edenhall Hotel provides bar meals and there is a children's play area opposite

Bowlees

WALK 78
CO DURHAM
NY908283

High Force, two miles to the west of Bowlees, is the highest waterfall in the country, but it is impossible to explore it in safety. This walk uses the excellent parking/picnicking area of Bowlees as the pivot for two short walks, leading beside the tumbling waters of the River Tees and Bowlees Beck to more accessible waterfalls.

START
The little hamlet of Bowlees lies three miles north-west of Middleton-in-Teesdale on the B6277. The entrance to the large car park and picnic area lies just to the east of the scatter of farms and cottages, on the east side of the beck.

DIRECTIONS
There is a wardens' office at the back of the car park with a nearby notice for orientation. For the walk upstream of the Bowlees Beck, follow the path between the beck and the office, bear left at a fork and continue past the toilet block to a footbridge. It is possible to cross to the far side here and explore the shallow, stony stream at its safest point. There are cascades and pools and the banks are covered with wild flowers. Cross back and continue upstream, up a series of steps with a pretty waterfall on your left, then with woodland to your right. You are on the land of the Raby estate and the path is accessible with their permission. Through a gate, the path is broad and passes a grassy bank before entering trees again and leading eventually to Summerhill Force. Behind the waterfall is Gibson's Cave. Retrace your route back to the car park.
For the walk along the Tees, start at the car park and cross the back by a low concrete bridge, then go up a flight of steps to the Visitor Centre (the old Methodist Chapel). Left of the Centre, walk down the track straight ahead, with a meadow on your right, to the road. Turn right and cross the road, then go through a gate on the left side of the pasture. Cross two fields, with a gate between, then cross a stone stile and drop down a path through woodland. The path leads to the Wynch Bridge, a little suspension bridge over the River Tees. On the far side turn right. The waterfall to your right is called Low Force. The current can sometimes be fierce here and some of the pools are deep,

Pied wagtail

What to look out for

Wild flowers are abundant in the meadows of Teesdale and along the river.
During the early summer, look for yellow rattle, eyebright, meadow saxifrage, common sorrel, common spotted orchid, globeflower and marsh marigold.
Birds are plentiful too – dippers, grey wagtails and common sandpipers along the banks, redshanks and curlews on the fields and peregrine falcons high overhead.

Low Force Waterfall on the River Tees

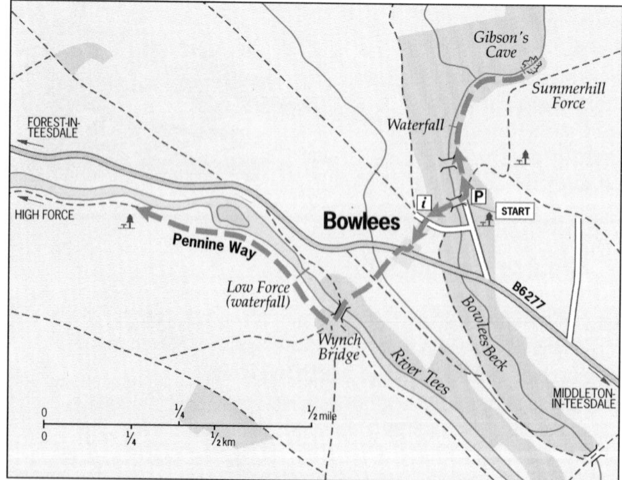

Information

There are two halves to the walk, each a mile long

Both walks have some steps and stiles, but the Gibson's Cave walk is easier

The Tees walk crosses a road

Refreshment facilities at the Visitor Centre

Picnicking is possible at many places on the banks of the streams

Toilets at start of the first walk

but by continuing upstream along the clear gravel path you soon reach quieter waters with good picnic places. Return by the same route.

Hay Meadows

In July the meadows of Teesdale are cut for hay. These days most British farmers make silage, putting fertiliser on their fields and cutting their grass when it is still very green and juicy. This means that wild flowers can never compete with the grass or set their seed. Farmers in the Pennine dales still use more traditional methods and cut hay a little later, by which time the wild flowers have finished their growth, and though the grass crop is not so heavy, this has kept the countryside colourful.

Gibson's Cave

Gibson was on the run from the law in the 16th century when he found the perfect hiding place – behind a waterfall!

WALK 79
TYNE AND WEAR
NZ398649

Marsden Rock

Information

The walk to the lighthouse is about two and a half miles
Clear level path, but vertigo may be a problem along the cliffs
No stiles or gates
No road walking
Marsden Grotto serves pub food, with access to the beach and a refund on the price of the descent in the lift
Ice cream kiosk in the car park

There are coast walks in either direction from Marsden, both of unexpected richness considering the closeness of industrial Tyneside – sea cliffs, islands alive with seabirds, miles of clean golden sands, rock pools, smugglers' caves, and a lighthouse at Lizard Point.

START
The village of Marsden lies on the coast just to the south-east of South Shields and two miles north of Whitburn. Start in the large car park (pay-and-display in summer) at Marsden Bay, on the seaward side of the A183.

DIRECTIONS
Facing the sea from the car park, turn right along the clear cliff path. (The walk can be extended along the cliff path to the left.) It is impossible to get lost, but

The rocky coast near Marsden

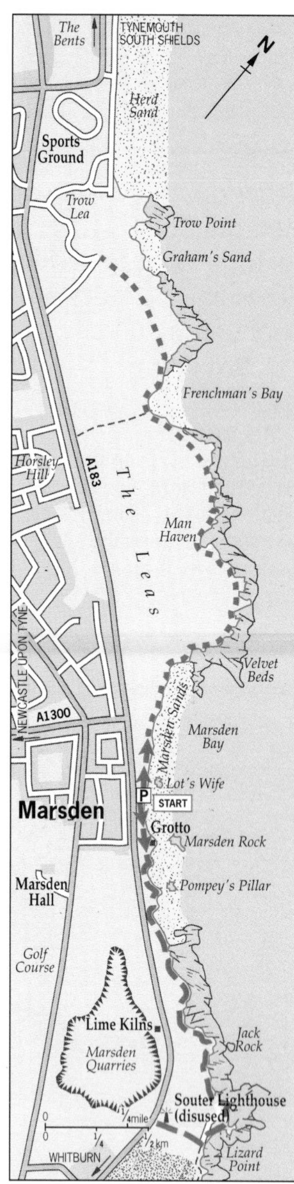

What to look out for

The islets, arches, pillars and stacks are impressive, composed of magnesian limestone 245 million years old. The main island is 91 feet high. Most of the islands throng with nesting seabirds in the spring. Rocky cliffs are chosen by many species because they are inaccessible to predators and give easy access back to the sea. Marsden provides some of the closest and safest viewing of their nesting sites – and the noise and the smell are unique!

Kittiwakes, ocean-going gulls, are the most numerous, making nests of seaweed which they manage to stick to vertical clefts and crevices on the rock. By contrast, herring gulls – seaside scavengers which rarely go far from land – make much bigger nests, usually on the grassy cliff-tops of the islands. Cormorants are inshore specialists too, roosting on the islands, safe from foxes. Fulmars are the most aerial of the Marsden cliff-nesters, sailing on the updraft of air along the cliff edge, often eye to eye with walkers on the path. Out to sea, gannets, skuas, shags, terns, guillemots, eiders and a host of other birds can be seen passing to and fro, following the rhythm of tides and seasons.

The clifftop vegetation includes thrift, sea plantain and scurvy grass, with rock rose, thyme and autumn gentian on the limestone outcrops.

Fulmar

don't be tempted off the path, which could be dangerous. The main features to look for along the way include the rock stack called Lot's Wife, Marsden Grotto, then the main seabird island of Marsden Rock, after which come the smaller stacks of Pompey's Pillar and Jack Rock, and finally the Souter Lighthouse on Lizard Point. The return route is by the same path.

Marsden Grotto

What looks like an ordinary pub perched on the clifftop is just the start of an adventure. The grotto was established in 1782 by a character called Jack the Blaster and was intended to service the needs of tourists and smugglers, who used a cave to the south of the grotto. Access to the foot of the cliff is much easier today than it was in Jack's time; he built the flight of steps but there is now an electronic lift which, for a very modest charge (you only pay on the downward journey), takes you down to the beach and the pub which is set into the base of the rock face. At low tide it is possible to walk out to Marsden Rock, which dominates the sea view.

Souter Lighthouse

Though no longer a working lighthouse, this red-and-white striped tower is open to the public.

Dunstanburgh – The Castle Above the Sea

From the tiny little harbour at Craster, Dunstanburgh Castle away to the north is perched high on a hill, with sheer cliffs on the seaward side. Its keep and towers, although fairly battered, seem just about capable of withstanding one more siege.

WALK 80
NORTHUMBERLAND
NU256198

Information

The walk is three miles long
Mainly level, easy walking on grass
No stiles but several kissing-gates
Dogs must be kept on leads over grazing land
Pub in Craster serves bar meals and there is also a restaurant
Lots of grassy areas for picnicking along the coast near the castle

START

Craster is on the coast six miles north-east of Alnwick. From the A1 Alnwick bypass take the B1340 then follow signposts to Craster on unclassified roads. There is a large National Trust car park in the old quarry at the western edge of the village.

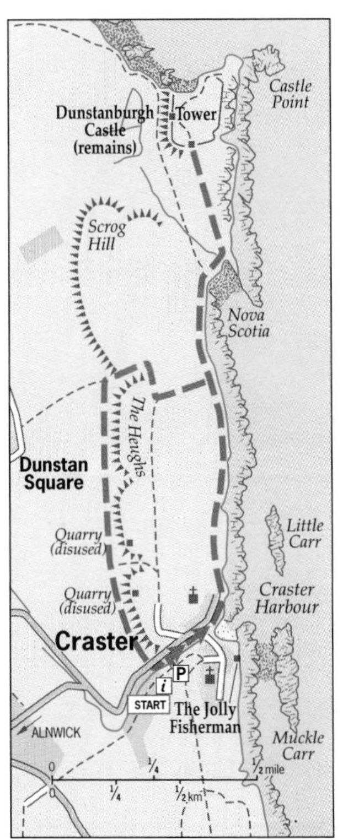

DIRECTIONS

Turn right out of the car park and walk to the harbour, then turn left along the sea front. Go through a kissing-gate and follow the path north along the edge of the rocks. There are two more kissing-gates. After the second, take the path to the right round the head of an inlet. Surprisingly, although so tiny and now partially marsh-filled, this used to be a port from which warships sailed. The path then winds uphill to the castle entrance.

From the castle retrace the outward route as far as the second kissing-gate, after which turn right and follow the fence uphill and through a gate. Turn right along the edge of the field to another gate, then left along a track through a shallow gap in the ridge. At the bottom of the slope turn left through a kissing-gate and follow the path running below 'The Heughs', the craggy ridge on the left. The best route keeps to the left immediately below the slope, arriving at another kissing-gate. The path then goes through a short stretch of woodland to emerge at the road opposite the car park.

Dunstanburgh Castle

Thomas, second Earl of Lancaster, founded the castle in the early 13th century. In the 1380s its defences were strengthened by John of Gaunt, Baron of Embleton, who led an invasion of Scotland from here, but his action did not stop constant

The harbour at Craster

raiding by the Scots. His son, Henry of Bolingbroke, succeeded him in 1399 and later that year usurped the throne to become King Henry IV. Thus Dunstanburgh became a royal castle and was a Lancastrian stronghold during the Wars of the Roses. Seiged, counter-seiged, captured and recaptured, in 1464 it finally fell to the Earl of Warwick to be held for Edward IV. The poundings taken during many battles wrought great destruction which was never fully repaired. Now an English Heritage property, the castle is open to the public and has a small information centre in the grounds.

Craster Kippers

Craster has long had a fine reputation for its kippers (still smoked in the traditional way over oak chippings), which are sent far and wide from the smokehouse near the harbour.

Herring gull

What to look out for

Look out for seals and cormorants offshore. Many other seabirds can be seen from the coast path, particularly eider duck. In the nesting season, the cliffs on the north side of the castle are alive with kittiwakes, fulmars and shags.

A lovely display of wildflowers includes thrift and bird's-foot trefoil, and lots of butterflies may be seen along the coast and on the return route. The scrub along the Heughs provides a landfall for exhausted incoming birds, especially in autumn. Birds such as warblers and chats rest and feed here, recovering from their flight across the North Sea.

Bamburgh and Budle Bay

WALK 81
NORTHUMBERLAND
NU184349

Bamburgh is a pretty seaside village and its huge Norman Castle dominates the landscape for many miles around. The walk starts at the Castle, crosses a lovely stretch of heathland to a serene sheltered bay, taking in one of the best stretches of coast in the country.

Information

The walk is three and three quarter miles long
Mostly level on grass or beach with some easy rocks to cross; at some high tides it may be difficult to get past Black Rock – see alternative in route directions
Pubs, cafés and restaurants in Bamburgh
Good picnic sites along most of the route, although the dunes in Budle Bay are probably the best

START
From the north, Bamburgh is reached via the B1342, leaving the A1 just beyond Belford. From the south, 12 miles beyond Alnwick, the B1341 leads to Bamburgh. There is a large car park at the east end of the village opposite the castle entrance.

DIRECTIONS
From the car park turn left, walk back along the road and take the path along the edge of the cricket field below the castle crag. At the end of a ruined wall bear left, then right beside a fence, to join a road leading north from the village. Follow it, turning right at the top of the hill,

Bamburgh Castle

through an informal parking area and down through the dunes. Go left along the beach, heading for the inland side of the lighthouse at Stag Rock, and take the path up the bank past a lifebuoy to the golf course entrance.

Take the path westwards across the golf course and, 50yds before reaching a drystone wall, bear right on the green path winding along the edge of the heath above the dunes. Continue along the edge of the fairway then descend to a ruined concrete gun emplacement overlooking Budle Bay. Go left behind it and descend again towards the caravans, then bear right through the dunes to the old pier.

Follow the beach to the right, skirting Black Rock below Budle Point (if tide is very high, use the path running just above the beach instead). Continue along the beach then head towards the north end of the castle, keeping just to the right of a lifebuoy. A path then runs south along the seaward side of the castle beside a fence. At the south end fork right, away from the fence up towards the castle entrance. Start down the access road then fork left on to a path leading directly back to the car park.

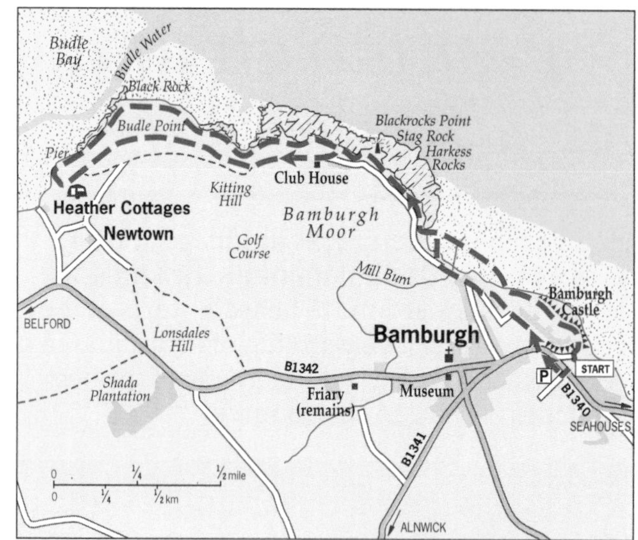

Bamburgh Castle

For 900 years the great Norman Castle of Bamburgh has towered above the sea on its basalt crag, and for 500 years before that it was the royal centre of the Kingdom of Northumbria. But the 'golden age' of Bamburgh began in the 7th century with the arrival of Christianity, when King Oswald established the monastery on nearby Lindisfarne (Holy Island) which would become a great centre of learning.

The Victorian Heroine

In 1838 Bamburgh again became famous, courtesy of Grace Darling, daughter of the keeper of the Longstone Lighthouse. During a storm which had driven the *Forfarshire* on to Harcar Rocks, she and her father risked their lives to row a fishing coble to rescue the survivors. Her bravery caught the imagination of the whole nation and inspired many songs and stories; people flocked to the area from all over the country to catch a glimpse of her – she even became a national heroine in Japan! The cottage in which she was born is now a small museum, and among the exhibits is the rescue boat.

What to look out for

Northumberland is the only English county where eider ducks nest and there are usually great flotillas of them around Stag Rock, as well as many other seabirds and waders along the coast. At low tide Budle Bay has a fantastic display of lugworm casts. In spring and summer the heathland near the golf course has a beautiful array of wild flowers, and is alive with butterflies including grayling and common blue.

The Town Walls of Berwick

WALK 82
NORTHUMBERLAND
NT997531

This is a short and easy walk along the ramparts that defended Berwick for centuries during prolonged border disputes between the English and the Scots .

START
Berwick-upon-Tweed is just off the A1 in northern Northumberland. Follow the signs for the town centre and park in the large car park in the old cattle market, immediately north of the Scots Gate.

DIRECTIONS
From the car park go back to the road, left through Scots Gate, cross over and walk along the south-east side of the Walls. With a statue (of Lady Jerningham) in view turn sharp right up a ramp then left up steps to Meg's Mount, the start of the circuit. Go back down the steps and north-east over Scots Gate. The higher path on the left gives the better views.
At the next great bulwark, Cumberland Bastion, the tunnels in the walls which gave access to the flankers for men and ammunition can be seen below. Continuing around the ramparts, Brass Bastion at the north-east corner provides a splendid viewpoint from which most of the fortifications can be seen.
The walls run south-east now over Cow Port, the only gateway through the walls surviving in its original form. There is a path down to it on the town side and the Barracks are only a few yards away.
Still heading south-east, Windmill Bastion stands at the most easterly point in the defences. (It did originally have a windmill on top, but in Victorian times and in both world wars guns were sited there for coastal defence.)
Now go due south to Kings

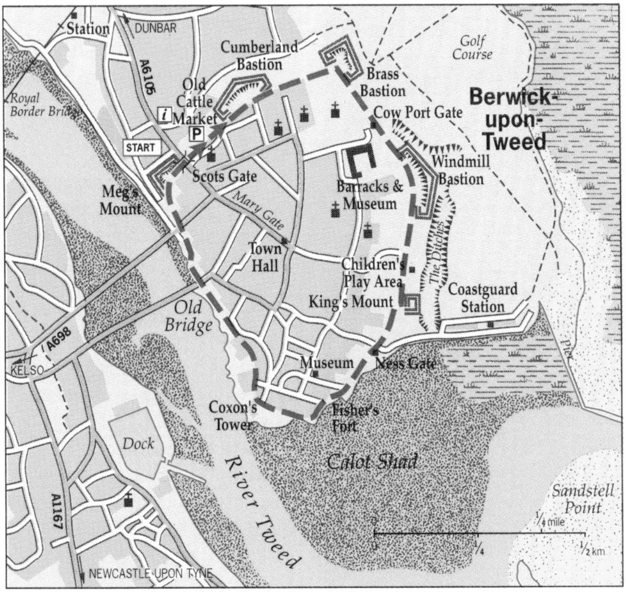

Information

The walk is just over one and a half miles long
Mainly on level, hard-surfaced paths; one short (avoidable) section over steps and steep grassy slopes. There are hidden sheer drops along the ramparts
Dogs should be kept on leads
Pubs, cafés and restaurants in Berwick
Several grassy areas for picnics on the first half of the route

Mount. From this point the planned Elizabethan fortifications along the river-side were never completed and the medieval walls are joined.

The path descends along the sea wall past Black Watchtower, and over two more access points, Ness Gate and Fisher's Fort, to Coxon's Tower above the river. The arched doorway on the town side of the tower leads to a tunnel inside the walls. The tunnel is not open to the public.

Continue upstream along the Quay Walls to the 300-year-old river bridge. Cross the road and go along Bridge Terrace. After the gun emplacements at the next corner bear right uphill, passing under the new road bridge to arrive back below Meg's Mount.

What to look out for

The walk gives close-ups of some elegant town houses of Berwick, with magnificent views over the town and the surrounding area. Coastal birds such as herring gulls, kittiwakes and fulmars can sometimes be seen surprisingly far inland over the town.

Above, the river bridge, and left, the bastion

Turn right, and head back towards the Scots Gate and the car park.

A Battleground

Berwick has had a turbulent history, and was for centuries a major prize in the struggle between the English and Scots. During countless battles over about two hundred years, Berwick changed hands thirteen times, but has been part of England since 1482.

The immensely strong battlements constructed in the reign of Elizabeth I clearly illustrate the continuing strategic importance of the town.

Peel

WALK 83
ISLE OF MAN
SC248844

This energetic walk climbs steadily to give impressive views of Peel Castle, continuing upwards to a height of some 500 feet above sea level at Corrin's Folly. There are spectacular views of the rocky coastline, which is a haven for sea birds.

Information

The walk is about three miles long
Steady climbing, steep in places
No road walking, except on extended walk
No stiles, but some kissing-gates
Snack bar near castle
Picnic area by car park, also grassy area by tower
Toilets near castle

START
Follow the road round the harbour towards Peel Castle. On the left before the causeway is the fairly large car park.

DIRECTIONS
Go up the steps to the right of the car park entrance. At the top of the steps follow the track straight up the hill. It joins a wider gravel track which swings round to the right. Follow this round the headland. Continue, passing two shallow but quite dramatic disused slate quarries. The track runs out by the second of these, but you will see a steep path up the hill to the right. (Children and dogs should be strictly supervised at this point.) Head up towards the summit of

The view over Peel

Thistle Head. When you reach three large blocks of granite, take the right-hand track. Follow this until you reach the wall, go through the gate, signposted '*Raad Ny Foilian*' (coast path). Continue along the path, which becomes rocky with a severe drop to the right (spectacular views of the coastline). When the track divides, take the right fork. Continue until it divides again, go left this time. Head towards the dry stone wall (view of the Milner Tower on Bradda Head, and the Calf of Man). Keep left at the next two divisions,with the walls on your right (view of Corrin's Hill and Folly). Where the path divides, keep right, climbing steadily up towards the tower. From up here you can see Peel, Port Erin and the Calf, St Johns, and to the north-east, Jurby Head. Follow the wide grass track north, descending towards Peel. Head towards the wall, go through the kissing-gate and continue straight on to the crest of the next hill, where you will find the remains of three tumuli (breathtaking aerial view of Peel Castle, the harbour and bay). Follow the path straight down the hill to rejoin the original gravel track, and retrace your footsteps to the car park. To extend the walk, a footpath starts near the castle entrance and goes round the exterior of the castle walls. There are good views of Peel Hill and the coastline, and the path will bring you round to the harbour wall.

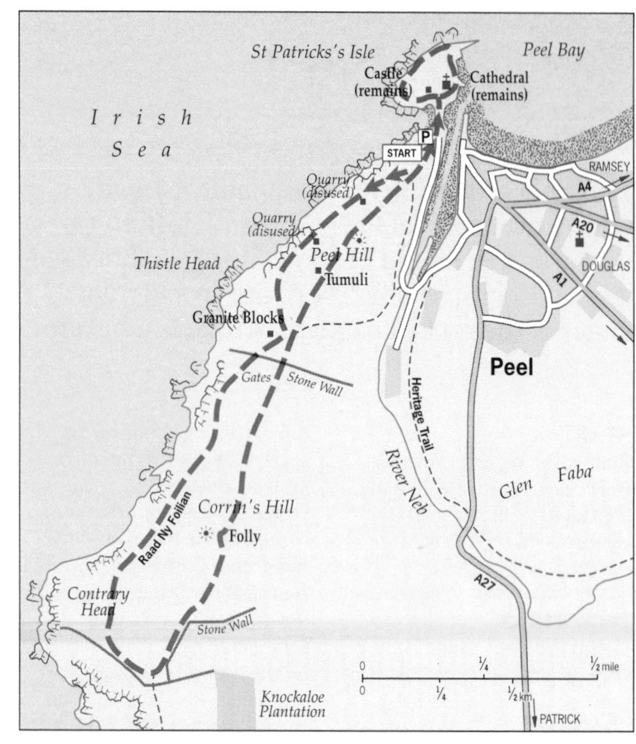

Corrins Hill and Folly
Constructed in 1806 by Thomas Corrin as a memorial to his family, the tower is 50ft high and built on the highest point, some 500ft above sea level.
The four corners of the tower are aligned with the four points of the compass. Corrin, his wife and their child are all buried nearby.

Peel
Though primarily a fishing port, Peel is, in fact, a city with two cathedrals: one in the centre and one within the castle. The castle was built to protect the cathedral of St German's, possibly founded by St Patrick, and is said to be haunted by a black dog. The castle is open from Easter to September.

What to look out for

St Patrick's Isle is a popular haunt for grey seals which escort the fishing boats into harbour, and look out in summer for the harmless basking sharks.
Stonechats and meadow pipits haunt the coastal scrub.
There are many butterflies, and among the wild flowers are harebells, self heal, ling and thrift.

Drumlanrig Castle and Country Park

This is an absorbing walk through woodlands, with lots of ornate stone bridges and a special wheelchair and pushchair nature trail. The castle and grounds are only open during the summer, but the park is open all year round.

WALK 84
DUMFRIES & GALLOWAY
NX851993

START
Drumlanrig Castle is off the A76 three miles north of Thornhill. The walk starts at the car park to the west of the front of the castle, and is one of three waymarked woodland walks.

DIRECTIONS
Follow the red directional signs opposite the woodland walk map board, up through the beech wood to Beech Loch, a small and peaceful man-made lochan. Turn right and then first left, following the red arrows down a forest track to Coldstream Loch, a smaller loch which is gradually silting up.
From the loch walk down to the left to reach Montague Bridge, a pretty, stone bridge over the burn. Take the path almost directly ahead of you, on the left hand side of the bridge beside the burn, again following the red arrows. At the next bridge, cross over the burn and continue straight on. At a picnic area turn right along the wheelchair trail at Druids Loch, where there are several seats.
At the head of the loch turn left (with red arrows) and cross the main drive, then in about 100yds cross a wooden footbridge into forest. At a

Drumlanrig Castle from the Forest Walk

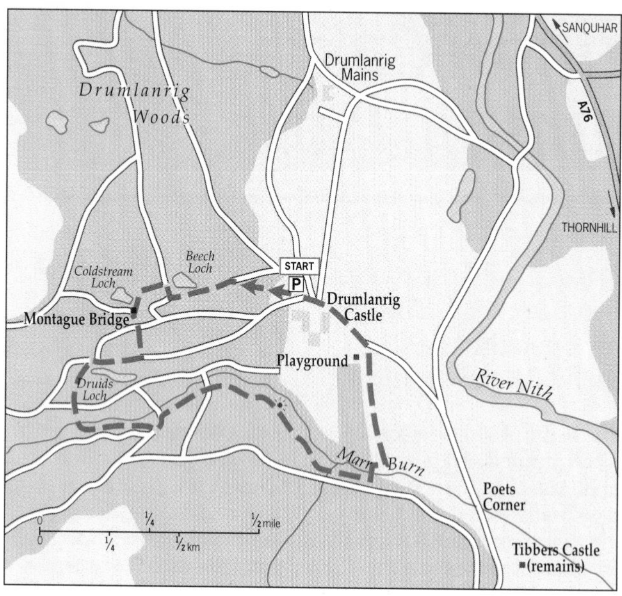

Information

The walk is two miles long
Mostly on woodland paths; many seats en route, including tiny plastic seats for children
Dogs must be kept on leads
A few stiles
Café-tearoom at castle (summer only)
Grassy area around castle suitable for picnicking

clearing turn left and follow the path down through mixed woodland, turning left at the end down a rough stone drive. Turn right before you come to a stone bridge through spruce trees and follow the burn, passing a small waterfall.

Continue along the burnside path through a clearing and then into larch woods (passing a wooden seat which affords a superb view of the south side of the castle through a gap in the trees).

Turn left over footbridge and then sharp right at a metal gate. Cross a stile to your left and go up the side of the field, crossing another stile, then continue over parkland before returning to the car park.

Drumlanrig Castle

The castle, the home of the Duke of Buccleuch, is nicknamed 'the Pink Palace' and is a fine example of 17th-century Renaissance architecture. It has an internationally famous collection of priceless art treasures, including a Madonna by Leonardo da Vinci and works by Rembrandt, Gainsborough and Holbein.

The drawing room has a unique inlaid cabinet, which King Louis XIV presented to Charles II, and there is a portrait of William III, which bears a slash mark. The culprit was one of Bonnie Prince Charlie's troops, who rested at the castle in 1745. There are also relics of Mary, Queen of Scots, and Flemish tapestries and Victorian summerhouses. The castle is open May to August (closed Saturdays), the grounds are open May to September daily.

What to look out for

In the grounds there is a tree planted by Neil Armstrong, the first man on the moon, as well as one of the country's first ginkgo trees, and Britain's oldest Douglas fir. A massive sycamore is listed in *The Guinness Book of Records* as Britain's largest.
Woodland birds include great spotted woodpeckers, nuthatches, chaffinches and treecreepers. The park has a beautifully landscaped garden, and there are brown trout in Coldstream Loch.

WALK 85
BORDERS
NT331354

Traquair House

This is a lovely short walk through woodlands within the grounds of Scotland's oldest inhabited house. Other attractions here include a maze, a brewery, historical displays and a delightful old tearoom. The walk is only accessible from April to September.

Information

The walk is around a mile long; one and a half miles if you include the maze
Easy ground
No road walking
One stile
Cottage tearoom at Traquair House
Picnic area near the car park
Toilet facilities at Traquair House

Weasel

START

Traquair House is off the B709, six miles south-east of Peebles, near Innerleithen. Start the walk just outside the courtyard gates next to the garden. There is a car park next to the 'wineglass lawn' (charge for entry to house and grounds).

DIRECTIONS

Come out of the courtyard and turn left. Proceed through a stone doorway straight ahead, past garden and beech hedge and a croquet lawn on your left. Turn left after the wickerwork summerhouse and two huge horse chestnut trees.
When you reach the Quair Burn, veer left through some lovely old yew trees and massive firs. Continue left along the bank of the river. Go through a swing gate and bear left diagonally across the meadow until you come to a stile (across the meadow on your right you can see where Quair Burn flows into the River Tweed). Cross the stile and turn right. Walk up the side of the fence with the River Tweed on your right. After about 50yds turn left into woodland. Follow the path through woodland across three footbridges. After crossing the third footbridge turn left.
On reaching the drive by the house turn right, passing the

What to look out for

Look out for the famous Bear Gates at the end of a long tree-lined avenue, near the entrance. They were closed in 1745 after the Jacobite Rebellion, when the fifth Earl of Traquair promised that they would remain shut until the Stuarts regained the throne.
Traquair has extensive ancient woodland. There are stately beeches which allow nothing to grow under their canopies, old oaks which support more species of insect than any other trees, and numerous ancient firs and yew trees. A row of poplars next to the maze is particularly striking.
In winter bramblings and chaffinches feed on the woodland floor, especially under the beeches. Grey herons and kingfishers may be seen along the banks of the Tweed.

library and a fine collection of tapestries, family relics, antiques and paintings. There is a restaurant, a tearoom, gift shop, art gallery and craft workshops.

Traquair's 18th-century brewery produces up to 60,000 bottles of beer each year and is open to visitors. There is also a maze to explore and a fascinating collection of toys. The house is open daily from the end of May to September; limited opening Easter to May. The grounds are open April to September.

Above and left, the house and grounds

brewery on your left and the Well Pool on your right. At the junction turn left, back towards car park.

Traquair House

Romantic Traquair House, dating from the 10th century, is steeped in history. This is where Alexander 1 signed a charter, and William the Lion held court here in 1209. It was visited by 27 kings and queens, among them Mary, Queen of Scots. Many kings and nobles used to visit the estate for fishing, hunting and hawking.

The house has a splendid

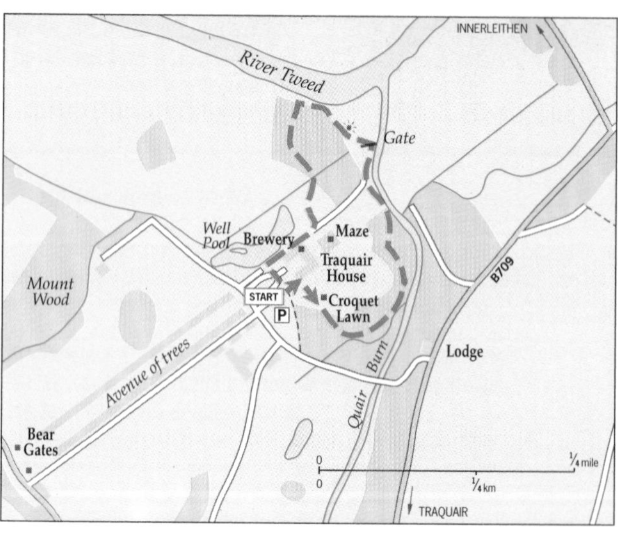

Gullane Bay

WALK 86
LOTHIAN
NT476831

Seaside walks are always fun and this one is no exception. It goes along an excellent sandy beach beside the broad Firth of Forth, with views across to Fife, and returns beside the famous Muirfield golf course.

Information

The walk is about two and a half miles long
Good paths, but soft going across the sand dunes
Dogs can run on the beach, but should be kept on leads by the golf course
Pubs and cafés in Gullane
Toilets near the car park

START
Gullane is 15 miles east of Edinburgh. Turn off the A198 in Gullane at the sign 'To the Beach' and park at Gullane Bents car park.

DIRECTIONS
From the car park walk down the tarmac path to the beach, reached by a gap through the dunes. There is a play area to the left.

Turn right and walk along the beach on the firm sand. The view extends from Edinburgh over to the Fife Hills and round towards the Bass Rock.

When you reach the rocks go up to the right and walk along the shore path, passing concrete blocks placed here in World War II as tank traps, then over a shingle beach. The path goes through the dunes (soft sand and harder going) then improves to run outside a fence to reach the scant remains of an old chapel.

The dunes at Gullane Bay

The path winds inland following the line of a stone dyke. Continue up a broad grassy path, keeping the wood on your right. The path swings right to start the return journey, passing along the edge of Muirfield golf course. Pass through a fence beside a gate (note the warning about keeping dogs under close control because of rabbit snares).

Cross the end of the road over the golf course and pass to the right of a green shed. Turn left at wooden gatepost and continue with the fence on your left. At a junction fork left, at the next junction go left, and at an open area head for a signpost about 50yds ahead. Turn right on a broad grass path to wind through the dunes and return to the beach.

What to look out for

This is a superb area for nature study. Over 200 species of birds have been recorded here and at Aberlady Bay to the west, including many waders and seabirds. In winter thousands of common and velvet scoters and brent geese are seen. The area is also rich in interesting plants including autumn gentian, burnet rose and northern marsh orchids. Grey and common seals are often seen offshore, especially near the Hummell Rocks, at the west end of Gullane Bay.

Muirfield golf course

Gullane Bents

Considerable work has gone on here to restore the dune system, which suffered in the 1920s and '30s from vehicles being driven down to the beach, and between 1941–5 from military training – the area was used as a practice ground for the Normandy Invasion in 1944. Information boards give details of how the restoration has taken place.

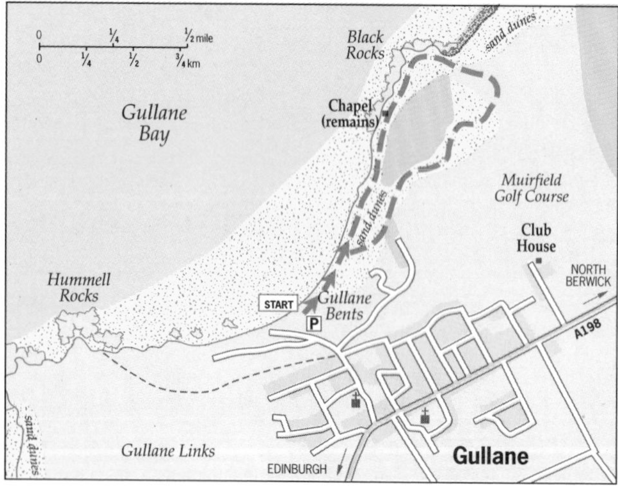

Muirfield Golf Course

Muirfield is one of the famous 'links' courses on which the British Open is played, when the world's best golfers pit their skills against the natural hollows, knolls and traps.

WALK 87

LOTHIAN
NT006746

Beecraigs and Cockleroy

Information

The walk is about three and a half miles long
Tracks and paths mostly have good surfaces, with one short stretch of open grassy hill
Two sets of steps at the deer farm
Dogs should be kept on leads
A range of information is available at the Park Centre
Refreshments available at the centre
Cafés in Linlithgow
Picnic tables at Balvormie near an attractive pond
Toilets at the park centre, at Balvormie and in Linlithgow

Fox

Beecraigs Country Park offers a wide range of activities, including a climbing wall and target archery course. The walk takes in a wonderful viewpoint, a trout farm and a deer farm.

START

Beecraigs Park Centre is two miles south of Linlithgow. Take a minor road from the west end of Linlithgow, signed 'Beecraigs Country Park', then follow signs for Beecraigs Loch, turning left then right to reach the Park Centre.

DIRECTIONS

From the Centre, return past the entrance, cross the road and take the track opposite, signed 'Balvormie Walk'. In 100yds take left fork past a gate on to a forest track. Follow the track for nearly ½ mile to reach the 'trim track'. Just beyond this is the Balvormie car park. Cross the road, signed 'Cockleroy Walk' and take the path immediately in front of the toilet block to re-enter the woods.

About 250yds after the toilets, where a blue waymark points back the way you have come, turn right onto a narrower path down across a small stream and continue to a junction. Turn left to reach a road, cross over (the Cockleroy car park is on the right) and continue on the path opposite (another blue waymark).

At the edge of the wood, cross a stile and walk up to the summit of Cockleroy (cairn and a viewpoint indicator). When you have enjoyed the view, return to the stile and retrace your steps to the Cockleroy car park, across the road, and back to Balvormie. Cross the car park and from its right side cross the stream and turn left along a wide track fringed by fine broad-leaved trees. Keep on this track for about ½ mile, to reach the next road. Turn left for 50yds and turn right on the road to the trout farm. Pass the anglers' lodge and reach the trout farm, leaving

What to look out for

The Cockleroy view stretches from coast to coast. In the woods you may see roe deer, rabbits, brown hares and perhaps a fox, and birds include great spotted woodpeckers.

On the summit of Cockleroy

it by crossing the bridge and climbing the steps to the top of the dam. Turn right along the dam and then left in the woods, keeping the loch on your left. Part way along the loch at a junction, turn right, signed 'Deer Farm'. Climb and descend steps to enter the walkway through the deer farm, continuing round to the left, then climb and descending more steps to return to the Park Centre.

Cockleroy

Cockleroy, which has remains of an ancient fort, is only 912ft high, but commands an exceptional view. On very clear days you can see Goat Fell on Arran, the Bass Rock to the east, Edinburgh, and across the Firth of Forth. The viewpoint indicator will help you to identify all the places you can see.

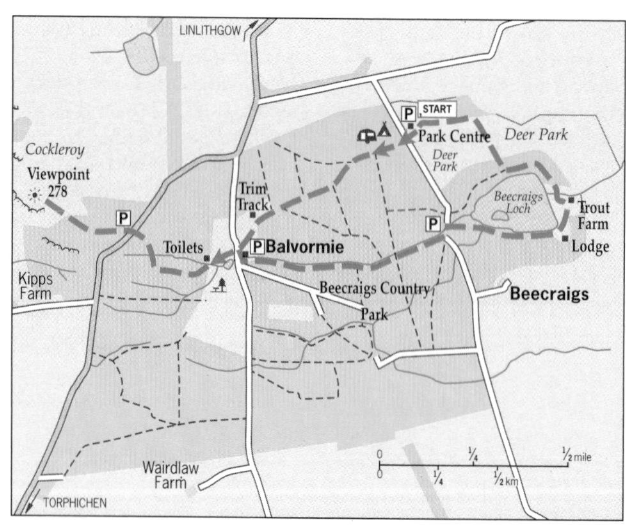

The Trout Farm

The fish bred here are used for stocking rivers and lochs in the area, providing sport for anglers, and trout can also be bought for the table.

The Deer Farm

Red deer, our largest native mammals, are bred here for their meat, which can be bought at the park centre. The stags have been 'de-antlered' to save them injuring themselves or the hinds. Young are born in June, and in October during the 'rut' the stags can be heard roaring as they prepare to mate.

Culzean Country Park

Set in Scotland's first country park, in the grounds of a fine castle, this walk takes in some splendid scenery and covers a variety of terrain – cliff tops, sandy beach, a walled garden, woodland, ponds and a disused railway line.

WALK 88
STRATHCLYDE
NS230098

Information

The walk is just under three miles long
Mostly easy ground
No road walking
No stiles
Dogs must be kept under control
No pub, but there is a tearoom (seasonal) at Swan Pond Cottage and a coffee house at the visitor centre
Picnic places at Swan Pond and Port Carrick

START

Culzean Country Park is off the A719, four miles west of Maybole and 12 miles south of Ayr. There is an admission charge to the park. Start the walk in the car park next to the walled garden at the heart of the park.

DIRECTIONS

From the car park turn downhill towards Happy Valley, with the walled garden on your left. At the southern point of the walled garden bear left following the line of the wall. At the first fork turn right. Continue to Happy Valley pond and bear left. Turn left again onto a gravel path and then take the first path on the right through woodland. Where the woodland path joins a track, turn left and continue to a crossroads. Turn right and go uphill along a drive. Turn sharp right after a row of cottages and down past Sunnyside Mill, an old meal-mill.

From the mill continue uphill under an old railway bridge and then right up onto the disused railway line. Follow the line for ½ mile to Morriston Bridge. Take the steps up onto the bridge and turn right onto a track. Continue down the track through the 'Cat Gates', where an impressive old beech hedge forms an attractive canopy overhead. In about 50yds fork left. At junction turn left, following the path with Hogston Burn on the right. At Carse Pond turn left along Piper's Brae towards the Swan Pond Cottage and Aviary.

From the cottage go to the edge of Swan Pond and turn left, following the edge of the pond. Pass the play area in the trees and take the path on the left, signposted 'Port Carrick'.

From the coast retrace your steps to the pond-side path and turn left over a footbridge. Turn left again

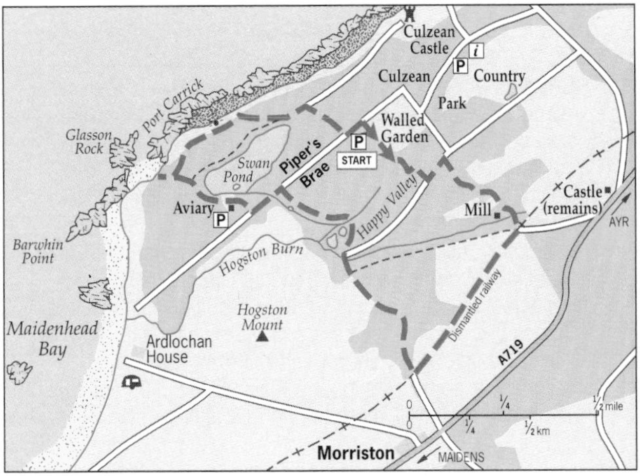

Looking down the coast, with Ailsa Craig in the distance

up along the cliff-top path, then cross the next old estate road, back onto Piper's Brae. Turn left and then take the first right to return to the start point.

Culzean Country Park
Culzean (pronounced 'Kullane') Country Park and the nearby castle, both in the care of the National Trust for Scotland, together provide one of Scotland's most popular days out. The park covers 563 acres and has a wide range of attractions, from beautiful woodland walks to an adventure playground. There is a visitor centre with various facilities, and this is also the base for the ranger naturalists who provide guided walks. A number of events are held in the park each year.

The Walled Garden
The garden is in the shape of a blunt diamond to allow the fruit trees to enjoy maximum sunshine. The kitchen garden was established in 1815 and the pleasure garden is over 200 years old.

What to look out for

The cliff-top path affords superb views of the Clyde, the Isle of Arran, Ailsa Craig and the Mull of Kintyre.
Given the range of habitats, the Country Park is a great place for wildlife of every description. The heathy cliffs support flowers such as thrift, sea campion, ling and formentil. At low tide, search the rock pools for sea urchins, anemones and limpets, and great northern divers, eiders and long-tailed ducks are seen offshore in winter. The Happy Valley woodland has many old, gnarled trees and exotic shrubs, including fine specimens of western hemlock, wellingtonias and Scots pines. Two mighty sitka spruces ('Adam and Eve') are among the oldest in Britain. The old railway line, which ran from Maidens to Dunure, also has plenty of wildlife. In the cliffs are two cave systems where herald moths hibernate.

Glenashdale Falls

WALK 89
STRATHCLYDE
NS047253

The island of Arran has been called 'Scotland in Miniature'. It is a very popular holiday area and contains superb mountains, lovely coastline, historic buildings – and Glenashdale Falls, justly famed for their beauty. The walk also visits the Giants' Graves, an ancient chambered cairn.

Information

The full walk is about four miles long; about three miles if Giants' Graves are missed out
Good paths and tracks, but steep, sometimes slippery climbs to Giants' Graves and the upper part of the path to the falls
Dogs must be kept on leads
Cafés and pubs in Whiting Bay
Toilets in Whiting Bay

START
The ferry from Ardrossan on the Clyde coast (daily service all year round, several boats a day) arrives at Brodick. The walk starts from the village of Whiting Bay, ten miles south of Brodick. In summer, with Arran's excellent bus services, the walk could easily be done on a day trip without taking your car on the ferry; buses are less frequent out of season. If you do take the car, park opposite the youth hostel in Whiting Bay.

DIRECTIONS
From the youth hostel follow the path signposted to the falls up beside the Glenashdale Burn. Go through a gap in the fence and in another 100yds turn left up the path signposted

Glenashdale Burn

'Giants' Graves'. Climb up a long flight of steep steps and at the top turn left along a broad path. Part way along this section there is a seat with a lovely view back across Whiting Bay to Holy Island. Reach the clearing containing the Giants' Graves (there is some 100-year-old carving on the stones – Victorian graffiti). Return down the (slippery) steps to the path in the glen and turn left.

The path climbs steadily towards the falls, crossing two bridges over side streams. At a sign go right and down to a viewpoint below the falls, which tumble impressively over a series of rock steps and are deafening when the falls are in spate. Return to the main path and continue up to the top of the falls, crossing the burn above them by a footbridge (with a rather different but still impressive view of the falls).

Follow the path right to start the return journey. At a wall go through the gap and turn right, continuing along the path through a gap in another wall, and follow the sign 'Iron Age Fort'. The path then twists sharply back up to the left, through the wall again, and turns right on a broad track.

Leave the forest at a gate and continue down the track, passing through two kissing-gates, to South Kiscadale. Carry on downhill to reach Whiting Bay and at the main road turn right to return to the start of the walk in 400yds.

Glenashdale Falls

The falls are the highest on Arran, tumbling for over 120ft in a triple cascade over rock steps into a narrow, wooded gorge. Above the falls the stream is called the Allt Dhepin; below them it becomes the Glenashdale Burn.

The Giants' Graves

Arran is very rich in prehistoric remains, including standing stones, circles and cairns. The chambered cairns, early tombs, follow a common pattern, with a shallow grave in a chamber, originally topped with a large rock slab. The whole grave was often covered with a cairn of boulders several yards high. Sometimes groups of tombs occur in rows. Most of the cairns date from about 2500–3000BC.

Turnstone

What to look out for

In spring and summer the trunks and branches of the trees are festooned with lichens and mosses. A variety of woodland birds such as garden warblers and chiffchaffs may be seen in summer, as well as year-round residents such as squirrels and deer.

Dùn na Cuaiche – an Inveraray Viewpoint

Dùn na Cuaiche is a noted viewpoint high above the town of Inveraray and is part of the estate of the famous Inveraray Castle, which can be visited before or after completing the walk.

WALK 90
STRATHCLYDE
NN097093

The spectacular view down Loch Fyne from the hilltop

Information

The walk is about four miles long
Good tracks and paths, steep in places
No stiles but some steps
Dogs should be kept on leads
Café at the castle (seasonal) and in Inveraray
Toilets at the castle (seasonal)

START

Inveraray is 24 miles north-east of Lochgilphead and 25 miles west of Arrochar. Park at the castle car park, reached by turning off A83 at the signed entrance at the north end of the village.

DIRECTIONS

The walk is one of the three waymarked routes on the hill. For this walk follow the blue waymarks from the car park, passing a monument marking the execution of 17 Campbells by the Marquis of Atholl in 1685, then crossing the River Aray by Frew's Bridge (designed by John Adam and built in 1758). Over the bridge fork right, following the blue waymarked path up through woodland. Pass through a kissing-gate and continue uphill across open meadow to a gate, then follow a track through woodland, passing the remains of an old lime kiln (point 4) and a huge western red cedar tree (point 5), believed to have the largest girth of any such tree in Scotland. About 50yds after the tree turn right and continue climbing steadily. Where the path meets a track turn right and later turn left up a flight of steps with a rope handrail.

The path crosses a rock fall (fine view down Loch Fyne over Inveraray) and a little care is needed at this point. The path then turns left to climb steeply towards the top of the hill (point 12). This section of path may well be muddy and quite slippery. The hollow before the summit (point 13) is Glac a'Bharaille ('hollow of the barrel'). From here a good track leads to the summit and its little lookout tower, at a height of 813ft. The view over the castle, town and loch is quite superb and well worth the effort of the climb. The easiest way down is to return to point 13 (see * below) and turn left down a broad grassy track which takes you back to point 6 on the trail. From there retrace your steps to the car park.

*It is possible to extend the walk from point 13 by turning right (take care on the slippery section between points 13 and 14). At point 12 fork left downhill. At point 16 turn right and continue down the track to point 17 then turn left. On reaching the main track again at point 18 (at the 'Sweetie Seat') turn right. Between points 18 and 20 the walk follows 'The Grand Approach', constructed around 1775 as the principal entry to the castle. Continue until you meet the outward route and turn left to retrace your steps to the start point.

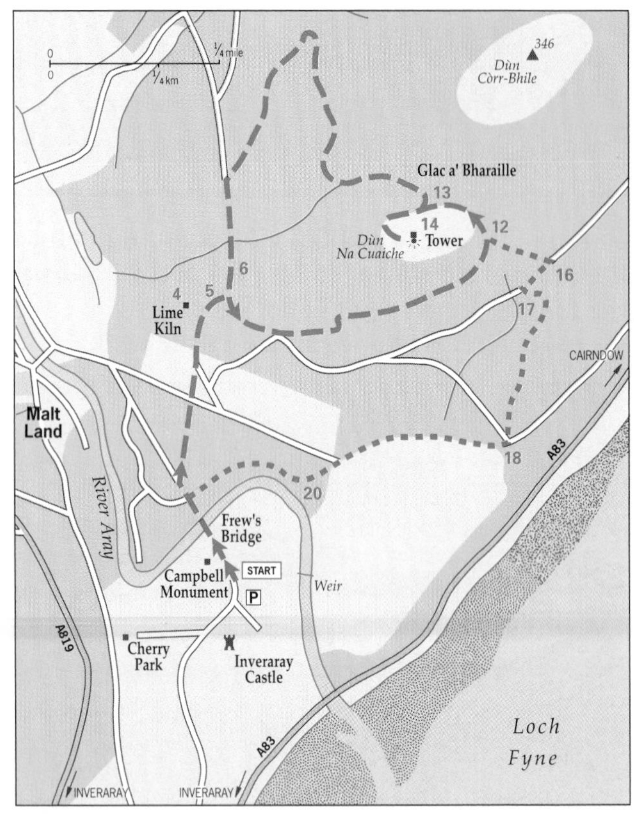

Inveraray Castle

The castle is the seat of the Duke of Argyll, Chief of Clan Campbell. It was built in the late 18th century to replace an older castle and at the same time the entire town of Inveraray was replanned and moved to its present position. Castle and town were planned together by Roger Morris and form one of the best preserved groupings of their kind anywhere in Britain. The castle is open from Easter to October (closed on Fridays).

The Lookout Tower

Dùn na Cuaiche means 'fort of the cup', possibly from the hollow near the top of the hill. The tower was designed by Roger Morris and William Adam and was built in 1748 for the grand sum of just £46. The roof was restored in 1989. The tower is sited so that it appears in silhouette when viewed from below, and is a popular local landmark.

Cherry Park

The block of buildings known as Cherry Park, in the castle grounds, holds an exhibition on the work of the Combined Services Operations unit that was based at Inveraray during the years of World War II.

What to look out for

The woods on Dùn na Cuaiche contain many fine trees: the excellent walks leaflet available at the castle will help you to identify them. There are woodland birds and also ravens and buzzards, and mammals include rabbits, squirrels and foxes. From the hilltop on a very clear day you can see the dam on Ben Cruachan, 20 miles away to the north.

The Highland Edge

This walk is from a forestry visitor centre near Aberfoyle, in an area where massive geological forces produced a major fault line millions of years ago. The walk uses forest tracks and paths, passing a fine waterfall.

WALK 91

CENTRAL
NN521014

Information

The walk is about four miles long
Good paths and tracks, with some steep sections
No stiles
David Marshall Lodge has good displays and an audio-visual show
Café at David Marshall Lodge
Picnic sites at the Lodge and at various places on the walk
Toilets at David Marshall Lodge

Down the rocky valley

START

David Marshall Lodge is on the A821, a mile north of Aberfoyle.

DIRECTIONS

From the left of the main entrance to the lodge follow the path signposted 'Waterfall Trail'. Go left at the first junction and right at the next. After crossing the raised wooden walkway turn right and soon cross the line of an old droving trail (Rob Roy operated around here, holding people to ransom for the original 'black mail'). The path winds down to the

'Waterfall of the Little Faun', 55ft high. As you approach the burn turn right. Turn left over the footbridge, then right and immediately left along a forest track (note information board on the production of slate in this area). At the next junction turn left, climbing steadily. Turn left onto a path for a short distance to see another waterfall, and soon rejoin the forest track. Continue uphill along forest track, with the burn on your right. At a junction of tracks turn right and contour round the hill, climbing again to a fine viewpoint, and continue along the track up the west side of a deep gully which is right on the fault line. On reaching the clearing at the top where the track ends, turn right on a delightful path, descending steeply. This is the route of a former 'inclined railway' used to take limestone from the quarry on Lime Craig to the kilns below. Continue downhill crossing one forest track, then meeting another. Turn right, with Dounans Camp below and the site of the lime kilns nearby. Cross the fault line again and in a further ¼ mile, at sign 'Trail End', turn left. Follow the path across a footbridge over the burn and turn right. Continue for 120yds with the burn on the right, then follow path to the left alongside a wooden handrail for the return to the lodge.

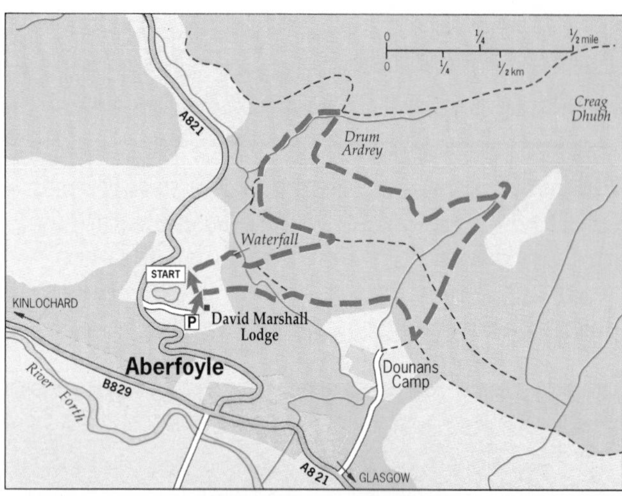

The bridge over the burn

The Highland Edge

This great fault runs right across Scotland from the Clyde estuary to Stonehaven and it is possible to see how the rocks were shaped and bent by immense forces. The types of rock which can be seen include leny grit, sandstone, dolerite and slate.

David Marshall Lodge

The lodge is the main visitor centre for the Queen Elizabeth Forest Park and has a great deal of informative literature, including a leaflet on the Highland Boundary Fault Trail. Among the displays are items showing how writers such as Wordsworth and Scott attracted early tourists here and ensured the lasting fame of the Trossachs.

What to look out for

The information boards along the trail give lots of information about the geology, history and wildlife of the area, showing how the forest has evolved and what birds you can expect to see and hear, including buzzards.

Dollar Glen and Castle Campbell

WALK 92
CENTRAL
NS964989

This is an exciting walk up a dramatic glen with waterfalls rushing down between cliffs, leading to a superbly sited castle.

Information

The walk is about a mile long
Rough in places, and some boardwalk; fairly steep climb up to the castle
No stiles
Dogs should be kept on leads
Café (seasonal) at the castle; pubs and cafés in Dollar
Grassy area around castle suitable for picnics
Toilets at castle

START

Dollar is about 12 miles east of Stirling on the A91. Follow signs from Dollar to Castle Campbell, and park in the car park part way up this minor road.

DIRECTIONS

From the car park cross the road, pass through the gate and take the path and then steps down into the glen. Turn right up the glen and after the first stretch of boardwalk, go down left to the Long Bridge. Cross the bridge and follow the path through a narrow gap between cliffs, with several fine waterfalls. Follow the path to the left and then up steps on the right as it winds up the glen. Recross the burn higher up and climb up to Castle Campbell.
After visiting the castle, return by turning right through the gate by the castle drive and going down a long flight of steps into the glen. Keep to the path, to rejoin the outward route at the steps leading up to the path back to the car park, signposted 'Lower (quarry) car park'.

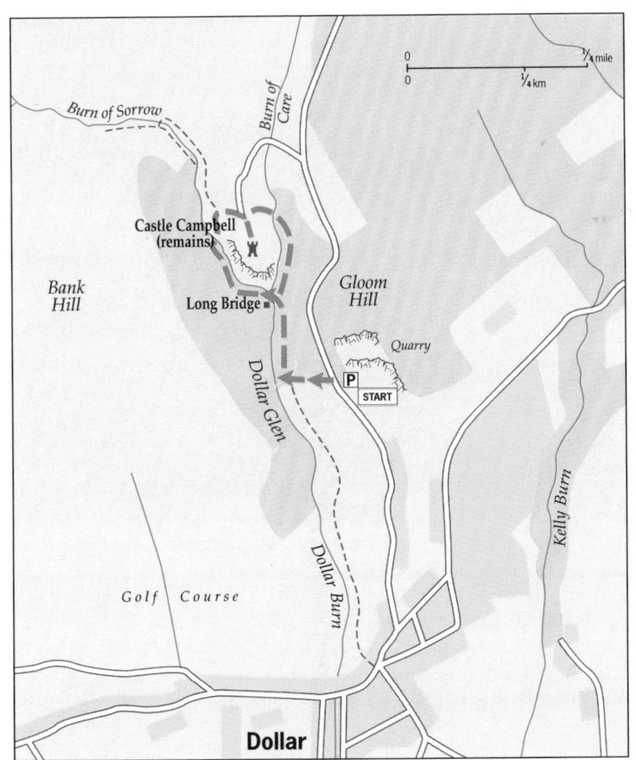

Dollar Glen

Dollar Glen is the most dramatic of the steep-sided glens that thrust into the southern scarp face of the Ochil Hills, east of Stirling. Two streams – the Burn of Sorrow and the Burn of Care – rush down the glen, crashing over rocks in

tumbling waterfalls. The path twists and climbs up the glen, winding excitingly under cliffs and close to the falls.
The glen has been in the care of the National Trust for Scotland since 1950. In the lower, open part is a grassy area with children's play equipment.

Castle Campbell
Castle Campbell has everything a castle should have: battlements, a tower with winding stone stairs and dark underground rooms. The castle is documented as far back as 1426 and was used by the Earls of Argyll as an eastern lowland stronghold until the 17th century. The name dates from 1490, before which it was called Castle Glume or Gloom, supposedly named by a princess who was imprisoned here; the two burns – Care and Sorrow – would seem to have been named at the same time. True or not, it is a good story!
The castle's importance waned after the mid-17th century, and it passed through various ownerships until acquired by the National Trust for Scotland in 1948. It is cared for by Historic Scotland on behalf of the Trust and is open all year. The view south from the castle is extensive.

The imposing Castle Campbell, above Dollar Glen

What to look out for

The glen is geologically very interesting – indicator boards give more information. Fine oak trees support a varied birdlife, and beneath them grow wild flowers such as lesser celandine.

The Earl's Tower

WALK 93
TAYSIDE
NO136235

This walk near Perth visits a tower set high on a cliff with superb views, and takes in fine woodland with excellent wildlife.

The Earl's Tower is in a superb cliff-top setting

What to look out for

The woods are rich in bird life and many species, from chaffinches to tawny owls, have their homes here. There are also roe deer and you may see the flash of a white rump as one bounds across the path.

Information

The walk is about two and a half miles long
Mixed paths and tracks, with some climbing and rough ground
No stiles
Nearest refreshment and toilet facilities are in Perth
The Stone Table area is excellent for a picnic

START

From Perth, cross the Tay by the old Perth Bridge (A85) and at the traffic lights on the far side go straight ahead up a steep hill. Follow signs for Kinnoull Hill Woodland Walks to go right at the hospital, and right again to the Corsiehill car park.

DIRECTIONS

From the car park take any of the small paths up the hill to the indicator at Corsiehill viewpoint (superb panorama of mountains). Turn half-left towards the cottage, walk up beside the fence and at the end of the fence turn left on a small path which soon broadens. At a cross path go straight over.

Just past a brown waymark turn left on to a path with a yellow waymark and continue through fine open woodland for about ¼ mile to a broad track (marker 13).

The stone table

Turn right and continue on this track below tall pines, then at a fork in about 600yds go right, signposted 'Tower'. Follow the track round to the right and uphill to reach Kinnoull Tower on the cliff edge, with a stunning view across the River Tay. From the tower follow yellow waymarks ('Children's Walk') to wind round a deep gully (can be icy in winter and muddy any time after rain) and climb again to the top of the hill and the Stone Table. A few yards on is the actual summit with another viewpoint indicator.
Return to the Stone Table and turn right along the cliff-top path. Follow the path downhill through gorse and whin bushes. The path soon opens out.
Cross one junction and at the next, nearly ½ mile from the summit, turn right on a clear path. At a fork keep right and at the next junction turn left (yellow waymark) to return to the car park.

Kinnoull Tower
Contrary to its appearance, the tower is not a real ruin, but was built this way by the Earl of Kinnoull in the 18th century. He was inspired to build the folly, so the story goes, after visiting Germany and seeing the romantic castles on cliffs above the Rhine. There is another similar tower on Binn Hill a mile or so to the east.

Stone Table
This feature of the hill was also built for the earl, so that he and his friends could sit here and enjoy the view, just as we do today. He did not, of course, have the M85 motorway interchange directly below.

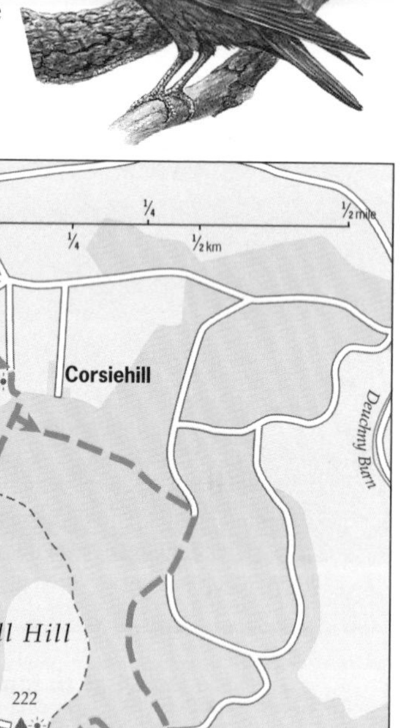

Rook

Around Glen Lednock

An attractive and varied walk which includes fine woodland and a lovely waterfall. A diversion can be made to a viewpoint tower. The walk is particularly good in spring and autumn when the colouring is at its best.

WALK 94
TAYSIDE
NN773221

START
Comrie is seven miles west of Crieff. The walk starts from the car park just off Dundas Street (the A85).

DIRECTIONS
Walk up Dundas Street and where it swings left go straight ahead into Monument Road. Shortly take the signposted path on the right. Continue along the path, keeping the fence on your right, through fine woods of beech, oak, larch and birch. Cross a small burn. The path enters the woods proper and broadens out to give excellent walking. In ¼ mile fork right to the Little Caldron viewpoint, continuing to rejoin the main path, which narrows, and runs alongside the road. The path becomes a wooden boardwalk before plunging in flights of steps to the Deil's Caldron (Devil's Kettle) waterfalls.
Climb steps to join the road, and continue carefully along it. (In 200yds a diversion can be made to the left to climb the hill to Lord Melville's Monument.) Carry on with the glen opening up. At a left-hand bend in the road go

Information

The walk is about four miles long
Good paths with some boardwalk and steps; some climbing, especially to the Melville Monument
A few stiles
Dogs must be kept on leads
Nearest refreshments and toilets are in Comrie
Good picnic areas in the woods and by the Shaky Bridge

Looking across the glen

What to look out for

There are lots of different trees to identify, and woodland birds such as finches, tits and treecreepers. Moorland birds can also be seen on the open stretch. Mammals include rabbits and possibly roe deer and foxes in the woods.

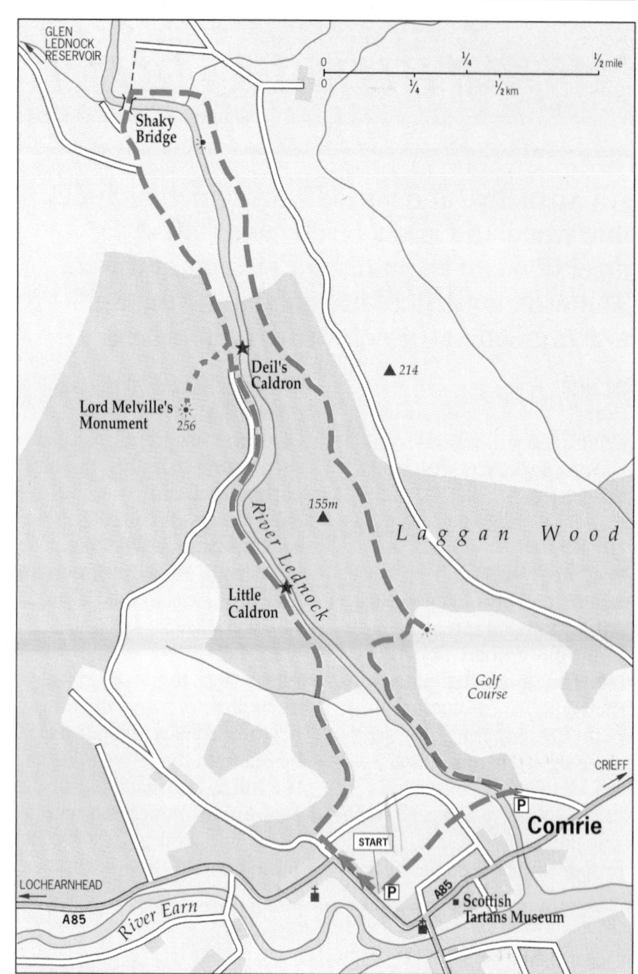

ahead on a track signposted 'Laggan Wood' and follow yellow waymarks to the Shaky Bridge (its far end is ingeniously balanced in the fork of a sycamore tree). Over the bridge turn right along the path beside the river. Cross a stile and climb steps to join a lovely grassy path with a good view of the monument. The path climbs gently above a wet meadow to enter Laggan Wood by a stile, and before long starts the descent towards Comrie. Ignore the sign 'Forest Walk' on the right.

At a fork turn right down steps (a short diversion left leads to a viewpoint with a splendid panorama of Comrie and Strathearn). The path continues down to rejoin the burn and passes a weir before re-entering Comrie by the cricket ground. Turn right over the bridge and follow the path right and left (now following an old railway line). At a cross path go straight on between fences to return to the car park, or divert left into the village to visit the Scottish Tartans Museum.

The Deil's Caldron
The falls are an impressive sight, tumbling out of a narrow gorge between cliffs and over rock steps to a deep pool (the Caldron) some 100ft below.

Lord Melville's Monument
The monument, 73ft high, was built in 1812 in memory of Henry Dundas, first Viscount Melville. He was Lord Advocate of Scotland for many years and had an estate at Dunira, west of Comrie. From the monument there are superb views all around.

Scottish Tartans Museum
In the main street of Comrie, the museum includes displays on the history of tartan, how it evolved, how dyes were made from plants and vegetables, and much more. There is a reconstructed weaver's cottage and a special children's corner. The museum is open Easter to October daily.

The Pass of Killiecrankie

The Battle of Killiecrankie in 1689 was one of the first victories for the Jacobite rebels. Learn about the battle at the National Trust for Scotland visitor centre, and then walk down into the lovely pass to see the site for yourself.

WALK 95
TAYSIDE
NN917627

START
The National Trust for Scotland Visitor Centre is at Killiecrankie on the B8079, three miles north of Pitlochry. The car park is open all year; the centre is open daily from Easter to late October.

DIRECTIONS
Walk round the back of the Visitor Centre, following signs 'Pass and the Soldier's Leap'. Go down steps and across a wooden bridge over a burn. This is Trooper's Den, where the first shot of the battle in 1689 was fired. Continue down the path (a seat gives a splendid view of the pass), descending a long curving flight of steps to turn sharply left for a few yards and then right, signposted 'Soldier's Leap'.
Return to the signpost and continue on the riverside path, soon passing the fine 1863 railway viaduct by Joseph Mitchell which is 510ft long and 54ft high at its highest point.
The path continues through splendid mature woodland, with the River Garry below. This stretch is particularly fine in the autumn when the trees are at their most colourful. In about ½ mile pass Balfour's Stone, where Brigadier Balfour, a Dutch commander in the government force, is said to have been killed in the retreat after the battle.
Join the old road from Tummel Bridge to Blair Atholl, noting the fine milestone on the left, and soon turn right on the footbridge over the Garry. Look back here for a splendid view up the pass, framing the soaring peak of Carn Liath, part of the Beinn a'Ghlo massif. Return by the same route to the Visitor Centre.

The view from the bridge

The Soldier's Leap, where a desperate man jumped to safety

Information

The walk is about two and a half miles long
Good paths, with a long flights of steps from the Visitor Centre down into the pass
Dogs should be kept on leads
Snack bar at Visitor Centre
Plenty of picnic places and seats along the way
Toilets at Visitor Centre

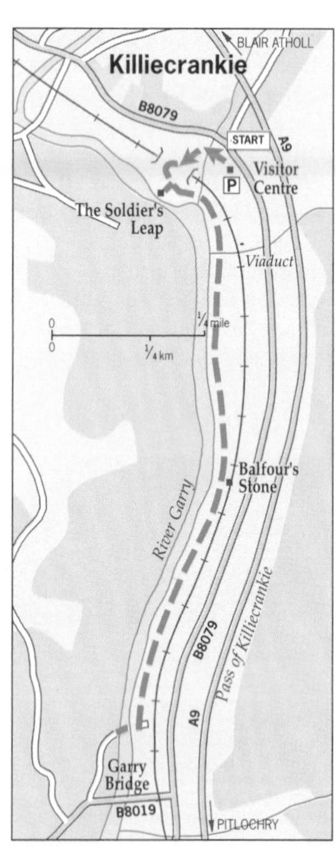

The Battle of Killiecrankie
The aim of the Jacobite rebels was to overthrow the Hanoverian William of Orange and restore the Stuarts to the British throne. Here, on 27 July 1689, they met government troops. Led by John Graham of Claverhouse – 'Bonnie Dundee' – the Jacobites won a rapid and total victory. Unfortunately Graham was killed and without its charismatic leader the rebellion fizzled out.

What to look out for

Look out for birds such as great spotted and green woodpeckers among the oak and birch. Ferns grow in profusion on the forest floor. Regular guided walks from the Visitor Centre.

The Soldier's Leap
The story here is that one Donald MacBean, fighting on the government side, ran into the pass in an attempt to escape. Coming to this point, as he told, 'I laid down my gun and hat and jumped, and lost one of my shoes in the jump'. At 18 feet across, it would be a very respectable distance for a trained athlete of today, and shows what a desperate man can do.

Dunnottar Castle

WALK 96
GRAMPIAN
NO878855

This splendid short walk goes from the attractive.harbour at Stonehaven to one of Scotland's most dramatic castle ruins, standing on a cliff-top promontory, and returns across a pebble beach.

Information

The walk is about three miles long
Good paths, but a long flight of steps at the castle, and pebble beach on the return
Some road walking
Several stiles
Dogs should be kept on leads
The Marine Hotel at the harbour is open all day and welcomes families
Cafés in Stonehaven
Ladies toilets at Dunnottar Castle; others in Stonehaven

START

Stonehaven Harbour is 15 miles south of Aberdeen, reached by turning off the A94 into Stonehaven and following signs to the harbour. There are parking spaces at the harbour.

DIRECTIONS

From the harbour walk up Wallace Wynd (a wynd is a lane) and turn left into Castle Street. Where the road ends, continue ahead on a path which climbs steeply to the left to meet another road. Turn left and in a few yards, where the road bends sharply right, go ahead on the path between fences, with a fine view back over the town, harbour and the cliffs beyond. (The war memorial on the prominent knoll to the right is worth the short diversion through a gate and over the grass. An imposing rotunda, it is inscribed around the inside: 'One by one Death challenged them. One by one they smiled in his grim visage and refused to be dismayed.' Return to the gate and turn right.)

Continue along the cliff path. Cross two stiles, walk across a field (usually of turnips), cross two more stiles and walk along the edge of another field. Cross one more stile to reach Castle Haven. The path winds round the bay to reach the castle. On reaching Dunnottar, turn left down the steps and go across to the entrance and ticket booth. After visiting the castle, start back by turning right, down on to the pebble beach of Castle Haven. At the far end of the beach climb up the path ascending the grass

Stonehaven Harbour

What to look out for

This is a very good area for seabirds, with an RSPB reserve at Fowlsheugh, to the south. From May to July, watch for razorbills, guillimots, fulmars, kittiwakes and great black-backed gulls. Puffins and eiders also come to Fowlsheugh to breed.
Keep a look-out for peregrines, which may be glimpsed hunting along the cliffs.

Dunnottar Castle

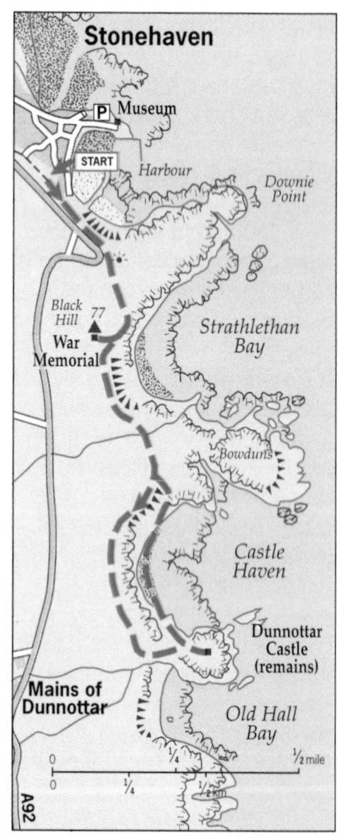

slope on the left (not the very steep gully just left of the cliffs) to regain the cliff-top path. Retrace the outward route back into Stonehaven.

Dunnottar Castle
The castle was started in the late 14th century and has 15th- and 16th-century additions. It was besieged several times, notably in 1652 when it held out for eight months before surrendering to Cromwell's forces.
The considerable remains are very impressive, both on the approach towards the castle and on closer inspection. A guidebook can be bought on entry, and all the main buildings are clearly labelled. Its dramatic setting has made Dunnottar a popular choice as a film location, and it was used in Zefferelli's recent remake of Shakespeare's *Hamlet*. The castle is open daily (but limited hours in winter).

Stonehaven
Stonehaven is an attractive town with a good sandy beach beyond the harbour. On the old pier is the Tolbooth Museum of local history. It is housed in the oldest building in Stonehaven, which was built as a store for Dunnottar about four hundred years ago.

Duff House and Bridge of Alvah

WALK 97
GRAMPIAN
NJ690633

Duff House, near the attractive seaside town of Banff, is considered to be one of William Adam's very finest works. This walk follows pleasant tracks through the woodland of its extensive policies, passing an 18th-century refrigerator, a mausoleum and a beautiful old bridge.

Information

The walk is about four miles long
Good track or path all the way
Dogs should be kept on leads
Cafés and Tourist Information Centre in Banff
Toilets at the Duff House car park and in Banff

START
Duff House is just off the southern outskirts of Banff, signposted from the A98. The walk starts from the car park.

DIRECTIONS
From the car park turn left and walk around the edge of the sports field to reach the Fife Gates, named for the second Earl Fife, who was largely responsible for laying out the park in the mid-18th century. Pass through the Fife Gates and follow the track south. At a fork keep left (the right fork goes to 'The Orchard' where honey can be purchased). In a further 100yds take the small path on the left,

The imposing Duff House

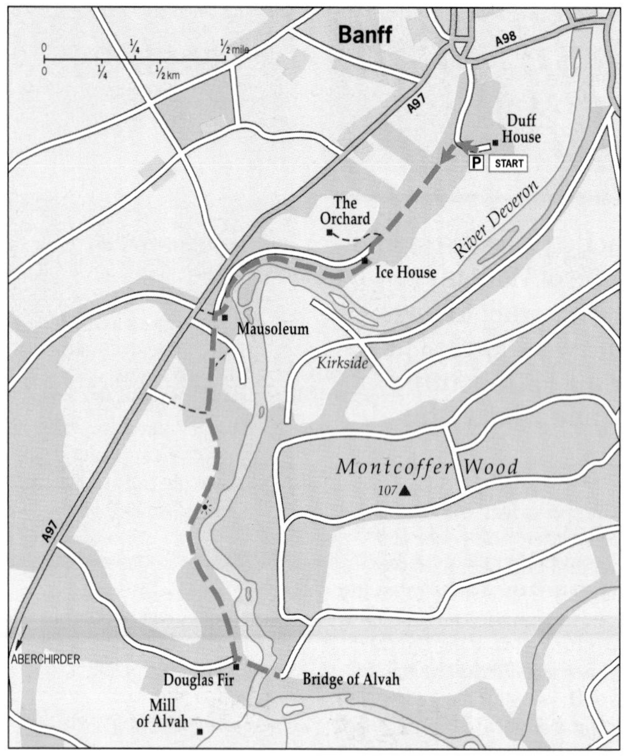

signposted 'Woodland Footpath'. Immediately on the right, down a few steps, is the former ice house for the estate. Continue along the winding path, with the River Deveron on the left. The path rejoins the main track at the Duff Mausoleum, built on the site of a former Carmelite chapel. Turn left along the track and at the next fork go straight ahead.

At a triangular junction keep left, with fields on the right and, at one point, a fine view of the river through a gap in the trees on the left. Reach a junction with a fine old Douglas Fir ahead (said to be a 'wishing tree' – if you stick a coin in the tree, spin round three times and make a wish, your wish should come true). Turn left here, steeply down the track to reach the Bridge of Alvah. Return to Duff House by the same route.

Duff House

The house was designed by William Adam for William Duff, who became the first Earl Fife. Work began in 1735, but for various reasons, including a protracted lawsuit over Adam's fees, was never completed. The house fell into disrepair, but considerable restoration work is now under way. It is open to visitors in the summer.

The Mausoleum

There was a mausoleum in the original plans, but it was not until 1791 that work started at the instigation of the second Earl Fife, then aged 62. The mausoleum is in rococo Gothic style and contains a monument to the first Earl, whose body was brought here when the building was completed. The second Earl was so proud of his Banffshire roots that he had soil from the area taken to London and spread on the ground where he was building a house, so that he could say that he 'lived on Scottish soil'.

The Bridge of Alvah

The bridge was rebuilt in 1772, replacing an even older crossing of the river. A graceful single-arch structure, it complements its fine setting perfectly. The section of our walk which leads to the bridge was originally a carriage drive, intended to show off the fine park of Duff House to visitors. The scenery was considered at the time to be an ideal representation of how the landscape should be 'arranged'.

What to look out for

The woods and fields here have interesting birdlife. Look for pheasants and grey partridges, and grey herons down by the River Deveron – a fine trout and salmon stream. There are plenty of rabbits and you may spot deer if you are lucky.

Loch an Eilein

WALK 98
HIGHLAND
NH898085

This is a beautiful walk around what is considered to be one of the most picturesque lochs in the Highlands, set amid one of the finest remnants of the ancient Caledonian Pine Forest with the massive Cairngorms as a dramatic backdrop.

Information

The walk is just over three miles long
Mainly level, easy ground
Dogs should be kept on leads as this is a Nature Reserve
Lovely picnic areas around the car park and Information Centre, and at the north end of the loch

START
Loch an Eilein is three miles south of Aviemore. Follow the B9152 from Aviemore turning left to Inverdruie, then right on to the B970. After a mile or so turn left, signposted 'Loch an Eilein'. Park in the car park at the end of the road.

DIRECTIONS
Leave the car park by the footpath and after 100yds or so reach the information centre. Go straight ahead to join a footpath which encircles the loch. Head anti-clockwise around the loch. Go left at the first fork and continue on the footpath, passing the ruins of Loch an Eilein Castle on its island on your left. Soon you will pass Loch an Eilein Cottage on your right and pass through a gate into ancient Caledonian Pine woodland.

Keep to the main path with the waters of the loch on your left. Beyond some fallen trees, where the path splits, take the left branch, passing the head

Loch an Eilein Castle

of the loch and climbing a short steep hill. From the top of the hill continue through more woodland and cross a small wooden footbridge over the stream. Once over the footbridge, continue to the left, slightly downhill, crossing some stepping stones over another narrow stream and continuing on the obvious footpath.
Continue on the footpath with Loch an Eilein still on your left for about 1½ miles, ignoring a narrow path which turns left towards the loch.
At the next path junction, keep ahead across a footbridge. Continue on the main path, up a long, easy hill, through a gate, and past a cottage on the right. Continue through woodland. Take the next left fork downhill over a footbridge and return to the car park.

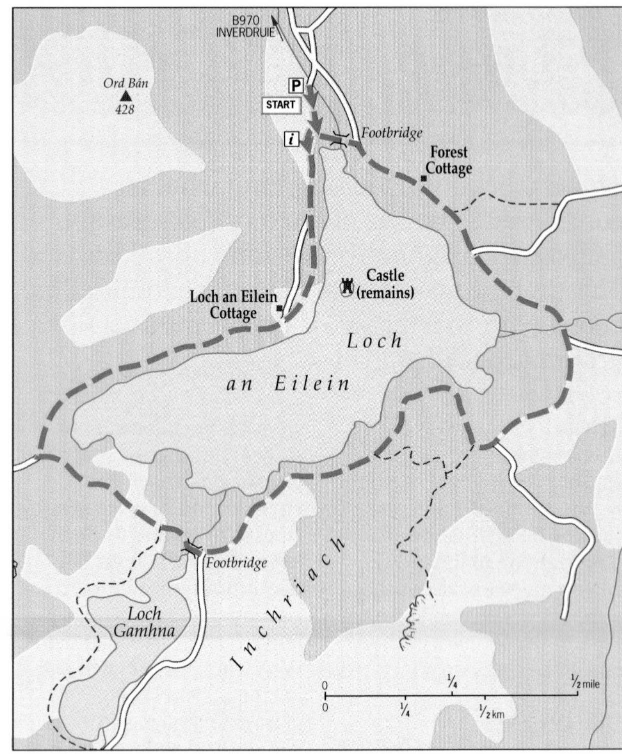

Loch an Eilein Castle
Dating from the 14th century, local legend claims that the castle was once the lair of the notorious 'Wolf of Badenoch', otherwise known as Alexander Stewart, the grandson of Robert the Bruce, who was eventually excommunicated by the Church for burning down Elgin Cathedral. The castle was once reached by a causeway of flagged stones, now covered by the waters of the loch, and only rarely is the water level low enough to reveal the stones.

The Loch
At the east end of the loch, near the car park, there is a broad bay offering fine views of the castle island and the hill beyond. The waters are safe, but bathers beware – they stay very cold until well into July.

What to look out for

The castle ruins were used by one of the last native pairs of ospreys to breed in Scotland, before the old Scottish stock became extinct earlier this century. The re-introduction of the osprey to Scotland is one of the great environmental success stories, and you can often see these magnificent fish-hawks hunting over the waters of the loch, although none now breed on the castle ruins.The loch area is part of the Cairngorms National Reserve, and many rare species of birds and mammals live and breed here, including red squirrels, crested tits, Scottish crossbills and capercaillie. More about the history and wildlife of the area can be learned from the Information Centre.

WALK 99
HIGHLAND
NH498205

The Fabulous Falls of Foyers

Information

The walk is about three miles long
Mainly level, easy walking on narrow woodland paths, but care needed at the falls
Some road walking
No stiles
Dogs should be kept on leads near farm buildings

Of the Falls of Foyers, the poet Robert Southey once said, 'everything is beautiful, and everything – woods, rocks, water, the glen, the mountains and the lake below – in proportion'. The walk also offers tantalising glimpses across the deep and mysterious waters of Loch Ness.

START

Foyers is about 13 miles east of Fort Augustus via the B862, turning onto the B852 just north of Whitebridge. Park at the car park or layby on the roadside, close to the telephone box and post office (Foyers Stores).

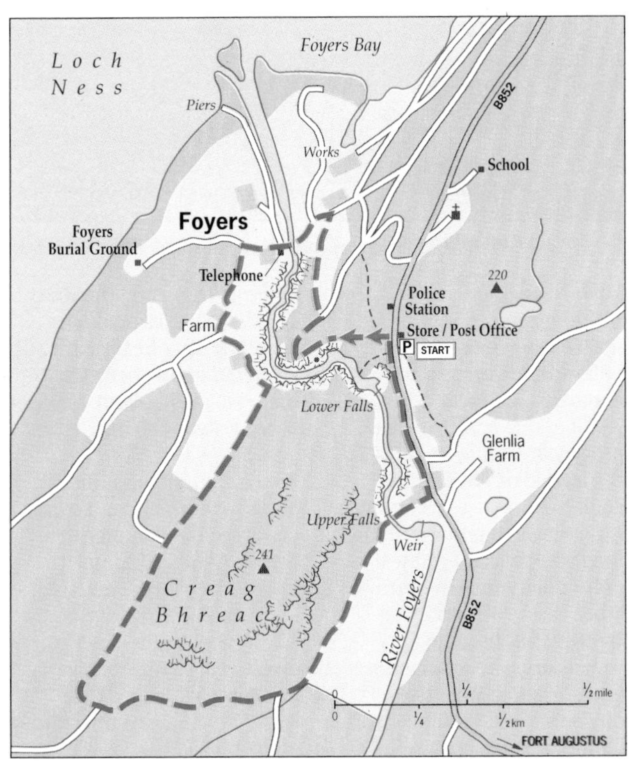

DIRECTIONS

Pass through the gate opposite the post office and shop and turn left down the footpath. After about 40yds turn right down to a wooden fence and then left again. The path winds steeply downhill. At the next junction turn left and proceed downhill, later taking the narrow path around the left side of a large rock to the falls viewpoint. Retrace your steps uphill. At the junction go straight ahead across a footbridge and along the cliff edge. Follow the path alongside the fence. At the next fork, bear right on the path through the trees. Turn left at the next junction and continue along this path, crossing a car track and descending a steep narrow path towards houses and the road. Turn left onto the road. On reaching a tight right-hand bend, turn left onto the 'no through road' and cross the river on the old road bridge. Continue straight ahead past the telephone box and follow the road past the entrance to Foyers Burial Ground. Continue along the road to reach some farm buildings. Go through the farm and bear left through a gate onto a track up towards the forest. Pass through another gate and turn right onto the forest track. Continue straight on, climbing uphill. In about ½ mile, at a junction on the brow of the hill, go straight ahead.

After about another ½ mile reach a junction of forest roads and turn left, then go through the gate onto a track leading out of the forest. Cross a bridge (view of Upper Falls) and continue past some cottages uphill to the road. Turn left and return to the starting point.

What to look out for

The Loch Ness Monster, of course – but there is a great deal of wildlife in this area which is more easily seen. You may spot a buzzard circling above the forest, and on the bridge over the River Foyers look out for salmon jumping – especially when the river is in autumn spate. Roe deer can often be seen in the fields, particularly in the early morning and evening.

The view from the path to the Falls of Foyers

Loch Ness

The longest loch in Scotland, Loch Ness extends for 21 miles from Inverness to Fort Augustus. Its great depth – 754ft at one point – of dark peaty waters has encouraged the legend of 'Nessie', the Loch Ness monster. The story is not new – it is claimed that a sighting was made by St Columba in the 6th century. Since the 1930s, monster spotting has become something of a boom industry in the area, with Nessie museums and visitor centres doing great business.

Falls of Foyers and the River

The Falls are particularly dramatic after heavy rain. From a narrow rocky lip, the main fall drops about 100 feet down a steep cliff into a dark pool below.

To the right of the stone bridge over the River Foyers you'll see the remains of British Alcan's original hydro-electric scheme, used in the making of aluminium. The flow of water was diverted above the bridge into pipes which fed the factory turbines at the bottom of the hill.

Durness and Balnakeil

WALK 100
HIGHLAND
NC403678

Starting from the most north-westerly village on the Scottish mainland, this walk includes impressive limestone cliffs, a beautiful beach of sparkling white sands and, on a clear day, a view of the Orkney Isles.

START
The Sutherland village of Durness is some 15 miles north of Rhiconich on the A838. The walk begins at the car park just opposite the Parkhill Hotel in the village.

DIRECTIONS
Leave the car park opposite the Parkhill Hotel and turn left. Follow the road and after ½ mile pass the Balnakeil Craft Village. Continue along the road for about another ½ mile. At a churchyard wall, the road turns left. At this point bear right onto the beach and continue along the sands with the sand dunes on your right. After ½ mile rejoin the road and continue, turning right just before a cattle grid and crossing grassland

Information

The walk is about four miles long
Mostly flat and easy, with a section along the sands; care needed close to the cliffs
Some road walking
No stiles
Dogs should be kept on leads where there are sheep in the fields
Tea shops in Balnakeil and Durness

The ruined church at Balnakeil

What to look out for

Puffins breed on the cliffs just south of Durness and there are thousands of fulmars nesting on ledges on the limestone cliffs of Sango Bay. Also between April and July you are likely to see guillemots, razorbills and kittiwakes. Sango Bay has lots of rock pools which are always worth exploring.

towards the cliffs, with a stone wall on your left. Walk uphill, bearing right towards buildings on the headland. On the cliff top, bear right towards the next group of buildings. After ½ mile turn right on to a broader track and keep left at the junction with another track. Go through a gate in a wall and then follow the wall on your right.
Just past the corner of the field, turn right through another gate and walk across the field. Go through another gate and walk across the rough road between the fences. Go through a final gate onto the road and turn left to return to the starting point.

Balnakeil Craft Village
This was established in 1964, with Sutherland County Council funding, on the site of an old radar station. The Craft Village uses the former station buildings, and a community of craftspeople and artists have gathered here. There is a pottery, an art gallery and many other attractions, including a tearoom.

Balnakeil Churchyard
Celtic monks established a monastery here in the 6th century – Balnakeil means 'the place of the kirk'. Ancient Vatican records show that the church here donated 14s 8d towards the cost of the Crusades in 1274!
The graveyard has some fascinating and very old graves, including one, inscribed in Gaelic, Latin and Greek, to the Gaelic poet Rob Donn Mackey, the Bard of Reay. Another tomb contains the remains of one Donald McLeod who reputedly committed at least 18 murders. He bought his way in by contributing some money towards the construction of the present building, in 1619, on the condition that he would be buried in the graveyard.

Sango Bay
This bay, just below the caravan site in the village of Durness, boasts one of the finest beaches in the area. Brilliant white sands, limestone cliffs, deep green seas and the constant cry of fulmars and herring gulls make it a place to linger, especially when the sun shines. At low tide several limestone skerries appear, and on the outskirts of the bay there are lots of rock pools.

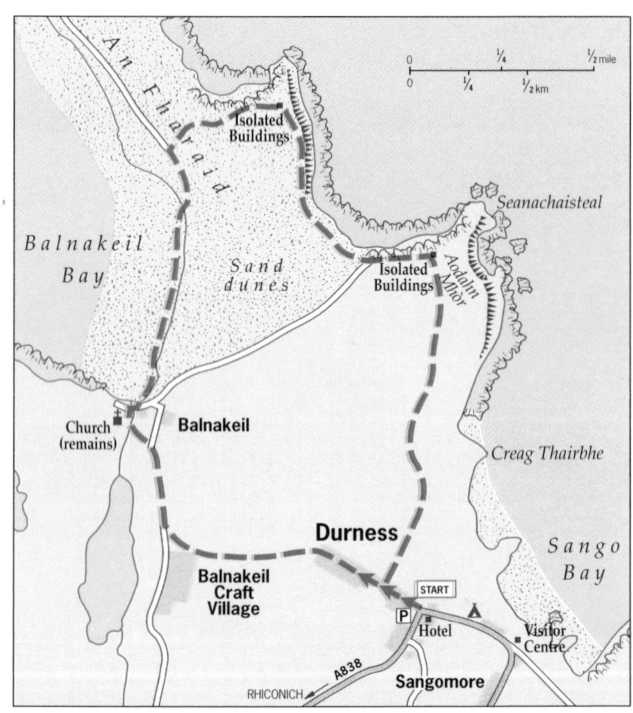

Notes

Notes

Index

Note: all numbers refer to walk numbers

A

B

C

D

E

F

Acknowledgements

All photographs are held in the Automobile Association's own photo library (AA PHOTO LIBRARY). The Automobile Association wishes to thank the following photographers for their assistance in the preparation of this book (numbers refer to walk numbers).

P Baker 20; V & S Bates 22, 36, 37, 38, 54, 55, 56, 61, 62, 63, 64, 116a, 117, 118, 119, 120, 121, 170; **J Beazley** 173; **M Birkitt** 64, 71, 98; **I Burgum** 110a, 110b, 111a, 111b, 112a, 112b, 113a, 113b, 114, 115, 116b, 126a, 127a, 127b, 128, 129; **J Carnie** 189; **D Croucher** 51, 53a, 53b, 122, 123, 124, 125, 130, 131, 132a, 132b, 133, 134, 135, 136a, 136b, 138, 139; **P Davies** 75b; **S Day** 190a, 190b, 191, 192, 193a, 193b, 198; **P Eden** 33, 34; **A Edwards** 100; **E Ellington** 194b, 195, 196, 197, 199, 200; **D Forss** 18, 19, 21a, 21b, 39, 40, 41, 42a, 42b, 43, 44, 45a, 45b, 46, 47, 48, 49, 50, 52, 65, 66, 67, 68, 69, 70, 71, 72, 73, 74a, 74b, 75a, 76, 77, 78, 79, 80, 81a, 81b, 82, 83, 84, 85, 86a, 86b, 87, 96, 99, 101a, 101b, 141, 142, 143b, 147, 148a, 148b; **P Goodrum** 2, 3a, 3b, 4, 5, 6a, 6b, 9a, 9b, 10a, 10b, 11a, 11b; **A Hopkins** 158a, 158b, 159, 160a, 160b, 161, 163a, 163b, 164, 165, 166, 167, 168, 169a, 169b; J Ingram 7a, 7b, 8a, 8b, 14; A Lawson 13b; **S & O Matthews** 24b, 162; **C Mellor** 88a, 88b, 90a, 90b, 95a, 95b, 97; **C Molyneux** 126b; **J Morrison** 144, 145, 146, 149a, 149b, 150, 151, 152, 153, 154a, 154b; **K Paterson** 171, 172, 174a, 174b, 175a, 175b, 176a, 176b, 177, 178, 179a, 179b, 180, 181, 182, 183, 184a, 184b, 185a, 185b, 186a, 186b, 187, 188a, 188b; **N Ray** 12, 13a, 15, 16, 17a, 17b, 25, 26; **P Sharpe** 156, 157; **M Short** 23, 24a, 27, 28, 29a, 29b, 30, 31, 32, 57, 58, 59a, 59b, 60; **A Stonehouse** 1; **M Trelawny** 143a; **A Tryner** 91, 93, 109, 140; **W Voysey** 32, 35; **R Weir** 194a.

Section titles:
H Williams The West Country; **D Forss** South and South-east England; **A Tryner** Central England and East Anglia; **C Molyneux** Wales and the Marches; **E Bowness** Northern England; **S Day** Scotland

Front cover (Ashness Bridge) and spine (Kersey): **Spectrum Colour Library**

Illustrations by Andrew Hutchinson
Introduction illustrations on pages 7,9, and 12 by Richard Draper and Ann Winterbotham